THE CARIBBEAN

MW01040680

North
Atlantic
Ocean

TURKS &
CAICOS

DOMINICAN
REPUBLIC

VIRGIN
ISLANDS

ANGUILLA

ST. MARTIN

BARBUDA

ST. KITTS
& NEVIS

ANTIGUA

PUERTO
RICO

MONTSERRAT

GUADELOUPE

Caribbean
Sea

DOMINICA

MARTINIQUE

CURAÇAO

ST. LUCIA

ARUBA

BARBADOS

BONAIRE

PETIT MARTINIQUE

ST. VINCENT &
THE GRENADINES

CARRIACOU

GRENADA

TOBAGO

Columbia

Venezuela

Guyana

TRINIDAD

KESHIA SAKARAH

CARIBE

Quadrille

CONTENTS

MONTSERRAT TO LEICESTER

'MUM, I WANT TO BE A CHEF!'

I remember the day I told mum I wanted to be a chef. It was a Saturday afternoon, I'd just left morning steel pan practice at the African Caribbean Centre, in Highfields, Leicester, and as always, we were taking grandma food shopping at Sainsbury's – she was loyal to them and her Nectar points. I was in the back, grandma in the front and mum was driving her purpleish, silver Fiat Picasso. I'm not sure what or why this was the moment I felt to bring it up, but I did. 'Mum, I want to be a chef,' I said. They were both quiet and only the radio was talking. She replied, 'A chef? Oh no, you can be something better than that.' Grandma said nothing. If only I could have seen the expression on her face; I imagine it was one of confusion. Her response wasn't what I had hoped for and we carried on with our Saturday as we did any other and it was all a bit of a blur after that.

At the time, food was the main thing that brought me joy and fed my curiosity, as it was present in so much of my life. By this age, I accompanied grandma to the market at every opportunity (not necessarily by choice, but I'm grateful for it now). I could tell a good yam or sweet potato from a bad one thanks to her, and others from the Caribbean community (mostly women) who nursed over them religiously, often peeling a little bit of the skin back with her thumb to check the flesh underneath before buying – of course, tremendously irritating the vendors. Not only that, I had been going to the garden (as they called it, an allotment to everyone else) with my maternal grandparents throughout school holidays. A first hand experience at growing, harvesting and eating seasonally – I planted the corn and rhubarb, picked the blackberries when they ripened, which often ended up in eve's pudding or crumble for Sunday dinner and harvested the abundance of 'peas' (rosecoco beans), which we later shelled together at the kitchen table, before freezing for rice and peas or Saturday soup.

There is something very sacred about the land for us as a community. We were taken from across the African continent and displaced throughout the Americas, with many never returning to their original soil. As said by Frantz Fanon – the Martiniquan revolutionary and Pan-Africanist thinker, '... for a colonised people the most essential value, because the most concrete, is first and foremost the land: the land which will bring them bread and, above all, dignity.' Historically, the land we worked was never ours, yet we understood it more than those who put us there. Having the ability to work it freely, by choice, is a revolutionary act in itself, and in some small way, my grandparents' garden was a small nod to this very idea.

As my maternal grandparents had retired, they cooked a lot and I loved to get involved. At the end of the long hallway of their terrace house was the kitchen, and when grandad opened the front door after he picked me up from school, the first sight I'd often see was grandma leant over the stove. I was my Grandad's favourite (much to my cousin's disappointment but it's true, sorry!). He taught me how to peel vegetables and use the grater, as they were often his jobs. I just copied him because I looked up to him for everything. My little hands using a peeler on a baking potato, which felt like half the size of my head, he'd watch and simply say, 'Min' yu don't cut yuself,' in his very calm and assertive manner. It was in these moments they often shared stories from the various chapters of their lives, which quietly informed me of the layers to my existence.

Grandma and I baked together often, as she had with her mother in Montserrat – here we'd make coconut tarts, black cake for Christmas or any other special occasion and roast bake for Sunday breakfast before Church. I was amazed by how she never measured anything, yet was so consistent. For context, my great-grandmother was born in the late 1800s, as one of the last generations during abolition when the islands of the Caribbean were slowly emancipating themselves from the depths and darkness of colonialism. She couldn't read or write as this right wasn't afforded to those of African descent, so very little was ever captured on paper from their perspective. As culturally, we often shared our histories orally, everything my grandma learnt was taught through show-and-tell. All these recipes I learnt in exactly the same way – by watching and observing. The fact that by the time she passed in 1968 she couldn't read or write, shows how close we were to that time and why we were encouraged to forever 'go pick up a book and read!' I didn't enjoy reading at all, but was always encouraged to.

My way around it was reading the odd, old school cookbook lying around – those ones that were over-styled, and often featured a super shiny turkey glazed within an inch of its life. I'd read them over and over like a novel, mostly just looking at the pictures, to be honest. Every food show possible on TV, we'd watch. Not that there were many in the late 1990s and early 2000s – *Ready, Steady, Cook!*, after school before *Countdown* was a favourite because Ainsley Harriot was on and the family were excited to see a fellow Caribbean on the screen. Years later, from all the absorbing, I knew this was what I wanted to do as I couldn't imagine anything else.

My mum saying no to me in the car that Saturday morning was not because she didn't believe in me – I was always encouraged to aspire high and achieve big. Her response was because working as a chef was not

a job, never mind a career, that was understood then. She too was born in Leicester and grew up in the 1970s and 1980s, when racism was even more overt than it is today, and it was becoming clear as day that the experiences of Caribbeans in Britain was systematic and institutional. She recalled stories from school, being told, 'You can only be (blank), because you're BLACK'. So of course, such derogatory remarks informed her advice to me, whilst highlighting the importance of her teaching me about our wonderful culture and history. Being of an immigrant community (although we're actually overseas British citizens), we came here with a purpose – to work hard, earn money and create better opportunities for ourselves, with the hope of eventually returning 'back home'.

I finally made it to the Caribbean at age 11, firstly to Barbados as my uncle and his family moved back there. On my second trip at 14, I visited one of my native islands, Montserrat. Montserrat is small and you can travel its entirety in a little over an hour. Only the northern third of the island is currently occupied, as the island is still recovering from the eruptions of the Soufriere Hills volcano between 1995 and 1998. It is sad to think that I will never see my grandparents' village, as it is covered in ash.

I loved how fresh the air was and the feeling of being surrounded by so much green. You could hear the branches brush one another in the breeze and the crickets chirp at night. Driving down from Gerald's to Salem, breadfruit trees flourishing in all their glory, hung over the roadside. I'd only ever seen them in piles on a market stall before. I never knew how tall they grew, nor did I know that these were once foods imported from Polynesia as fuel, exclusively for the enslaved. Mangoes would drop off their branches before they were ripe. I felt no shame in picking them up – never would there be another opportunity for free fruit (!), yet no one did, as it was so everyday for the locals.

Going back to reconnect has truly changed my life. Trinidad, Guyana, Guadeloupe, Tobago, St. Lucia, to name a few, have all spoken to me in numerous ways. Eating food from across these islands, I realised that the Caribbean recipes I cook in the UK are no less authentic, but speak to a particular time, place and generation of Caribbean peoples. The reality of being 'British Caribbean' no longer made complete sense to me. While I was British by birth, I have always felt my Montserratian and Barbudan heritage strongly in my heart and the two couldn't be disentangled. My family's history is quintessentially Caribbean and informs my approach to this cookbook, one that embraces the fluid nature and complexity of our cuisine as well as our identity, through our collective island community.

THE CARIBBEAN COMMUNITY IN LEICESTER – SMALL BUT MIGHTY

The Caribbean community in Leicester is mostly made up of Antiguans, Barbudans, Montserratians, Bajans and Jamaicans. With a few from St. Kitts, Kitts and Nevis, Grenada, Trinidad and Guyana. It's very much a collective of 'small island people', a common comment among us, often made by those from larger islands (like Jamaica!) – a little island-to-island shade you could say. In comparison to London, the experience of the Caribbean communities that settled in other cities such as Northampton, Bristol, Preston and Nottingham, to name a few, was somewhat different. Being that they were smaller, there were specific instances that allowed us to engage with the vastness of culture that remained. Whether it was Carnival, Church, community groups or the market, forming a strong, tight community was a way of protection and self-preservation, to deflect the indignities of racism, assert oneself in society, whilst controlling as many elements of your reality. Growing up in between Humberstone, where my mum and I lived, and Highfields – where my Montserratian grandparents and Barbudan nana lived, along with much of the remaining first generation of Caribbeans, there were a few distinct spaces that curated our community: Caribbean Court – a centre and safe space for elderly Caribbean citizens in Leicester; I'd go with my grandad sometimes whilst he played (more like slammed!) dominoes with other elder island men; Leicester Caribbean Cricket Club on Ethel Road was a hub for the community who bonded over the sport – my grandad loved cricket, so we'd go on Sundays to watch sometimes; the African Caribbean Centre, a cultural hub for the community, where my Saturday Steel Pan classes and Carnival activities were held; many Caribbean takeaways; and a Caribbean Supermarket that sold almost everything you needed from plantain to saltfish. The smell of dried, smoked herrings (kippers) hit you as soon as you walked in and became synonymous. We didn't have the same access to ingredients available in London, but this was good enough. Back in the 1970s, my grandparents' generation went on organised day trips to Brixton and Ridley Road Market in London, simply to stock up on the supplies they loved from back home. One takeaway shop in particular on Evington Road called 'Roti Hut', owned by a lovely Trinidadian lady called 'Pet' is one I'll always remember. She only sold roti on Fridays. Fridays were the day I saw my dad and when he didn't cook, we'd go to the roti shop and get takeaway for dinner. I'd have a fried bake as well sometimes, my first introduction to bakes, float style. My Barbudan nana mostly made fried dumplings, so that's what I was used to – a lot denser as opposed to the light, air pocket style of a fry bake. Fast forward to my teenage years, and my best friend at secondary school, whose grandmother had migrated from Guyana just like

ABOVE Mum and me, aged 4, cooking at home, Leicester
LEFT Othella, my Barbudan Nana.
BELOW William and Eleanor, my Montserratian Grandad and Grandma.

mine, taught me to make oil roti from scratch. I was always jealous that she could just get them at home, as that wasn't within our culture. One day when I went to their house, I asked if grandma (I called her grandma too) would teach me. It was such a lovely moment to share. Most of all, I found out years later that it was actually her who made the roti in the shop I used to frequent on Friday nights, with my dad.

SO HOW DID WE GET HERE?

The mass immigration of Caribbeans during the late 1940s to early 1960s was as a result of the end of World War Two and economic conditions throughout the islands. Jobs were scarce in the region and a budding, young ambitious generation from as far north as Jamaica, all the way south to Trinidad and Tobago, were eager to explore life beyond the tropics and aspire for more.

I wondered why both sides left all they knew, in this beautiful paradise they loved so dearly, to come to the cold and grey of Britain. Unfortunately, the Caribbean was experiencing its own economic depravity at the time and it was difficult for families to make ends meet. The official end of the sugar trade during the 1800s and the fact that compensation was only made available to plantation proprietors and enslavers, *not the enslaved*, meant the now free descendent African-Caribbean community struggled to establish their own economic stability while attempting to redefine their physical freedom from under colonial powers.

Their move to Britain was fuelled by an imagined understanding of having a rightful place within the British Empire, although having never actually engaged with the 'Mother Country'. Their collective perception of this place, although somewhat romanticised, was opportunity, royalty and progression. In Montserrat, the Union Jack hung on the side of buildings and the currency at the time was 'British West Indies dollars', so as far as they were concerned, they had every right to be here even though they were born thousands of miles away.

My Barbudan nana travelled on her elder sister's ticket on a whim, whereas my Montserratian grandma, just like many others, scraped cash together from family, friends and neighbours to 'pay her passage' (in her words), later meeting my grandad who had already left a few months earlier. Both of my grandmothers left their young, firstborn children (at the time) with family members to be looked after until they could join them in the UK. This was common, as understandably they didn't know who or what they were travelling to, however, the effects this later had on family was devastating across the community. Often termed 'Barrel Children', – first coined by Dr. Claudette Crawford-Brown, an academic at UWI (University of the West Indies), these children were later sent to be reunited with parents they no longer recognised or siblings they didn't know, sadly creating further fractures within families.

My Montserratian grandma recalls her two-week journey, stopping off in Puerto Rico as well as other islands to collect passengers or offload cargo before sailing north across the Atlantic, for England. November 1956, she reached the docks of Southampton in the depths of winter, having never experienced snow or even temperatures close to freezing. Like many others, on arrival, they made their way to various cities across the country, from Leeds to Bristol, Birmingham to London, based on the connections they had or jobs available at the time. In Leicester, there was a growing need for healthcare staff and new investments were being made in industrial factories, which attracted a small community of mostly Antiguans, Barbudans, Montserratians, Bajans (Barbados) and Jamaicans. This community has remained wonderfully tight for generations.

For both sets of grandparents, England was never meant to be forever. Although they came here as rightful citizens of the Empire, the racism, discrimination and marginalisation was incomprehensible, and it was clear, no matter how hard they worked, they would never be, and still aren't, made to feel equal in British society.

On arrival, the clear cultural differences and refusal of the home nation to accept these communities as their neighbours, meant life was significantly harder than it was ever expected to be or should have been. It was quickly realised that the dreams of '... streets paved with gold ...' and the open arms of the homeland was a myth. For many, this created a sense of failure, not through any fault of their own, but because of the pressures of making it and the expectations they had for life in Britain.

These sentiments naturally informed my upbringing and still ring true today. Among many things, to succeed here in England, in life, we had to be '... twice as good to get half as far ...', a line that is often said among us. Sadly, the effects of this on our community are immeasurable and I can only wish for an existence where we get to take our foot off the gas and breathe for a moment. As such, academics were considered the way to relieve ourselves of the oppressive, systemic injustices we faced and we were always encouraged to be doctors, barristers or bankers, with the hope of achieving things our grandparents never had the opportunity to. However, it's clear that climbing the ladder of social mobility isn't the entire answer. So when I do cast my mind back, and understand what moments of our past inform our present and future, I understand my mum's reaction to me, that Saturday afternoon in the car, all those years ago.

Due to our colonial past, laborious jobs that required hands-on work were often devalued, as they didn't represent freedom. Understandably, we had developed this unfortunate association with such work, therefore creative or skilled roles like carpentry or even farming were reduced to hobbies. I am of the belief these roles are undervalued and learning such skills can set you up for life.

Cheffing and kitchen work once fell into this category of manual labour, so when considering a career for a young Caribbean girl, beyond Rusty Lee and later, Lorraine Pascale, there weren't any consistent female chefs of African or Caribbean heritage on TV. You can't be what you can't see and there were no role models or anyone my mum or I could relate to and say, 'yes, I see this for you'.

The food world has long been dominated by British (White) male chefs, food standards judged by European contexts, and the kitchen culture has been known to be toxic in misogyny, often making it an unsafe space for women – very ironic when most family recipes and household kitchens are run like clockwork by the women, with their eyes closed! As such, the thought of me becoming a chef didn't compute, and in her mind this was not realistic or aspirational.

True to my personality, I did it anyway. The very fact I'm writing this book 18 years later is a testament to our continued determination as a community and I, along with many others of my generation, continue to be the people our younger selves needed to see and aspire to. Just weeks before my Montserratian grandma passed away in 2021, she saw me on prime time BBC One, guest judging *MasterChef: The Professionals*. I never revisited that conversation in the car with her, but after seeing all that I had done, one of the last things she said to me quietly, after watching it, at the very kitchen table I have sat for years, was simply, 'Yu did good'. She wasn't the most expressive emotionally, so for her to say that to me truly meant the world.

RETENTION AS RESISTANCE

Foodways belong to people, and for my elders, food created a path to stay connected to 'back home', with much of this being instilled within me from a very young age. I witnessed this quiet but powerful connection to ingredients and its invaluable integration within our culture, which later developed my deep love for cooking. They couldn't live off the land the way they used to – pick mangoes or breadfruit from trees or bush to make fresh tea – so they did whatever they could to create a living experience that met their needs. Caribbean cooking is complex with layers and ideas, steeped in tradition from the multitude of cultures that have contributed to it, due to its colonial past. My elders' stories told to me, much of which I have now pieced together as an adult, really helped me to understand our place in the world. Even the process of this book, while heavy at times, was still fascinating to me. The way both of my grandmothers prepared saltfish was passed on by our enslaved ancestors who learnt this method to be able to eat it without being poisoned by the high levels of sodium.

Where many cultural touchstones such as language, clothing and spirituality were once forcibly removed by colonists, cooking methods had the ability to remain for a number of reasons. The enslaved were tasked with cooking for their enslavers and held great responsibilities in the kitchen. They also had to cook for themselves where they could continue the skills they had on the continent (Africa) or were introduced to by the Indigenous communities (Taino, Carib, Siboney) that remained in the Caribbean. The ground provisions (or 'hard food') (vegetables) we love and went out of our way to source, were once the only foods we were able to grow ourselves, yet we still ate them with pride. We see this shine through in many recipes; 'kankie' or 'conkie' – steamed corn in banana leaves is an evolution of 'kenkey' – fermented corn steamed in corn husks; 'mofongo de fufu' – pounded fried plantain – evolved from pounded yam; and then of course there is rice and peas or rice and beans, a dish that has endured and evolved in a multitude of ways across the Caribbean and the world. My grandparents on both sides held on to their accents until the end. They arrived here in their twenties and by the time of their passing, had lived the majority of their lives in England. The fact they wore their accents with pride exemplified resilience and resistance to me.

I loved hearing it because it was another layer of our identity that remained. It helped me to connect to who I was and I often wished I could speak dialect like them because it felt like a marker of certifying my 'Caribbeanness'. By the time I was born in the 1990s, my Barbudan nana was still breaking the bank sourcing saltfish, yam and dasheen at a premium because 'English food nuh 'av nuh taste' and my Montserratian grandparents did their best to eat the foods they loved by growing their own. It takes real determination to stay connected to your own cultural traditions when you live on a foreign land. The cultural conflicts we often experience within, are that of identity politics and intersectionality. My cousins from Barbuda would sometimes try to hide theirs in order to conform to the confines of British culture that was often unaccepting, whereas I, having been born here, wanted to adopt as much as possible to stay affiliated to 'back home'. It's this feeling of knowing you belong, as you're born here, but not being fully accepted. Equally, feeling so connected to a place that you didn't grow up in, yet so much of your identity is of that place. I guess that's what it means to be of the diaspora, but what it feels like is a little more confusing at times. If the only thing that makes me different is the brown of my complexion, why aren't I considered British?

BACK HOME

Grandad often reminisced about Montserrat and had every intention to return. He had begun building a home in Dyers during the 1970s, the village he grew up in, and every so often, he'd fly out or send money for its gradual development. This was common, as again, deep down, many of that generation wanted to return one day. Unfortunately, Hurricane Hugo in 1989 destroyed around 90 per cent of the island's infrastructure, the active Soufriere Hills Volcano (1995–97), which made 70 per cent of the island inhabitable, and his own health battles meant he never got to return and live out his own dream. Although we never had the opportunity to go together nor did he live out his last years there as planned, I had such a vivid idea of the place through his stories when I finally returned at age 14.

The landscape of Montserrat is stunning, as the beautiful peaked mountains and low valleys surround you. He told me about how he used to milk cattle and catch mountain frogs – an Indigenous amphibian which is now endangered. These animals are similar to small garden fowls (chickens), and although he enjoyed eating them, they were seen as taboo among most, as they were associated with poverty. I found Montserrat was named after it was used in 1712 as the escape route by the French when they were, once again, driven off the island by the English. The ravine on the other side of the road, where the waters connect to the sea, is called Frenchman's Creek.

Plymouth, the island's capital located on the south-west coast, is now known as 'the buried city'. Sadly, the thick layers of ash and debris that engulfed the southern side of the islands has created a modern-day ghost town. During my grandparents' youth, it was the vibrant heart of the island and the main place they'd get the best produce. Everything from sugar apples, fresh coconuts and cashew fruits could be found there, and its close proximity to the coast meant there was an abundance of fresh fish such as marlin, dorado and wahoo, caught and sold daily.

Grandma shared her fair share of stories too, often about her days baking in the village, how there was a small convenience store next door that sold essentials such as rice and sugar, and the liquor store located a little farther up which sold rum exclusively. Here people would 'lime' (hang out), play music and have impromptu dances any time, day or night. I can well imagine this as it's still very much a part of the culture now.

CARIBBEAN BRITISH – BRITISH CARIBBEAN – DIASPORA

The communities of Caribbean people dotted across the city varied based on their size, location and access to the things that help us stay connected to our culture. On our trips to London, I could see and feel the culture more so because of the larger pockets of islanders across the capital. St. Lucia, Guyana, Trinidad, Grenada and even Guadeloupe all had a presence and contributed their own, unique subculture to the city.

To me, the Trinidadian community in London meant Carnival and the numerous roti shops dotted across boroughs. Whereas in Leicester, rotis were an occasional treat, so if you missed Pet on Fridays, you missed out for the week. Ridley Road market in Dalston where my great-uncle Gerry still lives had an abundance of stalls selling plantain and breadfruit, compared to the odd one or two in Leicester market. And Tottenham had some of the best Jamaican bakeries serving fresh hard dough bread and patties – a treat from my Uncle Franklyn whenever he picked my mum and I up from St. Pancras train station before we arrived at his house.

Even writing this is somewhat cathartic, as I'm able to make a little more sense of my own inner complexities. I've made peace with the layers within my identity, one I've realised is true for many within an immigrant community; as such, I'm a Caribbean woman, born and raised in Britain – specifically in that order. I've realised personally, which also quietly motivated me to write this book in this way, how the importance of accessing food and how proximity to the ingredients we know and love contribute massively to our survival. As I mentioned before, going to the market has been a big part of my life from young and still is today. Moving to London, specifically South London, was like this full circle moment. Whenever I had to search for somewhere to live, my main point of reference would be my proximity to buy plantain. Literally, not joking. At this stage in life, I'm away from home, building my own community away from family. Just like my grandparents, I've learnt to lean on the things that bring me comfort and joy and it was those little cultural details that helped me make the capital home.

I'm very grateful to have been afforded the opportunity to explore the world from a young age and now realise how a lifetime's travel has informed this book. So far, in the Caribbean, I've visited Montserrat, Barbuda, Antigua, St. Lucia, Trinidad, Tobago, Aruba, Barbados, Dominica, Guadeloupe, Martinique, Guyana, Jamaica and Puerto Rico, many of which I embarked on before this project was even an idea. On reflection, it was these trips that planted a tiny, but substantial seed, within me. One I couldn't ignore and had to be brought to life.

Whilst every island hasn't been included (as you can imagine, there was just so much information and not enough space), I've made every attempt to reference the majority, to give a broader context to this story and represent the region in its fullness.

As an ode to the indigenous communities who are the original fabric of the region, I've included the indigenous names of each island and their meanings within the chapter openers. These names existed before they were changed by the various European nations upon colonisation.

The beauty of history is that its ties to the past forever remain, as such, these names are still well known and exist within the cultural landscape of the islands.

INGREDIENTS

The ingredients used throughout Caribbean cooking are a blend of the 'old' and 'new' worlds coexisting and a crossover of all the communities that found themselves there over the last five centuries.

RICE

Growing up, I don't think there was ever a week I didn't eat rice. It was the centre of most dishes, so much so, it was always put on the plate first before adding the other components of a meal. Rice is an old world grain in the new world. The Hausa of Northern (present day) Ghana, were one of the many communities selected by colonists specifically for their knowledge and technology of rice production, as well as the Chinese and Indian communities who later followed. Across the Atlantic, the islands with naturally occurring wetlands such as Trinidad, Guyana and Jamaica, provided the perfect environment for complex rice production, which allowed the grains to provide sustenance and become one of the first real foods to be sold and consumed across the region. As such, rice continued and remained integral within the African diaspora in the Caribbean. Whether Cuban congri (page 55), Guyanese Chinese fried rice (page 85) or Jamaican rice and peas (page 125), they're a massive part of our eating culture.

CAPSICUMS: SCOTCH BONNET, WIRI WIRI AND SEASONING PEPPERS

Capsicums are Indigenous to the Americas in all of their varieties. It was the early arrival of the Portuguese and Spanish who brought them East from the West, introducing them into African cooking and beyond. Most common are the Scotch bonnets, said to have originally grown near the surrounding lands of the Orinoco river (today's Venezuela) and brought up to Jamaica by the Tainos. Wiri wiri peppers, tiny, cherry shaped with shades of reds and orange, are exclusively found on the South American mainland and used heavily in Guyanese cooking. My favourite are seasoning peppers, also known as pimento or ají dulces (Spanish Caribbean). They're so unique in their appearance and taste because they look very similar to Scotch bonnets but have zero heat and an abundance of flavour.

CALLALOO/DASHEEN/TARO LEAVES

Callaloo is an interesting leaf for many reasons. For centuries, and still sometimes today, the term is often used (even though incorrect) to describe the wide range of green, leafy vegetables used in cooking across the Caribbean. Then there's the cooking of 'a callaloo', which involves a big pot, green leafy vegetables, coconut milk and some form of protein – whether meat or fish. It also describes the mixing of cultures in the islands, especially in Trinidad. Just like the dish, which combines different textures and flavours of ingredients before being blended with a swizzle stick, the island's food culture has done just that, taking influence from the many people who have inhabited the space and evolved it even further. In Trinidadian folklore, callaloo is widely associated with Obeah, of Igbo origin. The 1939 calypso song 'I Don't Want No More Callaloo', by Errol 'The Growler' Duke, speaks of women hiding herbal substances in the callaloo to turn it into a love potion.

PIGEON PEAS, BLACK-EYED PEAS AND KIDNEY BEANS

Peas and beans are more than a legume, they're a foundational piece of the cultural foodways across the entire Caribbean. Before being braided into hair or worn as necklaces by those who travelled the middle passage, to ensure they had some sustenance on the other side of the unknown, black-eyed peas were commonly used in cooking on the continent by the Hausa of Northern (present day) Ghana, to make waakye (rice and beans). This method was well preserved, later incorporating kidney beans and coconut for rice and peas (page 125) in Jamaica or rice and pigeon peas (gungo peas) from the Bahamas and Anguilla. Pigeon peas (gungo peas) were also brought over and thrived in the drier climates of the Eastern Caribbean islands, such as Barbuda and Barbados, of which they were used to border sugar fields. Their high yielding capabilities in Barbuda makes sense as to why they're a favourite of my nana. She grew up with them and only ever used these to cook with – in her rice or mixed in fungee (page 208). I rarely see peas sold still in their pods these days, unless at a farmers' market. It immediately reminds me of garden (allotment) days with my grandparents. Almost every year, we harvested rosseco beans, then sat at the kitchen table watching *Countdown* or *Home and Away*, shelling them, before bagging and freezing them for the winter. These, along with black-eyed peas or kidney beans, would be cooked in rice weekly. Peas and beans have been a part of our journey for centuries and we still hold them dear.

CASSAREEP

Cassareep is a thick, bitter, aniseed-like syrup made from the juice of the cassava root sometimes known as manioc. The method of processing this was passed on from the Indigenous communities who originally inhabited the regions that make up present day Guyana and is still used in cooking today, most commonly in Guyana's national dish, pepperpot (page 88).

BREADFRUIT

One of the most famous stories of breadfruit is 'mutiny on the *Bounty*'. The story of the ill-fated voyage of HMS *Bounty* is a perplexing tale of mutiny, courage and deceit. In 1769, Sir Joseph Banks and Captain James Cook sailed to Tahiti and saw the potential these plants could have in the similar climates of the Caribbean. Plantation owners saw that the fruit grew fast, was high yielding and provided 'sufficient' food and sustenance for the enslaved – their priority was profit, and nothing else. King George III commissioned the journey, which was set to be spectacular. However, under the command of Captain William Bligh, an onboard mutiny saw the hundreds of breadfruit plants collected thrown overboard, never making the journey. Bligh successfully returned to Tahiti in 1791, introducing a few different varieties of the fruit to the botanical gardens of St. Vincent and Jamaica. The French also brought plants from the East to their colonies in the West. They collected breadnuts from the Philippines (1776) and another Tongan breadfruit variety called *kele kele*, was introduced to Martinique, Guadeloupe, and Cayenne, French Guiana by the late 1790s.

SORREL

I absolutely love Sorrel – especially with a splash of rum! It's one of those ingredients that has a multitude of names that I find so fascinating – *flor de Jamaica* in Mexico and Latin America and originally, *bissap* (Congo), *Sobolo* (Ghana) and *Zobo* Nigeria. With many other ingredients, it travelled the middle passage and continued to be prepared in the same way – boiled into a sharp drink with the optional addition of spices and fresh citrus juice remains. The only difference across the Caribbean today is that drinking it has become a tradition synonymous with Christmas due to its seasonality around this time of year. Once dried it can be stored and prepared all year round.

NUTMEG

Nutmeg is my favourite spice to cook with. Before you crack open its shell, in which the nutmeg sits, the bright red veins on the outside are also a precious aromatic: mace – a key ingredient in goat water (page 227). This spice was first introduced to the island of Grenada in 1843 by the Dutch following their colonisation of the Banda islands in Indonesia. The Banda population was annexed and the Dutch began exporting crops to their colonies in the Caribbean. They found it grew well in the climate, resulting in Grenada being known as the 'spice isle.' Nutmeg is now known as 'black gold' to the locals of Grenada because it was the largest producer worldwide.

MAIZE/CORN

Maize, Indigenous to the North American mainland, is an ancient grain which has been processed for centuries by the communities who took it to the Caribbean when they populated islands, centuries prior to colonisation. Corn was dominant in their cooking, and soon after became incorporated into the foodways of the African communities. My nana always cooked fungee (also fungi or cou cou), 'tun' cornmeal (meaning to beat until smooth) with added pigeon peas. My dad told me that when he was growing up, she'd serve stewed fish often but not often enough for him and his siblings because these ingredients were expensive when they first migrated to Leicester during the 1960s and 1970s. I learnt to make it by watching my nana and asking if I could turn the pan occasionally. The irony was that later in life when I said I'd make it, even after establishing myself as a chef, she'd ask 'Yu can tun' corn?', meaning, can you successfully beat the corn until it is smooth. It was and still is, this invisible measure of your cooking skills, predetermined by how well you can make cornmeal. Always made me laugh.

PLANTAIN

Although they are part of the banana family, they are worlds apart, almost like a distant cousin. Longer, thicker and way more starchy, they can be cooked when underripe (green), ripe (yellow with a little black blistering) and overripe (with more blackness than yellow). Green plantains are the basis of mofongo (page 72) and make the best tostones (page 37) when deep fried twice (Spanish Caribbean islands) also known as 'press plantain' in Jamaica or 'banann peze' in Haiti. Once ripened, they can be baked in their skin or boiled and fried once peeled. There's also the conversation about how it is pronounced, 'plan-tain' or 'plan-tin', very much a point of contention across the diaspora, but that's for another day.

SALTFISH
When they say foodways belong to people, I couldn't agree more. Both my grandmothers showed me how to prepare saltfish just like their mothers did, just like those before them. The way we have been preparing saltfish for centuries, descends directly from cooking on plantations during the colonial period to make it safe for consumption. With its mass importation from Newfoundland in the North Atlantic throughout the seventeenth and eighteenth centuries, saltfish has become a staple in the diets of Caribbean people on the islands and across the diaspora.

ANNATTO
Annatto is the Indigenous seed of the achiote tree, originally found across the Caribbean, Central and South America. It has a clay like texture with a slightly peppery, sweet taste on its own. Before it made its way to the islands, it was used as body paint by the Mayans. Now it is used in cooking, particularly as a natural food colour in dishes such as arroz con gandules (page 64).

BANANA LEAVES
Banana plants produce beautifully large, green leaves that have been repurposed for cooking for centuries. They're used to roll alcapurrias de jueyes (page 67) into long, round shapes, and they create a great seal and parcel effect around dishes such as ducana and kankie – cornmeal steamed in banana leaves (page 200). They're also used as a surface to serve the Guyanese celebratory dish of seven curries (page 94), if the traditional water lily isn't used.

PIMENTO
Also known as allspice berries, this plant was named 'pimenta' by the Spanish, which eventually translated to 'pimento' when they mistook the plant for pepper due to its spicy aroma. Bark from the pimento tree is traditionally what the Maroons used in Jamaica to roast meat on, which we now know as jerk, (page 128). Maroons were communities who successfully escaped plantations and lived in the mountainous parts of the island. The meat would be roasted in holes in the ground then covered with shrubs to ensure the smoke from the wood didn't reveal them to the colonisers.

OKRA
Okra is fundamental to cooking in the Caribbean and another ingredient that travelled the middle passage. It is said to have originated along the fertile lands of the River Nile between Ethiopia and Sudan, before making its way west across the African continent. There are stories of those who were captured on the continent and taken to the Caribbean, hiding okra seeds in their hair and ears, resulting in okra plants appearing on plantations sometime after. It's the foundation of dishes such as guiambo (page 208) from the Dutch Caribbean island of Aruba, an evolution of Nigerian pepper soup. Instead of being served with a traditional swallow (a pounded starch such as yam, formed into a light dough and eaten with stew), fungi/cou cou (turned cornmeal) evolved, sometimes with the addition of sliced okra, which is also part of the national dish of the British Virgin Islands.

CHADON BENI/CULANTRO/THAI PARSLEY/ BHANDANIA
Chadon beni is Indigenous to parts of the Caribbean and Central America and is used heavily in cooking in Trinidad and Tobago. Its flavour is a strong, fragrant cross between spring onion and coriander. The migration of East and South Indian communities from the mid-1800s introduced a new wave of foodways to the islands, especially Trindad, Guyana and Martinique where many of them settled. My favourite use of it is as a chutney (page 302), which I've always eaten with doubles (page 101) or the curry duck recipe on (page 118). It's fresh and naturally fragrant. You can buy chadon beni in Chinese supermarkets (often labelled Thai parsley).

TAMARIND
A part of Montserrat's beauty is a consequence of its devastation. The aftermath of the Soufriere volcanic eruptions and subsequent evacuation of two thirds of the island's population has meant that much of the natural flora and fauna grows in abundance and isn't exploited or disturbed by tourism. Driving along some of the bumpy, abandoned roads away from Garibaldi Hill (the highest and closest safe point before the exclusion zone on the West) are multiple tamarind trees, with their wonderful branches pouring over the roadside. On our drive back to Woodlands, my cousin and I spotted them, pulled up the car and jumped out to pick some, only to find they weren't ready to pick. If they were, I would have made a delicious chutney ready for doubles (page 302).

HAITI

AYITI
LAND OF HIGH MOUNTAINS

There's so much about Haiti that captivates me. The way the communities from across West and Central Africa preserved much of their traditions through their food and deep spirituality, has allowed it to remain until today. The quiet murmurs of *Vodou* (voodoo) continued to be practised among the enslaved, empowering the people in many ways. The religion was led by 'hougans' (priests or doctors) but wasn't given much attention by French colonists until the success of the Haitian Revolution in 1804, when it was realised that their strong spiritual beliefs manifested the largest uprising in the Caribbean since colonialism began. As the first independent, Black state established outside of Africa, it set the precedent for the path towards emancipation throughout the region. Haiti truly represents resilience in my eyes. Even though the country still struggles with vast poverty, political unrest and the effects of continuous natural disasters, there is still so much beauty in this place that is unlike anywhere else.

Bouyi [boo-yi] in Haitian Kreyòl means 'to cook' and Haitians themselves refer to their food culture as *manjé Kreyòl* (cuisine Creole). Following the end of the Haitian revolution, the foodways started to evolve to incorporate ingredients that were once restricted or inaccessible to the people of African descent, like *joumou* (pumpkin), reclaimed as the main ingredient for the independence dish of soup joumou (see page 33). In the depths of servitude, the *'Code Noir'* – French for *'Black Code'* – was a set of regulations used across the French Caribbean from 1685 to 1789, which restricted and rationed foods that were to be provided to the enslaved.

Just like the diet of the Tainos, who first inhabited the land, Indigenous fruits such as *ananah* (pineapple) and *guayaba (*guava), as well as *batata* (sweet potato), *aji* (hot pepper), *maiz* (crops of maize), *kowosòl* (soursop), *kenèp* (guinep), and *manioc* (cassava), are grown abundantly across the island and still used within the cooking today. There are so many plants and fruits grown throughout the regions, that each season of the year boasts a vast range of local roughage.

Today, street food is the heart of Haiti's eating culture. The roads of Haiti's capital, Port-au-Prince, are lined with *marchants* (merchants) selling freshly cooked goods – morning, noon and night – with the majority of the ingredients taken straight from the abundant lands. Fresh pâté kode (see page 251) – deep fried pastries, stuffed with meat, eggs or fish, are served for breakfast with traditional Haitian coffee, roasted with sugar, then hand ground in a giant, waist high pilon, before being brewed in a *gref* – a cheesecloth shaped like a sock. The aromas are beyond anything experienced in a coffee shop. Lunch is when the cornmeal, stews, rice and beans come out. *Tchaka* [t-cha-ka] is a stew or casserole made from hominy corn (maize), beans, pumpkin, and salted cured pork. It is used as an offering to the *loa* (pronounced lwah) or deities in Haitian Vodou. Through the coalescence of African gods and goddesses and European religion – the spiritual powers of deities often manifested themselves with the imagery of Catholic saints during the depths of colonialism. As night falls, the array of *fritay* (fried food; see page 37), hits the streets for the evening.

Beyond the food, there is so much tradition that is simply a part of life. *Krik? Krak!* – the folk storytelling *(tire kont)* between generations has long been a way to preserve stories, especially when writing was once forbidden. The legacy of Haitian food has travelled far beyond the boundaries of the island. Following the end of the Haitian revolution, many of the remaining 'free Blacks' and deserted plantation owners on the island who chose not to return to France, travelled north to the closest French colony in the Americas, Louisiana. New Orleans is often described as 'the most northern Caribbean island' due to the heavy influence of Haitian culture on the food historically. Today, Haitian communities in New York and Miami's 'Little Haiti', have evolved their cuisine within their diaspora communities in wonderful ways. The first recipe in this book had to be soup joumou, because it commemorates and symbolises African liberation within the Caribbean, and Haiti's importance in this.

RIGHT Vendor lady selling green plantain chips on the road side, Roseau, Dominica.
BELOW Enjoying snow cones with a friend in Stabroek Market, Georgetown, Guyana.

SOUP JOUMOU
HAITIAN INDEPENDENCE SOUP

SERVES 4

During seventeenth- and eighteenth-century in Haiti, known then as Hispanola, under French colonial rule, the enslaved were not just forced to work in the sugar cane fields or coffee plantations, they were also craftsmen and women, responsible for skilled roles such as cleaners, ironmongers, carpenters and most importantly cooks. *Joumou* is the Haitian Kreyòl word for pumpkin, and the main ingredient of this dish. Historically, *giraumon* (turban squash), a species of pumpkin that was once grown abundantly by the Taino of Haiti, was used to make joumou. Those given the responsibility of cooking in plantation kitchens, would prepare this soup for French colonists who explicitly forbade them from eating it, as they believed it gave good fortune, which they wanted for themselves. The success of the Haitian revolution in 1804 and uprising by the enslaved was unfortunately long and violent. Upon reflection, many Haitians recalled the particular pumpkin soup that the French denied them from consuming.

It is said that when Marie-Claire Heureuse Félicité Bonheur Dessalines created the Republic of Haiti alongside her husband Jean-Jacques Dessalines, she was concerned about what people could eat to survive, no matter what happened after independence. She took soup joumou as a form of medicine but also as a message to their defeated oppressors. Every New Year's Day (January 1st), many Haitians commemorate this poignant event by eating joumou. It provides the community with a reminder of their strength and resilience when fighting for their emancipation.

Ingredients

500 g (1 lb 2 oz) skirt (flank) steak or braising (chuck) steak (or any cut that's good for stewing), cut into medium chunks

3–4 tablespoons Epis (see page 299)

4 teaspoons sea salt, plus extra as needed

1 teaspoon freshly ground black pepper

1.2 kg (2 lb 11 oz) pumpkin (such as Crown Prince, Delica or calabash), peeled and diced

30ml (1 fl oz/2 tablespoons) rapeseed (canola) or olive oil

2.2 litres (74½ fl oz/9¼ cups) good-quality beef stock

few sprigs of thyme

few garlic cloves, crushed

1 Scotch bonnet, chopped (or left whole if you prefer less heat)

1 onion, chopped

3 carrots, peeled and sliced

2–3 waxy potatoes, peeled and diced

2 small turnips, peeled and diced

150 g (5½ oz) long macaroni, broken in half (or any other small tube-shaped pasta)

200 g (7 oz) white cabbage, roughly sliced

Put the beef into a bowl and season with the epis, 2 teaspoons of the salt and pepper, rubbing it in so that the meat is well covered in the seasoning. Cover and set aside in the refrigerator to marinate for a few hours, or overnight.

The next day, remove the beef from the refrigerator. Bring a large saucepan of water to the boil and cook the pumpkin for 10–12 minutes until soft, then drain. Crush the pumpkin using a fork or potato masher to form a smooth-ish purée, then set aside.

In a separate saucepan, heat the rapeseed oil over a medium-low heat. Once the oil is warm (not smoking), add the seasoned beef and sear all over until lightly browned, turning occasionally. Next, add the stock, cover and simmer for 1½–2 hours or until the beef is tender.

Once the beef is tender, remove the pan from the heat and separate the meat from the liquid, reserving both. Pour the liquid back into the pan along with the pumpkin purée and bring to the boil. Stir occasionally to ensure the pumpkin blends into the stock. Once the soup is smooth, add the thyme, garlic, Scotch bonnet, onion and remaining salt. Cook for 5–6 minutes, then add the carrots, potatoes, turnips and pasta. Simmer over a medium-low heat for a further 10–12 minutes, or until the vegetables are tender. Finally, add the cabbage and the cooked beef for the last 5 minutes of cooking, then serve.

POUL AK NWA
CHICKEN WITH CASHEWS

SERVES 4

This recipe is a dish from the northern region of Cap-Haitien. In Haitian Kreyòl, *poul* means hen or chicken, *ak* means with and *nwa* means nut. (This type of slow cook would commonly use 'yard fowl' or 'hard chicken'. These hens are often roaming wild and are more lean, and therefore their meat is considered less flavoursome). The dish reflects regionality of ingredients on the island as cashew nuts grow abundantly in the North. Their widespread use is said to be following their discovery by the Spanish who went on to classify cashew nuts as 'food of the heart', which had special medicinal properties. For those who eat cashews as a snack rather than in cooking, it's more than likely they have been roasted, giving them a harder, dry and crunchy texture. However, this recipe would traditionally call for raw, fresh cashews, which are used straight after being picked from the trees, giving them a slightly softer but firm bite.

Ingredients

1.2 kg (2 lb 11 oz) chicken thighs and drumsticks

juice of 1 lime

6 tablespoons Epis (see page 299)

2 tablespoons sea salt, plus extra as needed

300 ml (10 fl oz/1¼ cups) water

75 ml (2½ fl oz/5 tablespoons) rapeseed (canola) or olive oil

120 g (4¼ oz) tomato purée (paste)

2 teaspoons ground cloves or 10 crushed cloves

5 garlic cloves, crushed

few sprigs of thyme

1 Scotch bonnet, finely chopped (or left whole if you prefer less heat)

1 onion, thinly sliced

2 (bell) peppers, thinly sliced

150 g (5½ oz/1 cup) raw cashews

1–2 tablespoons chopped parsley leaves

White Rice

250 g (9 oz /1¼ cups) long-grain, jasmine or basmati rice, washed

2 bay leaves

3 sprigs of thyme

1½ teaspoons sea salt

1 teaspoon golden granulated sugar

To serve

Banann Peze (see page 35)

Start by marinating the chicken. Put the meat into a bowl with the lime juice, 4 tablespoons of the epis and the salt. Rub the marinade into the meat so that it is well coated, then cover and set aside in the refrigerator to marinate for a few hours, or overnight.

When you're ready to cook, transfer the chicken to a large saucepan and add the water. Bring to the boil, then reduce to a simmer and cook over a medium heat for 30–40 minutes until cooked through and tender. Remove from the heat and separate the meat from the broth, then set both aside for later.

Next, in the same pan, heat the oil over a medium-low heat. Once the oil is warm (not hot), add the tomato purée and remaining 2 tablespoons of epis and cook out for a few minutes. Next, turn the heat to medium, add the chicken and brown in the tomato mixture until there is a little colour on the meat. Add the reserved chicken broth, cloves, garlic, thyme, Scotch bonnet and half of the onion and sweet peppers. Cover and cook for 30–35 minutes over a low heat, or until the liquid has reduced and tomato sauce has started to thicken.

Meanwhile, put the cashews into a small saucepan and just cover with water, then bring to the boil. Once boiling, remove from the heat and drain. The cashews should feel a little softer. Set aside.

To make the rice, combine all the ingredients in a saucepan, adding enough water to just cover the rice. Bring to the boil, then reduce to a simmer and cook for 25–30 minutes, or until the liquid has been absorbed and the rice is tender.

In the last 10 minutes of cooking, check the chicken and stir to make sure it hasn't stuck to the pan, then add the cashews and remaining sweet peppers and onions. Once cooked, finish with the parsley, then serve with the *banann peze* and white rice.

LEGUME
AUBERGINE, SPINACH AND TOMATO STEW

SERVES 4

Legume is a rich, thick vegetable stew made with Epis (see page 299) and a combination of aubergine (eggplant), spinach, cabbage and chayote (chou chou) to the individual's preference. It's traditionally found in restaurants, casual eating spots and Haitian households, with the recipe often passed down through generations. It can also be cooked with a variety of meats such as goat, beef or sometimes blue crab or lambi (conch) to make it extra nice.

Ingredients

60ml (2 fl oz/4 tablespoons) rapeseed (canola) or olive oil

1 onion, diced

3 garlic cloves, crushed

3 tablespoons Epis (see page 299)

300 g (10½ oz) chopped tomatoes

2 tablespoon tomato purée (paste)

2 carrots, (approx 200g/7 oz) peeled and sliced thin

1 aubergine (eggplant), (approx 300g/10½ oz), finely diced

300 g (10½ oz) white cabbage, chopped thin

200 g (7 oz) spinach leaves

500 ml (17 fl oz/generous 2 cups) vegetable stock or 500ml hot water + 2 bouillon cubes

juice of ½ lime or 1 tablespoon apple cider vinegar

2½ teaspoons sea salt, plus extra as needed

¾ teaspoon freshly ground black pepper

Banann Peze
(twice-fried green plantains/tostones)

2 green (unripe) plantains

1 litre (34 fl oz/4¼ cups) vegetable oil, for deep-frying

To serve
White Rice (see page 34)

Heat the oil in a large saucepan over a medium-high heat, then add onions and garlic. Cook for a few minutes to soften, then add epis and cook for a few more minutes. Next add the chopped tomatoes and tomato purée, reduce the heat to medium, cover and cook for 4–5 minutes.

After this time the tomatoes, epis and onions should have cooked down well into the oil. Next, add the carrots, aubergine, cabbage and spinach. Take a minute or so to stir the veg well into the tomato base, ensuring everything is thoroughly mixed.

Next add the hot water and bouillon cubes or stock, turn up the heat to bring to a low boil. Once boiling, add the lime juice or apple cider vinegar, salt and pepper then reduce to a simmer, cover and cook for 40–45 minutes or until the vegetables are soft, the spinach has wilted and the aubergines have broken down. Check the pan often throughout the cook to stir the vegetables and ensure it doesn't stick to the bottom. Once the liquid has been absorbed, remove from the heat and set aside.

For the banann peze, use a sharp knife to trim the top and bottom of the plantains, then make a shallow slit from the top to the bottom of the plantain. Using the back of the knife, peel back the skin, ensuring no fibres from the inside of the skin are left on the flesh. Slice the plantains on an angle into 8–10 slices.

Fill a saucepan two-thirds of the way full with oil and heat to 175–180°C (345–350°F). Carefully lower the plantains into the oil and deep-fry for 8–10 minutes until golden brown all over, then remove from the oil with a slotted spoon and drain on paper towels.

Place the plantains flat between two pieces of baking parchment and use something heavy, such as a tin of tomatoes, to crush them, creating a flat disc. The edges will naturally break slightly. Return the crushed plantains to the hot oil and fry for a further 3–4 minutes until crispy. Remove from the oil and drain again on paper towels.

Serve the legume with rice and banann peze.

FRITAY: TASSO BEEF & GRIOT PORK WITH PIKLIZ

FRIED MEATS WITH SPICY PICKLED CARROTS & CABBAGE

SERVES 6

The early conquest of Haiti by the Spanish was brief in comparison to that of the British and French, but still left its mark on the food. *Fritay* loosely translates to fried food in Haitian Kreyòl. This array of fried meats such as *poul fri* – fried chicken, *tasso* – beef, goat or turkey and *griot* – pork, is made throughout households and sold on roadsides across Haiti.

Tasso is beef marinated in a combination of citrus juices and fresh seasonings then deep fried. The use of lime juice was introduced to clean meat when there was a lack of freshwater on the island, and the custom has remained, maintaining the zesty freshness throughout Haitian cooking. It bears major similarities to the Spanish dish *tasajo*. Specifically in the Spanish town of Toledo, tasajo is found in hunting regions and consists of marinated deer loin, smoked over a slow fire of holm oak wood. It was introduced to the Americas following colonisation and now refers to a cut of dried beef that is usually cooked over a wood fire. In Cuba, tasajo uses dried beef.

The *Griot* or *Griyo* (Kreyòl) movement was named after and pays homage to the 'Griot', a person of high standing such as a community leader, master of ceremony or spokesperson across the cultures of Nigeria, Senegal and Burkina Faso, to name a few. With unfortunate class divides ever-present in Haiti, it is said this dish was named as such because it was once reserved for the highest-class Haitian citizens, due to the premium cuts of pork meat used.

The assimilation of certain French values in Haitian culture, for example, colourism and classism, have halted progress on the island, years after emancipation. The Griot movement in the 1930s, when Haiti was under brief occupation by America, was formed by a group of forward-thinking Haitians of the emerging 'Black middle class' to achieve Indigenism. Lorimir Denis, Louis Diaquoi and Francois Duvalier shared ideas and spoke of upholding the cultural and spiritual values of their African cultures, such as *Vodou* (*voudou/voodoo*). Over time, more and more people cooked the dish, increasing its popularity internationally following the immigration of Haitians to America.

Both tasso and griot are usually served with *banann peze* – twice fried green plantain, sometimes *patat*, slices of sweet potato and *pikliz* (see page 305). Depending on where you are in Haiti will determine what selection of meat is available, so for this recipe I've gone for the ultimate and put together a combination of the options you could find, making it perfect for sharing. If you want to add a little heat, you can try Haiti's hot sauce – *ti malice* (see page 306).

Ingredients

500 g (1 lb 2 oz) boneless pork shoulder, (or another fatty cut) diced into large chunks
1 kg (2 lb 4 oz) chicken thighs and drumsticks
500 g (1 lb 2 oz) beef chuck or flank steak, diced or bone-in goat shoulder, diced into large chunks
10 tablespoons Epis (see page 299)
juice of 2 oranges
juice of 2 limes
2 tablespoons sea salt
2 teaspoons freshly ground black pepper
4 tablespoons rapeseed (canola) or olive oil
2 spring onions (scallions), sliced
3 garlic cloves, crushed
8 cloves
6 sprigs of thyme
2 Scotch bonnets, split in half if you prefer more heat
2 litres (68 fl oz/8½ cups) good quality beef or chicken stock
1 onion, sliced into rings
1 litre (34 fl oz/4¼ cups) vegetable oil, for deep-frying

To serve

Pikliz (see page 305)
Banann Peze (see page 35)

Put the pork and chicken into a large bowl and put the goat or beef into a separate large bowl. Add half of the epis, orange juice, lime juice, salt and pepper to each bowl, then mix well to rub the seasonings into the meat. Cover and set aside in the refrigerator to marinate for at least 2 hours, or overnight.

Once marinated, heat the oil in a large saucepan over a medium heat, then fry the chicken and pork (reserving any remaining marinade) for a few minutes to brown a little. Remove the meat from the pan and set aside, then add the goat and beef (reserving any remaining marinade). Fry for a few minutes to brown, then return the chicken and pork to the pan along with the spring onions, garlic, cloves, thyme, whole Scotch bonnet, remaining marinade from both bowls and stock. Place over a medium heat and bring to the boil, then reduce to a simmer, cover and cook for 40–45 minutes. After this time, remove the chicken and pork (it should be cooked through, if not cook until tender), and continue cooking the beef or goat for a further 35–40 minutes, or until tender.

Remove the pan from the heat, then remove the meat using a slotted spoon. Place onto a tray lined with paper towels, removing any pieces of onion or thyme that may have stuck to the meat. Leave to cool and dry thoroughly to ensure all moisture has been removed from the meat.

When the meat has cooled, heat the oil in a large saucepan until 180°C (350°F). Alternatively, you can test the oil by tearing off a piece of bread and dropping it into the oil. If it sizzles straight away and gradually turns golden brown, the oil is ready. If it turns brown quickly, it is too hot. Fry the meat in small batches for 6–8 minutes or until golden brown all over. Remove from the pan using a slotted spoon or tongs and drain on paper towels.

To serve, arrange the meat in the centre of a large plate, place the banann peze around the side, then top with the onion slices. Serve the pikliz on the side.

Note

You can use any combination of the meats you prefer as long as the total amount is 2 kg (4 lb 8 oz).

DOMINICAN REPUBLIC

QUISQUEYA
MOTHER OF ALL LANDS

espite the fact it shares land with Haiti, the Dominican Republic, culturally, geographically and historically, could not be more different. Deep inland sits a small border between the towns of Jimani (Dominican Republic) and Malpasse (Haiti), separating the two nations. The historical conflict between the French and Spanish, who occupied the east and western portions of the island, have kept these two nations apart for centuries. I was hoping to make this journey by bus to experience the crossing from one state into another but, that'll be for a future trip.

Although unfamiliar with sweet potatoes, cassava and maize, when the Spanish established their first settlement of 'La Isabela' on the eastern side of their western portion of the island, they had planned to survive utilising the skills of the Taino who already had well established hunting skills and crop generation. As an act of resistance, once it was clear the Spanish were reliant on them for their food supply, the Taino refused to plant the crops they were accustomed to, protesting the Spanish invasion and hijacking of their land. The effects were devastating for the Spanish, who underestimated the Taino's knowledge of the earth around them. Even though surrounded by guava trees and avocado plants, their fear of this unknown territory, clouded by their lack of knowledge, caused their starvation.

Despite this, the plan to conquer the 'new' world continued and the Spanish arrived better prepared on subsequent trips. They packed the keels of their ships with ingredients from the 'old world' that were recognisable to them, introducing wheat, coffee, soybeans, sugar, oranges and bananas, as well as livestock – cattle, goat and chickens – changing the face of the Americas. This mass movement of species is often described as the 'Columbian Exchange', which literally changed the face of flora and fauna across the globe. Not only were ingredients exchanged, but diseases were also, decimating crops and much of the Indigenous population. This opportunity of homogeneity and crossover set the pattern for exploitation and erasure of the land, literally inserting an old world into a 'new' one.

LOS TRES GOLPES (THE THREE HITS)

FRIED DOMINICAN SALAMI, FRIED CHEESE & EGGS WITH MANGÚ

SERVES 4

Mangú is a popular breakfast item in the Dominican Republic, usually served with *los tres golpes*, the trio of fried eggs, *salchichón Dominicano* (Dominican salami) and *queso frito* (fried white cheese). The deep-fried, crushed green plantain element of this dish, termed mangú, is said to have originated from the Congolese word *mangusi*, meaning to mash. Serve this plate with some freshly brewed coffee – it is a great dish to start the day with.

Ingredients

Mangú (crushed green plantains)

2 green (unripe) plantains, peeled and cut into 6–8 pieces

pinch of sea salt

3 tablespoons salted butter

1 tablespoon rapeseed (canola) or olive oil

2–3 salamis suitable for frying, such as Induveca or salchichón, thick frankfurter or smoked sausages, sliced 2cm thick

1 × 250 g (9 oz) block of queso frier, sliced (or another frying cheese, such as halloumi)

Quick-pickled red onions

30 g (1 oz/2 tablespoons) Demerara sugar

45 ml (1½ fl oz/3 tablespoons) apple cider or white wine vinegar

45 ml (1½ fl oz/3 tablespoons) warm water

¼ teaspoon sea salt

1 red onion, sliced into thin rings

To serve

4 medium eggs, fried

Start by making the onions. Whisk together the sugar, vinegar, water and salt in a bowl until the sugar and salt have dissolved. Pour the liquid into a small pan and add the onions. Place over a high heat, bring to a low boil then reduce the heat and simmer for 3 minutes. Remove from heat and set aside to marinate for at least 30 minutes before serving.

Next, prepare the plantain. Bring a large saucepan of water to the boil and add the plantains and salt, then cook for 10–12 minutes, or until soft. Once cooked, drain, reserving some of the water. Place the plantains in a bowl and mash with the butter, adding a little of the reserved water to create a smooth mash, then set aside.

Heat the oil in a frying pan over a medium heat, then add the slices of cheese and salami and cook for a few minutes on each side, or until evenly golden brown all over. Remove from the heat and set aside.

Serve the *mangú* with the red onions on top, alongside the sausages, *queso frito* and a fried egg.

Any leftover onions can be stored in an airtight container in the refrigerator for up to 2 weeks.

KIPES/QUIPES
DOMINICAN-LEBANESE KIBBEH

MAKES 16

Towards the end of the nineteenth century, a wave of immigration from the Middle Eastern countries of Lebanon, Palestine and Syria to the Caribbean took place by those escaping economic hardship and civil unrest. As these new immigrants from the East settled on the island, they introduced their cuisine into the landscape. *Kibes* or *quipes* are the Dominican version of the Lebanese *kibbeh*, which has been a staple across Assyria – present day Palestine – Jordan, Lebanon and Syria for centuries. The word *kibbeh* evolved from the word *kabbab*, an ancient Akkadian word, meaning 'to ball up'. As a result of the migration, they are now most commonly found in the Eastern and Southern parts of the Dominican Republic, substituting beef for lamb and often omitting mint, cumin and pine nuts and instead using oregano, olives and raisins, a reflection of the ingredients found in the local landscape.

Ingredients

Outer casing

80 g/2¾ oz/scant ½ cup bulgur wheat
250 g (9 oz) lean minced (ground) beef (no more than 10 per cent fat)
2 small onions, finely chopped
2 tablespoons roughly chopped parsley leaves
2 teaspoons sea salt
1 teaspoon ground black pepper
1 tablespoon Sofrito (see page 299)
1 litre (34 fl oz/4¼ cups) vegetable oil, for deep-frying

Filling

1½ tablespoons rapeseed (canola) or olive oil
125g (4½ oz) lean minced (ground) beef (no more than 10 per cent fat)
½ onion, finely chopped
½ sweet (bell) pepper, any colour, finely chopped
1 tablespoon Sofrito (see page 299)
1 tablespoon sea salt
2 garlic cloves, crushed
3 tablespoons tomato purée (paste)
1 teaspoon dried or finely chopped fresh oregano
60 g (2 oz/⅓ cup) green olives, pitted and roughly chopped
60 g (2 oz/½ cup) raisins, roughly chopped (optional)
1 tablespoon finely chopped coriander (cilantro) or chadon beni (culantro/recao) leaves
2 teaspoons sea salt
½ teaspoon freshly ground black pepper

Start by soaking the bulgur wheat. Place it in a bowl, then pour over cold water until it is just covered. Leave to soak and absorb the water for at least 4–5 hours.

While the bulgur is soaking, prepare the filling. Heat the oil in a saucepan over a medium heat, then add the beef, onion, chopped pepper, sofrito, salt, pepper and garlic. Fry for 8–10 minutes, or until the meat is almost cooked through and the vegetables are soft, then add the tomato purée and oregano. Continue to cook for a few more minutes until well incorporated, then add the olives, raisins and chadon beni or coriander. Stir through until well combined, then set aside to cool.

Drain any excess water from the bulgur using a sieve (fine mesh strainer), then transfer to a food processor along with the beef, onion, parsley, salt, black pepper and sofrito. Blend to form a slightly coarse paste. Divide the casing mixture into 16 pieces, then take a piece and spread it flat on the palm of your hand. Spoon about 2 tablespoons of the filling into the centre. Carefully encase the filling by closing the casing around it tightly, creating a cylinder shape and pinching the ends to seal. Ensure it is totally sealed so the filling won't fall out when frying. Repeat with the remaining filling and casing mixture, placing the *kipes* on a plate or tray as you go. Transfer to the refrigerator to chill for at least 1 hour before frying.

When you're ready to fry, pour the oil into a large saucepan over a medium heat and heat to 180°C (350°F). Alternatively, you can test the oil by tearing off a piece of bread and dropping it into the oil. If it sizzles straight away and gradually turns gold brown, the oil is ready. If it turns brown quickly It is too hot. Deep-fry the *kipes* in batches for 3–4 minutes or until they are brown all over. Serve warm.

SANCOCHO
MEAT SOUP

SERVES 6

Sancocho, usually found in the Spanish Caribbean or parts of the Americas that were once under Spanish rule, is a rich meat stew or soup that has been influenced by people and time. The word loosely translates from the Spanish verb *sancochar*, which means 'to parboil' and is said to have originated from the Canary Islands. Story has it, Canarian women would leave a large pot of the stew (originally using fish) simmering away until their men returned from work, ready to enjoy a hot and fulfilling meal. Soon after, farmers and other labourers took to the idea and would cook the stew themselves. As the Spanish were amongst the earliest colonists of the Caribbean and Americas, sancocho can be found in El Salvador and Belize in Central America and Venezuela on the South American mainland. Although the meats used vary based on the country, traditionally sancocho is always cooked with other root vegetables indigenous to the region, such as cassava, squash, and corn, then served with white rice, ripe avocado and lime. In the Dominican Republic, *sancoche de siete carnes* is the island's national dish, cooked using seven meats (beef, pork, chicken, smoked ham, longaniza (a type of pork sausage) and other offal, a recipe cementing 'new' and 'old' world ingredients.

Ingredients

500 g (1 lb 2 oz) ox cheek, beef flank or chuck steak, diced into medium chunks

500 g (1 lb 2 oz) skinless chicken legs, cut into 2 or 3 pieces

500 g (1 lb 2 oz) bone-in smoked ham hock, skin removed, then cut into medium chunks

juice of 1 lime

8 tablespoons Sofrito (see page 299)

a few sprigs of oregano

a few sprigs of thyme

3 garlic cloves, crushed

1½ tablespoons sea salt, or to taste

1 teaspoon freshly ground black pepper

2 tablespoons rapeseed (canola) or olive oil

2.5 litres (84½ fl oz/10½ cups) stock

300 g (10½ oz) pumpkin or butternut squash, peeled and diced

300 g (10½ oz) yam, peeled and diced

2 green (unripe) plantains, peeled and diced

300 g (10½ oz) cassava or eddoes, peeled and diced

2 corn cobs, cut into 1 cm (½ in) slices (optional)

10 g (½ oz) coriander (cilantro) or culantro (recao/chadon beni) leaves, finely chopped

To serve

Agrio de Naranja (see page 306)

Put the beef, chicken and ham hock into a large bowl and add the lime juice, sofrito, oregano, thyme, garlic, salt and pepper. Mix well, then cover and set aside in the refrigerator to marinate for a few hours, or overnight.

Remove the meat from the refrigerator. Heat the oil in a deep saucepan over a medium heat, then add the meat and brown for a few minutes. Next, add the stock, increase the heat and bring to the boil. Once boiling, cover, reduce to a simmer and cook for 1½–2 hours, or until the meat is tender.

Add the pumpkin, yam, plantains, eddoes or cassava. Cook for a further 20–25 minutes until the vegetables are soft. As the vegetables are cooking, they will naturally thicken the soup, but if you like you can cut a few of the pumpkin pieces a little smaller to ensure they break up and thicken the liquid. Add the corn cob pieces and coriander or culantro for the last 5–10 minutes and cook until they are soft. Serve hot with the *agrio de naranja*.

SHRIMP ASOPAO
SHRIMP & RICE SOUP

SERVES 4

This shrimp rice soup or shrimp rice pottage, as it is described by some, is a Dominican and Puerto Rican classic and just delicious! Elements of the recipe are very reminiscent of paella and *arroz al ajillo* (garlic rice) – the combination of a rich broth, seafood and rice. The exact beginnings of this dish aren't quite clear, however, the word *asopao* has evolved from the Spanish word *asopado*, meaning soup-like, which suggests the dish has some Spanish origins.

Ingredients

3 tablespoons rapeseed (canola) or olive oil

1 large onion, diced

3 garlic cloves, very finely chopped

1 (bell) pepper, any colour, diced

45 g (1½ oz) Sofrito (see page 299)

20 g (¾ oz) tomato purée (paste)

100 g (3½ oz/generous ⅓ cup) passata (sieved tomatoes)

600 ml (20 fl oz/2½ cups) good-quality hot fish or shellfish stock, plus extra as needed

2 teaspoons sea salt, or to taste

200 g (7 oz/scant 1 cup) short-grain rice, rinsed in cold water and drained

225 g (8 oz) raw shell-on king prawns (jumbo shrimp), deveined and one-third roughly chopped

40 g (1½ oz/⅓ cup) frozen peas

40 g (1½ oz) carrot, peeled and diced

2 tablespoons finely chopped parsley leaves

2 tablespoons Anatto Oil (see page 307)

Maduros (Fried sweet yellow plantain)

2 yellow-black (ripe) plantains

1 litre (34 fl oz/4¼ cups) vegetable oil, for deep-frying

To serve

2 limes, cut into wedges

Maduros or Tostones (banann peze) (see page 35)

1 avocado, sliced

Heat the oil in a large saucepan over a medium heat, then add the onions, garlic, pepper and sofrito. Cook for a few minutes until the onion and peppers have softened and the onion is translucent. Next, add the tomato purée and passata. Stir until the tomatoes have cooked out a little and the oil has started to separate from the sauce. Pour in the hot fish stock and add the salt, then bring up to a vigorous simmer, but not boiling. Taste and add more salt if needed.

Next, add the rice and stir well, then bring to the boil before reducing to a low simmer. Cover and cook for 15–20 minutes, or until the rice is tender. Stir occasionally to ensure the rice doesn't stick, adding more stock if needed to keep the liquid level above the rice. Once the rice is tender, add the whole prawns, chopped prawns, peas and carrots. Continue to cook for a further 10 minutes over a low heat, or until the prawns are pink. Check the seasoning again, adding more salt to taste, then finish with the chopped parsley and anatto oil.

For the maduros, use a sharp knife to trim the top and bottom of the plantains, then make a slit from the top to the bottom of the plantain. Using the back of the knife, peel back the skin, ensuring no fibres from the inside of the skin are left on the flesh. Slice the plantains on an angle into 6–8 slices.

Fill a saucepan two-thirds of the way full with oil and heat to 175–180°C (345–350°F). Carefully lower the plantains into the oil and deep-fry for 8–10 minutes or until golden brown all over, then remove from the oil with a slotted spoon and drain on paper towels.

Serve with the lime, maduros or tostones and avocado.

CUBA

COBAO
LARGE ISLAND OR PLACE

Cuba is the largest island of the Caribbean and one of the first settled along with Haiti and the Dominican Republic (Hispaniola) by the Spanish in 1511. By 1513, the *requerimiento* (the request) had been read to the native populations, a declaration by the Spanish monarchy, written by the Council of Castile jurist Juan López de Palacios Rubios, stating their land was no longer theirs and under Spanish rule, and justified as such through Catholicism. Food and spirituality have long been integrated among the customs of West and Central African ethnicities who eventually occupied the lands of the Caribbean. As a form of survival, spiritual marronage (religious protest) became a form of resistance against the confines of Western religions and allowed some of these practices to continue. The preservation of Yoruba culture, found in parts of Benin, Togo and Nigeria, through ritual observance, was strong. The Lucimi are a community of Afro-Cubans who descended from the Yoruba people. Their connection to deities are of great importance to their existence, whom they honour through the offerings of various foods. Descending from thousands of years of cropping and pragmatic experimentation, these communities in the Caribbean knew how to work the land and understood their foods with deep meaning. African rice was first cultivated in the Niger Delta, whereas white and black fonio were mainly cultivated across Senegal, Chad, Northern Benin, Togo and Nigeria. One of the most important crops of West Africa are yams, cultivated across the belt of fertile land from the Ivory Coast, through Ghana, Togo, Nigeria, Cameroon and Benin. Once transported to the Caribbean, they repurposed the skills to utilise the plants that were available.

The Lucimi of Cuba often presented white yam, cassava, cocoyam (malanga/taro root) as offerings to the Orisha. Although cassava was Indigenous to the Americas, it had been introduced to the Bight of Benin by the early Portuguese explorers in the Caribbean and became a significant staple within the diet along with other starches.

A popular *ẹbọ* named *amalá-ailá* was considered a favourite offering to Shango, the god of thunder, when Lucimi practitioners sought help and strength from their God. The name of the dish derived from àmàlà (pounded yam) being paired with *obe ila* (okra soup. Over time, this dish has transformed, now known colloquially as *amalá con quimbombó* (yam with okra), although the yam was substituted with cornmeal, the sentiment of the offering remained.

CONGRI
WHITE RICE & BLACK BEANS WITH SMOKED PORK

SERVES 6

The term *congri* (con-gris) meaning 'with grey' in Spanish refers to the off-white, greyish colour that forms within the pot when black beans and white rice are cooked together. Sometimes this dish is referred to as *moros*, an abbreviation of *moros y cristianos* and literally translates to 'Moors and Christians'. The black beans *(frijoles negros)* represent the Muslim Moors and the white rice *(arroz blancos)* signifies the Spanish Christians.

The dish commemorates the Reconquista – a period of conflict between the Moors and Christians who eventually came to coexist in the Iberian Peninsula. In 711 AD, the Iberian Peninsula (present day Spain and Portugal) was captured by a group of North African Muslims led by the Berber general, Tariq ibn-Ziyad. They named the region al-Andalus and it flourished culturally and economically. Over time, the Muslim state began to diminish, which allowed for the Christian groups who had resented their rule for centuries, to infiltrate. In 1492, Catholic monarchs Ferdinand II and Isabella I won the Granada War, successfully conquering the Iberian Peninsula, expelling the Moors from Spain. The subsequent invasions of Cuba in 1492 and 1511 saw this dish become a part of the food culture to commemorate the conquest.

Ingredients

150g (5½ oz/generous ⅔ cup) dried black beans, soaked overnight or
2 × 400g (14 oz) tins black beans, drained

½ teaspoon bicarbonate of soda (baking soda)

3 bay leaves

2 tablespoons rapeseed (canola) or olive oil

1 tablespoon ground cumin

½ green (bell) pepper, diced

1 medium brown or white onion, diced

3–4 garlic cloves, crushed

150g (5½ oz) smoked bacon, thick cut, diced

500 g (1 lb 2 oz/2½ cups) long-grain white rice

4 teaspoons sea salt, or to taste

a few sprigs oregano, roughly chopped

15 g (½ oz) coriander (cilantro) or culantro, roughly chopped

Begin by soaking the beans. Place the beans in a medium sized pot, fill with 1.5 litres (50¾ fl oz/6⅓ cups) of water and soak overnight. Once soaked, place the pan with the soaked beans over a medium heat, bring to a boil and add the bicarbonate of soda. As the bicarbonate froths, reduce the heat slightly, then scoop off any excess foam that forms from the top of the pot.

Then, add the bay leaves, then reduce the heat further to a high simmer, cover and cook for approximately 80–90 minutes or until the beans are soft. Once the beans are cooked, they're soft and can break easily when pressed in between your fingers. Drain the beans with a sieve (fine mesh strainer), reserving the liquid for later, set both aside. If using tinned beans, skip this step.

Next, add the oil to a separate pan and place over a medium heat. Once warmed add the cumin and cook in the oil for 30 seconds to a minute or to release the aromas; ensure it doesn't burn. Next add the green pepper, onions, garlic and smoked bacon. Cook in the oil for a few minutes until the onions are soft and translucent. Add the dry rice to the pan and mix into the cumin and onions. Next add the salt, oregano and cooked beans to the rice, followed by 500 ml (17 fl oz/generous 2 cups) of liquid (made up of the remaining cooking water and water) to just cover. Mix to ensure everything is combined well, turn up the heat a little to bring the rice to a low boil, then reduce to a simmer and cover. Cook for 20–25 minutes until the liquid has been absorbed and rice is tender.

Once the liquid has absorbed, give the rice a mix to loosen the grains, remove from the heat but keep the lid on to allow the steam to finish softening the rice. Finish with the coriander.

ROPA VIEJA (OLD CLOTHES)

STEWED BEEF WITH OLIVES & PEPPERS

SERVES 6

Originating in Spain at least five hundred years ago, the national dish of Cuba is *ropa vieja*, and of course it has a story. Meaning 'old clothes', this recipe has managed to stand the test of time. The Sephardic Jews who inhabited the Iberian Peninsula of Spain between 400 CE to 1492 CE, were not allowed to cook on the Sabbath (Saturday – religious day), and as a result, the Sephardi would slow-cook a hearty stew the night before. Others say, a very poor man who had nothing to feed his family, tore up some of his old clothes, put them in a pot and prayed over them, hoping his family would eventually have something to eat. His deep faith and devotion to his family, turned his pot of clothes into a delicious beef stew. Although a beautiful story, this one is slightly less believable.

Cuba's long and complex history is intertwined with its food landscape. In 1962, the Cuban Government, under the leadership of Fidel Castro, implemented a special food-rationing system, still in existence today, which dictated the amount and kind of products each household was provisioned based on their collective age, gender, and health status. Every time families visit state-owned supermarkets, *bodegas*, they would be required to present their state-issued ration book, known as La Libreta. Rations included rice, cooking oil, bread, beans, sugar, potatoes, bananas, a few eggs and a small quantity of meat (usually chicken). Families do have the opportunity to purchase additional 'luxuries', however, a monthly salary, a minimal $20, would barely cover a special family meal.

Ingredients

1.5 kg (3 lb 5 oz) skirt (flank) steak, cut into pieces

1½ tablespoons salt, plus extra as needed

½ teaspoon freshly ground black pepper

75 ml (2½ fl oz/5 tablespoons) rapeseed (canola) or olive oil

2 tablespoons tomato purée (paste)

450 g (1 lb/generous 1¾ cups) tinned chopped tomatoes, or passata (sieved tomatoes)

2½ tablespoons ground cumin

a few sprigs of fresh oregano or 1½ tablespoons dried oregano

2½ tablespoons sweet paprika

750 ml (25 fl oz/3 cups) good-quality beef stock

4 bay leaves

8 garlic cloves, crushed

1 Scotch bonnet, finely chopped (or left whole if you prefer less heat)

2 carrots, peeled and quartered

2 celery stalks, halved

3 onions, roughly sliced

3 (bell) peppers, any colour, roughly sliced

60 g (2 oz/½ cup) pitted green olives, roughly chopped

2 tablespoons roughly chopped parsley leaves

Black Beans

150 g dried black beans, soaked overnight or 2 × 400g (14 oz) tins black beans, drained

½ teaspoon bicarbonate of soda (baking soda)

3 bay leaves

1 medium brown or white onion, diced

1 green (bell) pepper, finely diced

5–6 garlic cloves, crushed

2 tablespoons rapeseed (canola) or olive oil

1 tablespoon ground cumin

2 teaspoons sea salt, or to taste

a few sprigs of oregano

½ teaspoon bicarbonate of soda (baking soda)

To serve

White Rice (see page 34), to serve

Season the beef all over with the salt and pepper. Heat 3 tablespoons of the oil in a large saucepan over a medium–high heat and brown the meat all over. Remove the meat from the pan and set aside, then add the remaining oil, tomato purée, chopped tomatoes or passata, cumin, oregano and paprika. Cook out for a few minutes, then place the beef back in the pan, along with the stock, bay leaves, garlic, Scotch bonnet, carrots and celery. Mix well and bring to the boil, then reduce to a simmer. Cover and cook over a low heat for 3–4 hours, checking and stirring occasionally, until the meat is tender and falling apart easily. Once the meat is soft, remove it from the stew and set aside, reserving the pan liquids.

Meanwhile, make the beans. Place the beans in a medium sized pan, fill with 1.5 litres (50¾ fl oz/6⅓ cups) of water and soak overnight. Once soaked, place the pan over a medium heat, bring to a boil and add the bicarbonate of soda. As the bicarbonate froths, reduce the heat slightly, then scoop off any excess foam that forms from the top of the pot before continuing.

Next add the bay leaves, then reduce the heat to a high simmer, cover and cook for approximately 80–90 minutes or until the beans are soft. Once the beans are cooked, they're soft and can break easily when pressed in between your fingers. Drain the beans with a sieve (fine mesh strainer), reserving the liquid for later, setting both aside. If using tinned beans, skip this step.

Next, add the oil to a separate pan and place over a medium heat. Once warmed add the cumin and cook in the oil for 30 seconds to a minute or to release the aromas; ensure it doesn't burn. Next add the onions and garlic. Cook in the oil for a few minutes until the onions are soft and translucent. Next add the salt, oregano and cooked beans to the pan, followed by 500 ml (17 fl oz/generous 2 cups) of liquid (made up of the remaining cooking water and water) to just cover the beans. Mix to ensure everything is combined well, turn up the heat a little to bring the beans to a low boil, then reduce to a simmer and cover. After 25 minutes crush one-quarter of them in the pan using the back of the spoon against the side of the pan to break them up and help them thicken the sauce. Continue cooking for a further 20–25 minutes until all the liquid has reduced by approximately one-third and thickened slightly. Set aside until ready to serve.

Next, fry the onions and peppers in the remaining oil until soft, then add to the stew base.

Using two forks, roughly shred the meat and add back into the pan with the olives. Simmer for 25 minutes, then finish with the parsley and serve with the rice and beans.

CROQUETAS

CROQUETTES

MAKES 24

The exact and specific origins of this dish are not quite clear, however, we do know that Spanish *croquetas* were originally French *croquettes* before they made their way to Spain. As Cuba has historically had a strong Spanish presence since colonisation in the sixteenth century, these have remained within the foodways.

The Spanish classic *croqueta de jamón*, simply uses a béchamel base combined with jamón (ham). During times of famine and ease of accessibility to wheat flour, with the addition of potatoes or milk and cheese, croquettes became an easy way to make a dish from very little. The dish has maintained the same sentiment even in Cuba and the diaspora community in Miami, with this dish creating a great opportunity to use leftover meat or create something with little ingredients.

Ingredients

500 ml (17 fl oz/generous 2 cups) whole (full-fat) milk

⅛ teaspoon freshly grated nutmeg

¼ onion

125 g (4½ oz) salted butter

75 g (2½ oz/scant ⅔ cup) plain (all-purpose) flour, plus extra for dusting

2 teaspoons sea salt

½ teaspoon freshly ground black pepper

70 g (2½ oz) ham (see page 140), or use shop-bought), chopped into small chunks

70 g (2½ oz) mature Cheddar or Manchego, grated

2 medium eggs, beaten

100 g (3½ oz/1⅔ cups) panko or fresh white breadcrumbs

1 litre (34 fl oz/4¼ cups) vegetable oil, for greasing and deep-frying

To serve

2 limes, cut into wedges

Combine the milk, nutmeg and onion in a saucepan and bring to the boil, then remove from the heat and set aside. Melt the butter in a separate pan over a low heat, then stir in the flour gradually, mixing well to avoid any lumps. Stir continuously for 4–5 minutes, ensuring the mixture doesn't catch and burn. Next, remove the onion from the warmed milk and then add a little at a time to the flour mixture, continuously mixing until you have a smooth, white béchamel. Season with the salt and pepper. Stir the ham and cheese into the sauce, ensuring the cheese melts completely, then transfer the mixture to a shallow dish to cool. Smooth the top to create an even layer, then cover with cling film (plastic wrap) so that it touches the top of the béchamel (this will stop a skin forming). Transfer to the refrigerator to chill overnight.

The next day, remove the béchamel from the refrigerator and lightly oil your hands. Divide into approximately 24 pieces, then roll slightly in your hands to create a log shape, transferring them to a lined baking sheet as you go. Chill the balls in the refrigerator for 30–60 minutes before frying.

When you're ready to fry, put the beaten eggs into a shallow dish and the breadcrumbs into a separate shallow dish. Keeping one hand for 'dry' and one for 'wet', dip the balls in the flour then the beaten egg, then roll in the breadcrumbs, ensuring they are coated all over. Pour the oil into a deep saucepan and heat to 190°C (375°F). Alternatively, you can test the oil by tearing off a piece of bread and dropping it into the oil. If it sizzles straight away and gradually turns gold brown, the oil is ready. If it turns brown quickly it is too hot. Carefully lower a few of the croquetas into the oil and deep-fry for a few minutes until crisp and lightly golden. Remove from the oil with a slotted spoon and drain on paper towels. Continue until you have fried all the croquetas. Serve hot with the lime wedges.

Note

Make a vegetarian version by omitting the ham and adding a little extra cheese.

MEDIANOCHE
MIDNIGHT SANDWICHES

MAKES 6

Medianoche is Spanish for midnight. During the early 1900s following the Spanish-American war in 1898, it is said a particular sandwich was created and started to gain popularity in Havana cafes. As it was often eaten at night after people finished partying at nightclubs, the sandwich subsequently adopted its name. It can be found all over Cuba, varying from place to place. The fundamentals of the sandwich are very similar to the 'Cubano' (Cuban sandwich), which is more commonly known outside of Cuba within the diaspora communities that settled in Florida (Tampa, Key West and Miami) in the 1860s following the establishment of mass cigar production. The key difference between the two is the bread. Cubanos use a harder style Cuban bread made with lard, whereas medianoche uses a softer, egg-based roll called *pan suave* (Cuban sweet rolls). To make this in the most classic way, the bottom bread gets a generous slather of butter, then it's topped with yellow mustard, dill pickles, Swiss cheese and meat. The meat used is either roast pork (such as *Lechon Asado* or *Pernil*, page 64) or ham (see page 140), sliced thickly. To cook this traditionally, you'll have to place the sandwich in a pan with another pan and a brick on top to weigh it down and compress all the filling. The sandwich can be served as it is but is best served hot and melted.

Ingredients

6 medianoche, long brioche or challah rolls
3 tablespoons Dijon mustard
200 g (7 oz) Swiss cheese, such as Emmental or gruyère, thinly sliced
250 g (9 oz) gherkins (dill pickles), thinly sliced
350 g (12 oz) honey roast ham, thinly sliced (this is great with leftover Honey Ham, see page 140)
250 g (9 oz) roast pork, thinly sliced or shredded (this is great with leftover Pernil, see page 60)
6 tablespoons salted butter, at room temperature

Split the bread rolls lengthwise, then spread the mustard on both sides. Add the cheese, pickles, ham and roast pork in layers, then close the sandwich tightly, pressing the top and bottom with your hands.

Heat a heavy-based frying pan over a medium heat. Brush the bottom of the sandwiches with half the butter, then place the sandwiches into the pan in batches. Place a sheet of baking parchment over the sandwiches, then use another heavy pan on top as a weight, to press them down. Cook for about 5 minutes, then remove the pan and baking parchment and brush the tops of the sandwiches with butter, turn over in the pan and repeat. Cook until they're evenly toasted on both sides and the cheese is melted. Repeat with the remaining sandwiches.

Once cooked, cut the sandwiches in half on an angle and serve hot.

Note

If you have a sandwich or panini press you can use those to make the sandwiches, but the traditional way is to use a pan and brick.

PUERTO RICO

BORIQUÉN
LAND OF THE BRAVE LORD

Unlike that of many other Caribbean islands, Puerto Rico's colonial past is quite a straightforward one. After settlement by the Spanish in 1508, it remained under their rule until 1898, when it was ceded to the United States of America.

Stemming from the Indigenous name of the island, Boriquén, as it was called by the Tainos, Puerto Ricans often refer to their food culture as *Boriqua*. It represents the many influences that have come to form the eating culture of Puerto Rico, from the Taino and multiple African communities, to the Spanish and other cultures, such as the Lebanese, that have later followed. *Mofongo* – crushed, fried plantains with pork fat and garlic (see page 70), is a direct evolution of *fufu* cooked by communities across West Africa, using fried starches instead of boiled ones and *kippes* – bulgur wheat fritters stuffed with meat and olives, was introduced by the Lebanese and have evolved to include local ingredients. The term Boriqua is said to embody more than just nationality; it encompasses ethnicity, referencing the generations within families that have resided in Puerto Rico and continues the mélange of cultural tradition that connects Africans, Tainos and the Spanish.

When I visited Puerto Rico to research this book, there was one thing I noticed and one food I knew I couldn't leave without trying. In the souvenir shops and hand luggage of many of my queue mates at Luis Muñoz Marin International Airport security I noticed bags and bags of homegrown, local and freshly roasted Puerto Rican coffee. Since the mid-nineteenth century, while sugar was the dominant export product for most Caribbean colonies, coffee was that of Puerto Rico. Coffee plants ruled the grounds of Puerto Rico's mountainous highlands and became a primary export for markets in Spain, France, Germany, Italy and Cuba. I made sure I sourced a bag to bring home with me.

Then there was *lechon. Lechon asado* (roast pork) is an official part of Puerto Rico's gastronomic heritage. The road to the town of Cayey within Guavate is known locally as *la ruta del lechon* (the pork highway). As you drive into the mountains, lechoneras – open air, rustic eateries, specialising in whole roasted pork, are dotted along Route 184. The Tainos, who once inhabited Puerto Rico and other parts of the Caribbean before Spanish invasion, used to slow roast meat over open fire – *barbecoa* – subsequently introducing the term 'barbecue' to the world. Upon one of the early expeditions to the Caribbean, it is said the Spanish brought with them pigs to ensure they had access to food when they returned, introducing pork into the food landscape which would later become an integral part of Puerto Rico's food landscape, lechon.

PERNIL
ROASTED PORK

SERVES 6–8

Pernil is a variation of lechon. Lechon is said to have been introduced to the Caribbean following the Spanish rule over the Philippines during the sixteenth and nineteenth centuries. Filipinos had their own style of roasting pork long before the arrival of the Spanish, however, the name derives from the Spanish word *leche*, meaning 'to milk', referring to the young suckling pigs that were used. As the dish gained popularity, fully grown pigs were used but the name remained.

In Puerto Rico, as well as Cuba and the Dominican Republic, there are key fundamentals to make lechon. First is the adobo. Adobo derives from the Spanish word *adobar*, meaning to 'marinate'. Prehistorically, vinegar was commonly used to preserve and store meat before refrigeration existed. Although many communities have done this in their own way for centuries, spaces where the Spanish colonised have subsequently adopted the term. Every lechonera has their own recipe, but the key ingredients include oregano, garlic, salt, pepper, annatto, and sometimes ají dulces, very similar to pimento or seasoning peppers, to which they are known on other islands in the region.

It's not usually possible to roast a whole pig at home, so instead people use a whole shoulder. This home-style version is called *pernil* by Puerto Rican families, who serve it for Christmas. It is very similar to lechon; however, it refers to the version cooked in the oven, rather than the whole pig cooked over coals. There are an abundance of sides it can be served with, such as, *guineos en escabeche* (pickled green bananas), *morcilla* (blood sausage), *maduros* (see page 48), *tostones* (see page 35), *tamales* as well as the *arroz con gandules* (rice with pigeon peas) and boiled yuca (cassava) with pickled red onions.

Ingredients

1 garlic bulb, cloves crushed
2½ teaspoons sea salt
2 tablespoons extra virgin olive oil
1½ teaspoons freshly ground black pepper
a few sprigs of fresh oregano, leaves picked, or 1½ teaspoons dried oregano
150ml (5 fl oz/scant ⅔ cup) sour orange juice (or juice of 2 oranges (120ml/4 fl oz/1½ cups) and 1 lime (30ml/1 fl oz/2 tablespoons)
4 kg (8 lb 13 oz) bone-in pork shoulder

Arroz con Gandules

150 g (5½ oz/generous ⅔ cup) dried pigeon (gungo) peas, soaked overnight in 1 litre (34 fl oz/4¼ cups) water (or 1 × 400 g/14 oz tin)
3 tablespoons Annatto Oil (see page 307)
1 tablespoon ground cumin
120 g (4¼ oz) smoked ham, pork or bacon lardons, cubed
2 tablespoons tomato purée (paste)
60 g (2 oz) Sofrito (see page 299)
500 g (1 lb 2 oz/2½ cups) long-grain rice, washed
2 bay leaves
2 teaspoons sea salt

Combine the garlic, salt, oil, black pepper, oregano and orange juice in a food processor or pestle and mortar and blend to a paste. Carefully partly detach the rind from the fat of the pork to create a gap that can be repositioned (you can ask your butcher to do this), then poke holes into the pork using the tip of a knife. This will allow the marinade to penetrate deep into the meat. Pour the marinade all over the pork and underneath the flap and rub in well. Place the pork into a baking dish, cover and set aside in the refrigerator to marinate for at least 2 hours, or overnight.

When you're ready to cook, preheat the oven to 160°C fan (350°F).

Remove the pork from the refrigerator about 30 minutes before roasting to allow it to come to room temperature.

Cover the pork loosely with foil, then roast in the oven for 2½–3 hours until the meat is tender and falling away from the bone. Check occasionally to make sure the liquid in the baking dish doesn't completely evaporate – add a little water if it does.

While the meat is cooking, prepare the rice. Pour the pigeon peas and their soaking water into a saucepan and bring to the boil, then reduce to a simmer, cover and cook for 60–70 minutes or until the peas are soft. Drain the peas and reserve the cooking water, adding extra water to the pea cooking water to make up to 600ml (20 fl oz/2½ cups), then set aside. Return the pan to the heat and add the annatto oil, cumin, ham or bacon, tomato purée and sofrito and cook out for a few minutes. Next, add the rice and stir to coat in the mixture. Add the drained peas and mix well, then add the pea cooking water. Top up with extra water if needed so that it just covers the peas and rice. Add the bay leaves and salt, bring to the boil, then reduce to a simmer, cover and cook for 30–40 minutes, or until the liquid has been absorbed and the rice is tender.

Once the meat is cooked, increase the oven temperature to 220°C fan (475°F) and remove the foil. Cook for a further 30–40 minutes until the skin is crispy. Serve hot with the rice.

ALCAPURRIAS DE JUEYES
CRAB-STUFFED FRITTERS

MAKES 6–8

Alcapurrias are sometimes described as deep fried *pasteles*, which are found across the Caribbean and central America in many different variations. The masa (outer casing) is mostly made from green bananas, eddoes or cocoyam (taro), but sometimes other ground provisions, blended raw, then seasoned with lard or oil and annatto for colour and spice. Their fillings are wonderfully varied, being stuffed with everything from minced beef, chicken, fish, even conch, before being deep-fried. You'll find them freshly prepared by the beach or on the roadsides in Puerto Rico.

Ingredients

Dough
300 g (10½ oz) taro root (cocoyam)

180 g (6¼ oz) green (unripe) bananas (about 2 bananas)

1–2 banana leaves, depending on size (optional; see method)

1½ tablespoons sea salt

2 tablespoons Annatto Oil (see page 307), plus extra for greasing

½ tablespoon cassava flour (optional)

lemon juice, for soaking the taro and bananas

Filling
1 tablespoon Annatto Oil (see page 307)

2 tablespoons Sofrito (see page 299)

10 g (½ oz) drained capers (baby capers), chopped

1 teaspoon sea salt

100 g (3½ oz) white crabmeat

1 tablespoon finely chopped parsley leaves

1 litre (34 fl oz/4¼ cups) vegetable oil, for deep-frying

Hot Pepper Sauce (see page 305), to serve

Start by preparing the dough. Fill a large bowl with water and add a squeeze of lemon juice. Peel and chop the taro and green bananas, then place in the lemon water to stop them oxidising.

Cut the banana leaves (if using) or baking parchment into 2–3, 10 cm (4 in) squares.

Drain the taro and bananas well, then transfer to a food processor. Depending on the size of your food processor, you may need to do this in batches. Pulse the vegetables until they are the consistency of a rough pulp, then season with the salt. Next, pour in the annatto oil and blend until smooth. The colour will change to a dark yellow. Add the cassava flour to the taro and banana pulp if it feels too wet and pulse again, as this helps to stabilise the dough, making it easier to shape. Remove the dough from the food processor, transfer to a bowl, cover with cling film (plastic wrap) and chill in the refrigerator for 1–2 hours.

While the dough is chilling, make the filling. Heat the annatto oil in a frying pan over a medium heat and add the sofrito and capers. Cook for a few minutes until the mixture is mostly dry, then season with the salt. Add the crabmeat and parsley, then cook for a further few minutes. Remove from the heat and allow to cool.

To assemble, brush a square of banana leaf or baking parchment with a little annatto oil, then add 2–3 tablespoons of the dough and spread it out, leaving a 1 cm (½ in) border around the edges. Next, place 2–3 tablespoons of the crab filling into the centre of the dough. Use the banana leaf or paper to help shape the fritter: fold one side over to create a semi-circle, then press the edges to seal. Continue with the remaining dough and filling, transferring the fritters to the refrigerator to rest as you go. Once finished, allow the fritters to chill for at least 1 hour.

When you're ready to fry, pour the vegetable oil into a deep saucepan and heat to 180°C (350°F). Alternatively, you can test the oil by tearing off a piece of bread and dropping it into the oil. If it sizzles straight away and gradually turns gold brown, the oil is ready. If it turns brown quickly it is too hot. Remove the fritters from the refrigerator and carefully lower a few into the oil. Deep-fry for 6–8 minutes, or until brown all over, turning occasionally. Remove from the oil with a slotted spoon and drain on paper towels. Leave to cool a little before you eat them as they are very hot. Serve with hot sauce.

MOFONGO
CRUSHED FRIED PLANTAIN

SERVES 4

Puerto Rican culture is a true hybrid of culture and is why I love the name of this dish. We can see it's rooted in the fabric of West African cooking as the term *fufu* originates from Twi (language of the Akan in present day Ghana) meaning 'to mash or mix' and describes the pounded starch (often plantain, cocoyam or cassava), which is then served alongside a stew. Before the Portuguese introduced cassava to communities across West African coasts, mostly plantain and cocoyam were used. Not only that, the word *mofongo* is said to be a direct evolution of the Angolan term *mfwenge-mfwenge*, meaning 'a large amount of something'. The technique for *mofongo fufu de plantain* (or *fufu de plátano* in Cuba) is the same as fufu would be made across West Africa, crushing and kneading starch-based vegetables, then adding fat or liquid to moisten and form into a round shape. In Puerto Rico, mofongo is traditionally served in a pilon – a wooden-style pestle and mortar with *ensalada de pulpo* (octopus salad; page 69) but can also be plated with the stew on the side such as *camarones guisados* (stewed shrimp; page 69).

Ingredients

1 litre (34 fl oz/4¼ cups) vegetable oil, for deep-frying, plus extra for greasing

300 g (10½ oz) pork skin, cut into 2 × 3 cm (1¼ x 1¼ in) pieces

4 green (unripe) plantains, peeled and sliced into 2–3 cm (¾–1¼ in) thick pieces

12 garlic cloves, crushed

120 g (4¼ oz) lard, cubed

2 teaspoons sea salt, or to taste

Pour the oil into a deep saucepan and heat to 190°C (375°F). Alternatively, you can test the oil by tearing off a piece of bread and dropping it into the oil. If it sizzles straight away and gradually turns gold brown, the oil is ready. If it turns brown quickly it is too hot. Add the pork skin and deep-fry for 6–7 minutes, or until the skin is crispy and golden brown. Remove from the oil using a slotted spoon, then drain on paper towels.

Next, prepare the plantains. Reheat the oil to 175°C (350°F). Add the plantain slices and fry for 6–7 minutes, or until they are slightly browned all over, then remove from the pan and drain on paper towels.

Next, prepare the garlic. Place the garlic and lard into a small saucepan over a low heat. Slowly cook the garlic in the lard for 2–3 minutes, ensuring it doesn't burn. Once the garlic has softened, remove the pan from the heat and set aside. Don't let it get too cool as it will solidify again. If it does, return to the heat briefly to melt.

Now make the *mofongo*. You may need to do this in batches depending on the size of your pestle and mortar. Place a quarter of the lard and garlic mix and quarter of the fried pork skins into a mortar with ½ teaspoon salt and crush to form a rough paste. Now add a quarter of the fried green plantains and pound further until you have a well blended mash. You may have a few crispy chunks of pork left, but that's fine. It is ready when the consistency is thick and dense and the *mofongo* forms a ball. Turn out into a small bowl greased with a little vegetable oil. Pack tightly to shape, then turn out. You should have a half sphere/mound shape. Continue until you have used all the garlic, pork skin and plantains, then serve.

CAMARONES GUISADOS
STEWED PRAWNS

SERVES 4

Camarones guisados is shrimp stewed in a creole style sauce with tomato, sofrito and seafood stock. It goes great with mofongo or can be served with white rice, tostones and avocado.

Ingredients

360 g (12½ oz) raw shelled king prawns (jumbo shrimp)
60 g (2 oz) Sofrito (see page 299)
3 teaspoons sea salt, or to taste
2 tablespoons olive or rapeseed (canola) oil
2 onions, finely chopped
1 (bell) pepper, any colour, finely chopped
4 garlic cloves, crushed
40 g (1½ oz) tomato purée (paste)
200 g (7 oz/generous ¾ cup) passata
300 ml (10 fl oz/1¼ cups) fish or shellfish stock
1 teaspoon Demarara sugar

To serve

Mofongo (see page 64) or White Rice (see page 34)

Put the prawns into a bowl with half of the sofrito and 2 teaspoons of the salt. Mix well, then set aside to marinate.

Next, heat the olive oil in a large saucepan over a medium–high heat, then add the onions, chopped pepper and garlic. Cook for 5–6 minutes until soft, then add the tomato purée and passata. Cook out for a few minutes, then add the stock and remaining sofrito, salt and sugar and cover and simmer for 15 minutes to reduce slightly. Finally, add the prawns and mix well to ensure they are submerged in the sauce. Cook for a further 8–10 minutes, or until the prawns are pink and opaque. Serve hot with the mofongo or white rice.

ENSALADA DE PULPO
OCTOPUS SALAD

SERVES 4

This octopus salad is so easy to make. The fresher the seafood the better, it can be made in advance and is perfect for sharing.

Ingredients

1 large red onion, halved and then half finely chopped
2 garlic cloves
3 bay leaves
1 teaspoon black peppercorns
2 teaspoons sea salt
1.5 kg (3 lb 6 oz) raw octopus, cleaned
1 sweet (bell) pepper, any colour, finely chopped
80 g (2¾ oz/⅔ cup) pitted green olives, sliced
2 tomatoes, seeds removed, then finely chopped
2 tablespoons finely chopped coriander (cilantro) or culantro (recao/chadon beni) leaves

Dressing

juice of 1 lime
90 ml (3 fl oz/⅓ cup) extra virgin olive oil
2 tablespoons apple cider or white wine vinegar
2 teaspoons sea salt, plus extra as needed

Bring a large saucepan of water to the boil and add the half red onion, garlic cloves, bay leaves and peppercorns. Dip the octopus in the water a few times using tongs, then fully submerge it in the water and cook over a low heat for about 1 hour, or until tender and with a little bounce to it.

Once tender, drain the octopus (reserving the garlic cloves) and set aside to cool. Once cool, dice the octopus into small pieces and set aside.

Next, prepare the dressing. Crush the reserved cooked garlic in a large bowl until it is mostly smooth, then add the lime juice, olive oil, vinegar and salt and whisk together. Add the octopus, the remaining chopped red onion, peppers, green olives, tomatoes and coriander. Toss the salad with the dressing, then leave to marinate for a few hours before serving.

GUYANA

GUIANA
LAND OF WATER

L and locked in between Suriname (formerly Dutch Guiana), Venezuela and Brazil on the South American mainland, a formation of three regions – Demerara, Berbice and Essequibo – Guyana is the home of pepperpot and cassareep. Although not an island, its shared colonial past along with neighbouring Suriname and French Guiana, has formally cemented the region as part of the wider Caribbean community. I always wondered how Demerara sugar gained its name, only to later learn Demerara is a river on the eastern side of Guyana, rising through the adjoining water networks of the central Amazon rainforests, running all the way north until it meets the Atlantic Ocean. These subtleties that still exist in our current realities, quickly connect us to the undertones of the colonial past.

Across the rich soils, just off the edge of these riverbanks, once sat sugar cane plantations set up by the Dutch, who were experts at developing smart irrigation systems to create functional earth from swampy wetland. Settling around the prime lands of the riverbeds for the best access to fertile soil, fresh fish and travel routes, was long practised by the Akawois, Warrous, Macushis, Wapishanas, Arecunas, Patamonas and Wai Wais, some of the many Indigenous groups who originally occupied the lands. They propagated native ingredients such as maize, brazil nuts and cassava – processing it by drying, grinding and roasting into a grain or flour, as well as creating a juice from the pulp making a thick, sticky, syrup out of the root, called cassareep.

The lengthy Dutch reign was briefly interrupted by French occupancy between 1782–1784, until the Dutch ceded to the British in 1803. By the early 1800s, the tone on sugar slavery was shifting, the Haitian revolution was in full effect and abolishment region-wide was near. Although enslavement in its current form had been abolished, an illegal intercolonial trade was developing at an exponential rate. As the lands of their current colonies, such as Barbados, Jamaica and Antigua, became more depleted, they set their sights on less 'developed' and rich, fertile lands of Trinidad and Guyana. Plantation owners were leaving the colonies as their insurance payouts covered their losses or they sought new lands to continue their enterprises. To prevent the old labour system from collapsing, a new one was curated. Indentured labour was not that much different from chattel slavery in terms of its conditions, however, those who worked were promised a piece of land or settlement at the end of their work period. In 1835, the first Portuguese labourers arrived in British Guiana from Madeira and later the Azores, Cape Verde and Sephardic Jews. Although these migrants were fleeing religious persecution and their own socio-economic challenges, the British wanted to increase the number of Europeans within the region, as they had been outnumbered for centuries by the African communities.

The first Chinese, all men, arrived in British Guiana on January 12, 1853 on board the *Glentanner* vessel, followed by 1838, when the first ship carrying East Indian indentured labourers arrived in Guyana. Since Guyana gained independence from Britain in 1966, the Chinese and East Indian communities made up large amounts of the population respectively, evolving the culture and cuisine beautifully. As such, the many cultures that have graced Guyana with their presence, are officially recognised within the six races – African, East Indian, Chinese, Amerindian, Portuguese and European and their corresponding foods – kankie (see page 198), dhal puri (roti; see page 237), fried rice (see page 83), pepperpot (see page 88) and pine tart (see page 266) –give a snapshot to all of the peoples that have made contributions to the land.

ABOVE Snow cones in Stabroek Market, Georgetown, Guyana.

Snow cones are a quintessential part of street food culture in the Caribbean; whilst the names may differ throughout the islands, the fundamentals are the same. Traditionally, vendors would cart out an enormous block of ice, slowly chipping away throughout the day using a metal hand scraper. The delicate flakes of ice shavings would be piled into a sheet of newspaper or plastic then covered with some form of sugar syrup. Nowadays the old newspaper has been replaced with plastic cups but the taste and experience is the same nonetheless.

DHAL

Lentils and pulses have a long deep history with India. Having been cultivated across the continent since the earliest civilisations inhabited there, the abundance of varieties such as masoor, chana, toor and moong, are unique in their appearance and subsequent preparation. During the journey across the Atlantic, (sometimes referred to as the *Kala Pani* – the belief within Hinduism that one loses their social respectability after crossing waters to foreign lands), migrants ate limited supplies of rice, dhal, dried fish, potatoes and onions. These rations, along with a few plant cuttings and seeds, often packed in a *jahaji* bundle (a piece of cloth often attached to a stick to carry prized possessions) continued on plantations for the early immigrants, which informed how existing foodways would evolve in the Caribbean. While only a few dhal varieties successfully popularised themselves in the islands, the key fundamentals of the cooking methods remained. When preparing dhal, the split peas are pressure cooked with turmeric, salt and maybe a little garlic, then are crushed or blended until smooth (traditionally using a swizzle stick). The next key historic technique is 'chunkaying' – the heating of the oil to toast extra spices and aromatics is crucial to the dish but varies from region to region. North Indian communities commonly use geera (cumin) seeds, green chillies and garlic, whereas South Indians use dry red chilli, mustard seeds, garlic and curry leaves. The tempered spices are poured over the hot dhal to create a silky, spiced emulsion on top. This technique is crucial and adds an extra aroma from the spices used, plus a silky, smooth, spiced texture that's created when the oil mixes with the dhal.

Ingredients

90 ml (3 fl oz/⅓ cup) olive oil
1 teaspoon ground turmeric
½ teaspoon ground cumin
1 teaspoon garam masala
1 small onion, finely chopped
4 garlic cloves, 2 crushed and 2 sliced
300 g (10½ oz/1⅓ cups) yellow split peas or yellow lentils
1 medium tomato, finely chopped
1.2 litres (40 fl oz/5 cups) water
1 Scotch bonnet or 2 wiri wiri peppers (split in half if you prefer more heat)
2 teaspoons sea salt, or to taste
1 tablespoon cumin seeds

First, toast the spices. Heat 3 tablespoons of the oil in a saucepan over a medium–high heat, then add the turmeric, ground cumin and garam masala. Cook for 30 seconds to release the aromas, then add the onion and crushed garlic. Cook for a few minutes until the onions have started to soften and the spices are clinging to the onion. Next, add the split peas and tomatoes stirring well into the spices and onion in the pan.

Pour over the water and add the Scotch bonnet or wiri wiri peppers and salt, then bring to the boil. Reduce to a low boil/ vigorous simmer, cover loosely and cook for 45–50 minutes, or until the split peas are tender and break easily when pressed in between your fingers. Remove the dhal from the heat and discard the Scotch bonnet or wiri wiri peppers, then blend until smooth using a hand-held blender or in a heatproof jug blender. Return the dhal to the pan and cook for a further 5–10 minutes, then remove from the heat.

Finally, chunkay the dhal. In a separate pan, heat the remaining oil over a medium-high heat. Once hot, carefully add the sliced garlic and cumin seeds – they will pop and splutter once they touch the oil, so be careful. Toast for about 1 minute, or until the majority of the cumin seeds and garlic have turned a slightly darker brown. Pour the hot oil and cumin seeds over the dhal. It will sizzle, so again be careful of any spitting. Serve immediately.

BUNJAL CURRY PRAWNS

SERVES 4

Bhunjal or *Bounjal* is described as a 'dry curry' that sears onto the vegetables or protein after most of the aromatics have evaporated in the pot. This style is contrary to common curry methods we know, where the ingredients are steeped in a sauce, often slow-cooked to absorb all of their aromas. The term *bunjal* is said to have evolved from the Bengali word *bhuna*, meaning to dry roast spices before adding moisture. 'Bounjaying' involves using the cuts of meat or fish made smaller as there is little moisture added. It will cook low and slow in its own juices until the remaining moisture has evaporated and residual aromatics have turned into a dried paste. Green (unripened) mango is also used in this recipe, giving a wonderful sourness and acidity to the dish, which works especially well with the fish. Any meat, fish or poultry can be 'bhunjaled', however, white belly shrimp is a popular choice in Guyana. This crustacean is a small variety that populates the nutrient-rich, muddy waters of Guyana's coastline, drained from the Amazon River. They come into season annually for a few months of the year, however, you can use any prawns (shrimp) you have access to. Serve with dhal (see page 77) and rice.

Ingredients

juice of 1 lime

50 ml (1¾ fl oz/3½ tablespoons) rapeseed (canola) or vegetable oil

3–4 curry leaves

1 Scotch bonnet or 2 wiri wiri peppers, seeds removed for less heat

1 tablespoon tamarind paste

2 tomatoes, diced

½ green (unripe) mango, skin left on, sliced into medium strips

60 ml (2 fl oz/¼ cup) water

1½ teaspoons sea salt, or to taste

2 spring onions (scallions)

Curry Paste

½ onion

3 garlic cloves

½ Scotch bonnet or 1 wiri wiri pepper

60 ml (2 fl oz/¼ cup) water

1 tablespoon Caribbean curry powder, such as Chief or Betapac

2 teaspoons amchar or garam masala

½ teaspoon cumin seeds

2 teaspoons tomato purée (paste)

To serve

White Rice (see page 34)

Dhal (see page 77)

Put the prawns into a bowl, cover with cold water and add the lime juice, then set aside.

Next, prepare the curry paste. Put the onion, whole garlic cloves, Scotch bonnet or wiri wiri pepper and water into a food processor or pestle and mortar and blend to a purée. Add the curry powder, amchar or garam masala, cumin seeds and tomato purée and blend again until combined, then set aside.

Heat the oil in a saucepan over a medium heat, then add the curry leaves – they will react with the oil a little. Fry briefly, ensuring they don't burn, then add the curry paste. Cook out the curry paste for a few minutes, again ensuring it doesn't burn. Next, add the tamarind, tomatoes, green mango and water and cook for about 10 minutes until reduced a little, stirring occasionally to ensure it doesn't stick and burn. Finally, drain the prawns and add to the curry. Cook for a further 5–8 minutes until the prawns are cooked through and coated in the spices and the curry is dry. Serve with the rice and dhal.

EGG BALL

MAKES 6

The clock tower bearing the words Stabroek Market (named after the president of the Dutch West India Company) stands tall in the centre of the hustle and bustle of Georgetown, still holding its original Dutch name. Just off the 'seawall' (a concrete wall separating Guyana's coastline and the Atlantic ocean), the market sells everything from plantain chips with or without mango sour (see page 307) to fresh coconuts, fresh sorrel flowers and wiri wiri peppers. A little walk farther down the seawall, away from the market, are a few snackettes (small roadside stalls) selling egg balls and cassava balls. A hard-boiled egg fills the centre, which is encased by a lightly seasoned, crushed cassava casing before being deep-fried. The use of cassava in Guyana and the wider Caribbean islands is said to have been originally cultivated by groups such as the Makushi, an Indigenous peoples of the Caribs, who still occupy the lands between the Branco and Rupununi rivers that border South Guyana and North Brazil and Guyana.

Ingredients

7 medium eggs, plus 1 egg, separated
400 g (14 oz) cassava, peeled and roughly chopped
200 g (7 oz) floury potatoes, peeled and roughly chopped
2 teaspoons sea salt, or to taste
2 garlic cloves, crushed
1 Scotch bonnet, finely chopped (deseeded if you prefer less heat)
2 spring onions (scallions), finely chopped
2 tablespoons salted butter, softened to room temperature
1 litre (34 fl oz/4¼ cups) vegetable oil, for greasing and deep-frying
200 g (7 oz/1⅔ cups) plain (all-purpose) flour

To serve

Mango Sour (see page 307)

Note

To make cassava balls, simply follow the recipe but omit the eggs. If you can't get fresh cassava, you can use potato and make potato balls instead.

Start by preparing the eggs. Place the whole eggs in a saucepan of cold water over a medium heat and cook for 8 minutes, then remove from the heat and cover the eggs in cold water to cool them down. Once cooled, remove the shells and set the eggs aside.

Next, prepare the cassava and potatoes. Bring a large saucepan of water to the boil, then add the cassava, potatoes and half the salt. Cook for 15–18 minutes, or until the vegetables are soft, then drain and set aside.

Meanwhile, combine the garlic, Scotch bonnet and spring onion in a blender or pestle and mortar and blend or crush to a paste. Scrape the onion paste into a large bowl and add the cooked cassava and potato. Mash with a fork, potato masher or ricer until smooth, then mix in the egg yolk, the butter and remaining salt and set aside to cool completely.

Once cooled, divide the cassava mixture into six portions. Rub a little oil on the palm of your hand, then take a portion of the cassava mixture and flatten it on your palm. Place one of the boiled eggs in the centre and then gently encase the egg with the cassava, forming a ball. Smooth the outside to ensure there are no cracks and the egg is fully covered. Repeat with the remaining cassava mixture and eggs, then place the egg balls in the refrigerator to chill before frying.

When you're ready to fry, pour the oil into a deep saucepan and heat to 175°C (350°F). Alternatively, you can test the oil by tearing off a piece of bread and dropping it into the oil. If it sizzles straight away and gradually turns gold brown, the oil is ready. If it turns brown quickly, it is too hot. Put the egg white into a bowl and the flour into another bowl. Dip each egg ball into the egg white and then into the flour, then carefully lower into the oil. Fry the egg balls in batches for 5–6 minutes until golden brown all over. Remove from the oil with a slotted spoon and drain on paper towels, then serve with the mango sour.

GUYANESE–CHINESE CHOW MEIN

SERVES 4

Chow mein literally translates to fried *(chow)* and noodles *(mein)* in Mandarin. The dish was curated by the people of Taishan in Guangdong near the Pearl River Delta, of which the community later found their lives in Guyana. The cooking of chow mein in Guyana can be attributed to the availability of ingredients that could survive the months-long journey from East to West. Soy sauce, dried noodles and a few spices were among the first and the later addition of cassareep and local fresh seasonings were added as the dish became more integrated into society.

Ingredients

400 g (14 oz) chicken thigh fillets, sliced

1 tablespoon cornflour (cornstarch)

1 teaspoon sea salt

2 tablespoons water

3 tablespoons vegetable oil

3 garlic cloves, crushed

1 Scotch bonnet, finely chopped
(deseeded if you prefer less heat; optional)

1 small onion, thinly sliced

3 spring onions (scallions), sliced into
4 cm (1½ in) pieces and green and white
parts separated

250 g (9 oz) dried egg noodles

1 pak choi (bok choy), thinly sliced

120 g (4¼ oz/1½ cups) beansprouts

2 teaspoons toasted sesame oil

Sauce

1 tablespoon light soy sauce

1 tablespoon dark soy sauce

1 tablespoon oyster sauce or mushroom
vegetarian stir-fry sauce

1 tablespoon cassareep

2 teaspoons raw cane sugar or
golden granulated sugar

Put the chicken into a bowl along with cornflour, salt and water. Mix well until sticky, then set aside.

Next, combine all the ingredients for the sauce in a bowl, stir well, then set aside.

Heat a wok or large frying pan until very hot, then add 1 tablespoon of the vegetable oil. Once hot, carefully add the chicken and fry for 8–10 minutes or until it is lightly browned all over and not sticking together. Remove from the pan and set aside. Add another tablespoon of oil to the wok, then add the garlic, Scotch bonnet, onion and white part of the spring onions and stir-fry for 1 minute. Remove from the pan and set aside. Next, add the remaining tablespoon of oil to the pan, then add the noodles. Stir-fry gently to ensure they are coated in the oil and warmed through but don't break up. Add the pak choi and beansprouts and stir-fry for a further 2 minutes. Finally, add the chicken, the cooked onion mix, the green parts of the spring onions and the sauce. Toss in the pan and mix well until everything is coated in the sauce and hot throughout. Finish with the sesame oil, then serve immediately.

Note

Feel free to add extra vegetables if you wish, such as cabbage or carrots, and substitute the chicken for tofu for a plant-based alternative.

GUYANESE–CHINESE FRIED CHICKEN & RED PORK WITH FRIED RICE

SERVES 4–6

'They say' some of the best Chinese food on the planet can be found in Trinidad or Guyana because of the cultural crossover that has taken place in the cooking. I can agree to this. As with many dishes that have evolved through their migration, this Guyanese fried chicken is a hybridisation and representation of the Chinese that settled in Guyana. By order of the British, 14,000 Chinese arrived in British Guiana between 1853 and 1879 from Hong Kong to fill the labour shortage on the sugar plantations following the abolition of slavery. Many of these communities came from the Guangdong province, introducing predominantly Cantonese foods into the culture.

It wasn't until the twentieth century, when migration hit its peak and trading became more advanced, that specific ingredients were able to be transported such distances. Rice, in particular, was not readily available during the early settlement of Chinese communities in the Caribbean. It was first mentioned in the 1895–96 *Blue Book* – British Guiana's government publication that noted the increase in rice production simultaneous with its establishment of the British Guiana Rice company. All of which was spearheaded by the Chinese and Indian communities who knew how to cultivate it. The growth of rice during this time can directly be linked with labour, skill, knowledge and demand for supply from these communities. Fried rice continued to be an easy way to utilise day-old rice and make a meal out of minimal ingredients. It originated in Yangzhou in the eastern Jiangsu province of China during the sixth century. Although a favourite of Emperor Yang of the Sui Dynasty, poorer communities also gravitated to the dish during times of economic inequality, and it remained within the foodways. In both of these dishes, the soy combined with cassareep and sugar give the dish its rich, sweet yet salty, tender flavour, representing the layers of Guyanese culture.

Ingredients

Red pork

2 tablespoons light soy sauce
2 tablespoons dark soy sauce
2 tablespoons Shaoxing rice wine
1 tablespoon oyster sauce
1 tablespoon toasted sesame oil
1 garlic clove, very finely chopped or grated
1 tablespoon finely grated fresh ginger root
½ teaspoon Chinese five spice
2 chunks of fermented bean curd plus 1 tablespoon of liquid from the jar
3–4 drops of red food colouring (optional)
2 tablespoons Demerara sugar
½ teaspoon ground white pepper
1 kg (2 lb 4 oz) boneless pork shoulder, sliced into thick lengths (or another fatty cut)

First, marinate the pork. Combine all the ingredients except the pork in a large bowl. Mix well, crushing the chunks of bean curd until smooth. Remove half the marinade and set aside, then add the pork pieces to the bowl and rub in the marinade, ensuring it is well covered. Cover and set aside in the refrigerator to marinate overnight.

When you're ready to cook the pork, preheat the oven to 190°C fan (400°F).

Place the pork pieces onto a grill tray (or a wire rack set over a baking tray (pan)), reserving any leftover marinade, then roast in the oven for 10–12 minutes. Add the water and honey to the remaining marinade for basting.

Remove the pork from the oven, turn the pieces over and brush with the remaining marinade, then return to the oven to roast for a further 10–12 minutes. Repeat this process three more times until the pork is cooked through and evenly coloured. Remove them from the oven and set aside to rest. Once rested, thinly slice the pork into short pieces.

Ingredients

Basting the pork

1 tablespoon clear honey	
1 tablespoon water	

Chicken

750 ml (25 fl oz/3 cups) water	
200 ml (7 fl oz/scant 1 cup) light soy sauce	
20 g (¾oz) fresh ginger root, sliced	
3 garlic cloves	
1 tablespoon pink peppercorns	
3 star anise	
4 tablespoons rice wine	
4 tablespoons Demerara sugar	
1 tablespoon sea salt	
2 spring onions (scallions)	
1 kg (2 lb 4 oz) chicken legs	
1 litre (34 fl oz/4¼ cups) vegetable oil, for deep-frying	

Fried Rice

250 g (9 oz/1¼ cups) jasmine rice, washed	
350 ml (12 fl oz/1½ cups) water	
1 teaspoon sea salt	
2 tablespoons rapeseed (canola) or olive oil	
50 g (1¾ oz) green beans, chopped	
50 g (1¾ oz) carrots, diced	
50 g (1¾ oz) white cabbage, shredded	
2 garlic cloves, crushed	
5 g (¼ oz) fresh ginger root, finely grated	
2 teaspoons toasted sesame oil	
2 tablespoons light soy sauce	
2 teaspoons Demerara or raw cane sugar (or whatever you have)	
2 teaspoons cassareep	
4 spring onions (scallions), sliced	

To serve

sliced cucumber	
shredded carrots	
shredded cabbage	
Hot Pepper Sauce (see page 305)	

For the chicken, begin by brining the chicken legs. Combine all the ingredients except the chicken and oil in a large bowl. Mix well until evenly incorporated, then add the chicken legs and submerge them in the liquid. Cover the bowl with cling film (plastic wrap) or transfer to an airtight container and set aside in the refrigerator to brine overnight.

To poach the chicken. Pour the chicken and all the brining ingredients into a large saucepan. Bring to the boil, then reduce to a simmer and cook for 25–30 minutes until the chicken is tender and mostly cooked. Remove the chicken from the pan and set aside to dry.

Once dry, fry the chicken. Pour the vegetable oil into a deep saucepan and heat to 160–170°C (320–340°F). Alternatively, you can test the oil by tearing off a piece of the bread and dropping it into the oil. If it sizzles straight away and gradually turns gold brown, the oil is ready. Carefully lower the chicken legs into the oil one or two at a time, depending on the size of your pan. Deep-fry for 10–12 minutes, or until golden brown all over. Once cooked, carefully remove from the pan and place on a wire rack or paper towels to drain. Repeat with the remaining chicken. Once all the legs are cooked and rested, slice the legs between the thigh and drumstick, then again to cut the thigh in half.

To make the fried rice, put the rice, water and salt into a saucepan. Bring to the boil, then cover and simmer for 10–12 minutes or until the rice has absorbed all the liquid. Once the water has been absorbed, remove the pan from the heat and keep covered to allow the steam to continue cooking the rice for a further 10 minutes, then remove from the heat and set aside.

Heat the oil in a large frying pan over a medium heat, then add the green beans, carrots, cabbage, garlic, and ginger and stir-fry for a few minutes, then add the cooled rice. Keep stirring to combine well with the vegetables, then add the sesame oil, light soy sauce, sugar and cassareep. Stir in well and continue to cook for a few more minutes until the vegetables are cooked but still have a little crunch. Finish with the sliced spring onions.

Serve the chicken and pork with the fried rice and a side of sliced cucumber, shredded carrots, shredded cabbage and hot pepper sauce.

PEPPERPOT

STEWED GOAT, SALTED PORK & COW HEEL WITH CASSAREEP & BROWN SUGAR

SERVES 4

Pepperpot is the national dish of Guyana and a traditional Christmas recipe that has been a part of the culture for decades. Although the exact origins of the dish aren't quite clear, the discovery of its key ingredient, cassareep, is attributed to the Arawaks – one of the Indigenous peoples of Guyana. Similarly to pepperpot, *tuma* is an Indigenous recipe cooked mostly by people of the Lokono nation, utilising the 'cassava water' – a broth that forms when boiling cassava to make cassareep. Cassareep is the reduced liquid extracted from the bitter root of cassava. Initially, it was said to have been discarded from the grated cassava prepared to make cassava flour. After being left in the sun, the white, floury liquid, turned into a dark brown lacquer with amazing preservative properties, and later came to be used in cooking. This process of producing cassareep still takes place in Guyana today. To ensure it is no longer poisonous, the liquid is boiled over coal fire, to remove the natural toxins, then clove, cinnamon and salt are added to enhance the flavour. Traditionally, this is served with plait bread (see page 241), or any bread you have.

Ingredients

800g (1 lb 12 oz) goat shoulder, bone-in, diced

300 g (10½ oz) cow heel (foot), cut into medium chunks

400 g (14 oz) pigs' tails, cut into medium chunks

1 tablespoon sea salt, or to taste

2 teaspoons freshly ground black pepper

2 tablespoons rapeseed (canola) or olive oil

180 g (6¼ oz/scant 1 cup) dark brown soft sugar or molasses

250 ml (8 fl oz/1 cup) cassareep

1.2 litre (40 fl oz/5 cups) water

2 Scotch bonnets or wiri wiri peppers, left whole (use 1 if you prefer less heat)

a few sprigs of thyme

2 small onions, halved

4 garlic cloves

4 cinnamon sticks

8 cloves

peel of 2 oranges

To serve

Plait Bread (see page 241)

Note

The quantity of meat doesn't have to be exact, so don't worry if it is a little over or under, just aim for 1.5 kg (3 lb 5 oz) in total. Try to ensure the pieces of meat are around the same size so they cook evenly.

Place the meat in a pan with cold water over a medium–high heat and bring to a boil. As the pan comes up to the boil, scoop off any scum that comes to the surface from the meat. Continue to boil for a further 5–6 minutes, then drain, discard the water and set the meat aside. Next, add the oil to the pan over a medium-high heat. Once hot but not smoking, carefully add the sugar or molasses. Try to ensure the sugar is flat in the pan not piled up, then allow it to cook in the oil and bubble into a caramel, this will take a few minutes. The heat needs to be high but if the heat is too high the sugar will burn too quickly. Once the sugar is caramelised, add the meat and brown in the sugar for a minute or so. Next, add the cassareep, water, scotch bonnets, thyme, onions, garlic, cinnamon sticks, cloves, orange peel, salt and pepper. Bring the pan up to a boil, giving a mix occasionally to ensure it isn't sticking to the bottom. Once boiling and bubbling, reduce the heat to a high simmer/low boil, cover and cook for 1 hour 50 minutes–2 hours or until the meat is tender and has liquid has reduced by one-third. Serve hot with plait bread.

PHOLOURIE
YELLOW SPLIT PEA FRITTERS

MAKES 30

The concept of *ahimsa* within Hinduism, means non-violence and compassion towards all beings. As a result, vegetarianism is common among worshippers, and meals are often prepared meat free. Subsequently, the Indian communities introduced an abundance of dishes to the Caribbean islands that were naturally plant-based – *pholourie* being one of them. Very similar to pakora, which are eaten throughout the Indian subcontinent, pholourie are soft, chewy, and savoury. These fluffy balls of deliciousness are made from a simple split pea batter before being deep-fried. In Trinidad, they're then steeped in a sweet, tamarind chutney (see page 300) or in Guyana, served alongside mango sour (see page 307).

Ingredients

5 g (¼ oz) fast-action dried yeast
1 teaspoon golden granulated sugar
250 ml (8 fl oz/1 cup) lukewarm water
100 g (3½ oz/⅔ cup) split pea or gram (chickpea/garbanzo) flour
200 g (7 oz/1⅔ cups) plain (all-purpose) flour
1½ teaspoons baking powder (baking soda)
½ teaspoon ground turmeric (optional, for colour)
2 teaspoons ground cumin
2 teaspoons sea salt
1½ tablespoons rapeseed (canola) or olive oil
2 tablespoons Green Seasoning (see page 299)
1 litre (34 fl oz/4¼ cups) vegetable oil, for deep-frying

To serve

Mango Sour (see page 305) or Tamarind Chutney (see page 300), **to serve**

Put the yeast and sugar into a bowl and add half the water, then mix and set aside in a warm place for 10–15 minutes to allow the yeast to activate.

Meanwhile, combine both the flours, the baking powder, turmeric (if using), cumin and salt in a large bowl.

Once the yeast mixture starts to bubble and froth, it is ready. Add the wet mixture to the flour mixture along with the remaining water, the oil and the green seasoning. Mix well to form a wet, sticky batter, cover with cling film (plastic wrap), then set aside to prove at room temperature for 30–60 minutes until doubled in size.

Pour the oil into a deep saucepan and heat to 180°C (350°F). Alternatively, you can test the oil by tearing off a piece of bread and dropping it into the oil. If it sizzles straight away and gradually turns gold brown, the oil is ready. If it turns brown quickly, it is too hot. Carefully drop spoonfuls of the batter into the oil, ensuring they don't touch each other, otherwise they will stick together. Fry for a few minutes until golden brown all over, turning often to ensure they cook evenly. Drain on paper towels. Continue until you have fried all the pholourie. Serve Guyanese style, with mango sour, or Trinidadian style, with chadon beni chutney.

Note

Traditionally, pholourie are dropped into the oil using your hands. For this method, rub a little oil on your hands, then scoop some of the batter into your palm and create a fist. With your thumb and index finger facing upwards, relax and contract your fist to allow drops of the pholourie batter to squeeze out of the bottom of your hand carefully into the oil. This recipe makes at least 30 pholourie depending on size.

SEVEN CURRIES

DIWALI CELEBRATORY MEAL OF SEVEN CURRIES

SERVES 6

Indian heritage has become an integral part of the culture across the region. May 30th and May 5th in Trinidad and Guyana, respectively, celebrate Indian Arrival Day to commemorate those who came from the East during the early 1800s. Diwali – the festival of light, known as Deepavali in Guyana and a national holiday in Trinidad – is the second largest festival in the country after Carnival. For the Hindu communities specifically from South India, seven curries have become the most important ritual food to be eaten at any religious or social function. The seven curries consist of *pumpkin talkari* (pumpkin cooked with cumin), *catahar* (curried breadnut), *baigan* and eddoes (aubergine and eddoes), *chana aloo* (curried potatoes and chickpeas), *mango achar* (curried green mango), *dhal* (split peas), *bhajee* (spinach), sometimes fried snacks such as *baiganee* (aubergine fried in chickpea batter) or *bara* (a fritter of split pea flour) and *bhajee* (spinach), all served with *paratha* (oil roti) and rice on a wonderfully green water lily or banana leaf, then finished with sweets such as *parsad*.

Ingredients

Pumpkin Talkari

1 tablespoon rapeseed (canola) or olive oil

2 teaspoons ground cumin

500 g (1 lb 2 oz) pumpkin, peeled and diced into medium chunks

1 small onion, finely chopped

2 garlic cloves, crushed

½ Scotch bonnet, deseeded and finely chopped

1 tablespoon Green Seasoning (see page 299)

2 teaspoons sea salt

Baigan and Eddoes Curry

6 garlic cloves

1 Scotch bonnet (deseeded if you prefer less heat)

3 tablespoons Caribbean curry powder, such as Chief or Betapac

2 tablespoons amchar or garam masala

1½ tablespoons tomato purée (paste; optional)

450 ml (15¼ fl oz/scant 2 cups) water

4 tablespoons rapeseed (canola) or olive oil

1 tablespoon cumin seeds

1 small onion, roughly chopped

2 spring onions (scallions), roughly chopped

1 tablespoon sea salt

3 tablespoons Green Seasoning (see page 299) or finely chopped chadon beni (culantro/recao) or coriander (cilantro) leaves

600 g (1 lb 5 oz) aubergine (eggplant), partly peeled and cut into small chunks

1 tomato, chopped

500 g (1 lb 2 oz) eddoes, peeled and diced into medium chunks

To make the pumpkin talkari, combine the oil and cumin seeds in a large saucepan. Heat slowly over a medium-high heat to toast the seeds. Once they start to pop and release their aroma, add the pumpkin, onion, garlic and Scotch bonnet. Stir to fry briefly in the oil, then add the green seasoning and salt. Reduce the heat a little and keep stirring for a few minutes to allow the pumpkin to release its own juices. Add 300ml (10 fl oz/1¼ cups) water, turn up the heat to medium–high and bring up to a low boil. Once bubbling, reduce the heat again to medium, cover and cook for 25–30 minutes or until the pumpkin is mostly soft, stirring occasionally. A few chunks for texture is fine, it shouldn't be like a purée.

To make the *baigan* and eddoes curry, crush the garlic and chilli in a pestle and mortar or blender. Transfer to a bowl, then add the curry powder, amchar or garam masala, tomato purée (if using) and 90 ml (3 fl oz/⅓ cup) of the water to create a curry paste, then set aside.

Heat the oil in a large frying pan or saucepan over a medium heat, then add the cumin seeds to toast for 1 minute. Add the onion and spring onions and cook for a further minute, then add the curry paste. Stir and cook out the curry paste for 3–4 minutes, or until the spices are fragrant and it starts to dry out a little. Next, add half the remaining water, the salt and the green seasoning, chadon beni or coriander and stir into the curry base. Cover and cook for 10–12 minutes until the oil has separated and it has thickened. Add the aubergines and mix well into the curry base, then cover again and cook for a further 10–12 minutes, stirring occasionally. Finally, stir in the tomato and eddoes and add the remaining water, then cover again and cook for a further 15–20 minutes, or until the eddoes are cooked and the aubergine is soft and cooked down.

Aloo and Channa Curry

150 g (5½ oz/generous ⅔ cup) dried chickpeas (garbanzos), soaked overnight in 1.5 litres (50¾ fl oz/6⅓ cups) of water (or 2 × 400 g/14 oz tins)

½ teaspoon bicarbonate of soda (baking soda)

3 tablespoons rapeseed (canola) or olive oil

4 teaspoons Caribbean curry powder, such as Chief or Betapac

1 teaspoon ground cumin

½ tablespoon amchar or garam masala

800 ml (27 fl oz/3⅓ cups) water

2 tablespoons Green Seasoning (see page 299)

2 garlic cloves, crushed

1 tablespoon sea salt

1 Scotch bonnet, split in half

400 g (14 oz) all-rounder potato, such as Desiree, peeled and diced into medium chunks

Bhajee

3 tablespoons rapeseed (canola) or olive oil

400 g (14 oz) spinach leaves or callaloo, chopped

4 garlic cloves, crushed

1 small onion, finely chopped

1 Scotch bonnet, deseeded and finely chopped

1½ teaspoons sea salt

75 ml (2½ fl oz/5 tablespoons) coconut milk

75 ml (2½ fl oz/5 tablespoons) water

Steamed Rice

200 g (7 oz/1 cup) basmati or jasmine rice

300 ml (10 fl oz/1¼ cups) water

½ teaspoon sea salt

1 teaspoon rapeseed (canola) or olive oil

To serve

Dhal (see page 77)

Curry Mango/Mango Talkari (see page 302)

Paratha/Buss Up Shot (see page 238)

For the aloo and channa curry, place the soaked chickpeas and their water into a large pan and place over a high heat. Once boiling, add the bicarbonate of soda then reduce the heat to medium–high. The water will froth on the surface initially, throughout the cooking you can scoop this off from the surface as the chickpea skins start to break down. Cover and cook the chickpeas for 50 minutes–1 hour or until the chickpeas are soft and can break easily in between your fingers if pressed together. If using tinned chickpeas skip this step.

Next, heat the oil in a large saucepan over a medium heat, then add the curry powder, cumin and amchar or garam masala. Cook in the oil for a minute or so to release the aromas, then add half the water, the green seasoning, garlic, salt and Scotch bonnet. Increase the heat slightly, cover and bring to a low boil for 5–6 minutes. Next, add the chickpeas and the remaining water and continue to cook for a further 15 minutes. Finally, add the potatoes, reduce the heat to medium, cover and cook for a further 15 minutes. After 20 minutes, the potatoes should have mostly softened. Using a large spoon, crush about a third of the potatoes against the side of the pan so that they break up and thicken the curry. Cover the pan again and continue to cook for a further 10 minutes, or until the remaining potatoes are soft.

To make the bhajee, heat the oil in a saucepan over a medium heat, then add the spinach, garlic, onion and Scotch bonnet. Cook for a few minutes, then add the salt, coconut milk and water. Cover the pan and simmer for 15–20 minutes until the liquid has evaporated and the spinach has completely softened, stirring occasionally to ensure it doesn't stick to the pan.

Finally, make the rice. Put the rice, water, salt and oil into a saucepan. Bring to the boil, then cover and simmer for 10–12 minutes or until the rice has absorbed all the liquid. Once the water has been absorbed, remove the pan from the heat and keep covered to allow the steam to continue cooking the rice for a further 10 minutes.

To serve, place a spoonful of the rice in the centre of a plate, water lily or banana leaf. Create a small well in the centre of the rice and pour in a few spoonfuls of the dhal, then add a spoonful of each of the curries around the edge. Serve with the mango talkari and paratha and eat with your hands.

TRINIDAD & TOBAGO

KAIRI
LAND OF THE HUMMINGBIRD

TOBAGO
TOBACCO PIPE

arnival is very dear to me. From a young age I have been making *mas* (costumes) and jumping (dancing) on 'de road' (as we say). It's a safe space that has always allowed me the freedom of expression, especially growing up within the hostilities of Britain – and as a part of the diaspora that allowed me to connect with my culture in such a special way. Notting Hill, Leicester, Leeds and Bristol carnivals, to name but a few, would not be what they are if it wasn't for the young Caribbean men and women, mostly from Trinidad and Tobago, who introduced Carnival celebrations to the cities they settled in the UK during the 1950s and 1960s (Windrush), who are now pioneers of the Carnival community.

The southernmost twin-island nation of the Lesser Antilles, sitting seven miles off the northern coast of Venezuela, is Trinidad and Tobago. The lands of Carnival, calypso and roti could be said to be the most ethnically diverse islands in the Caribbean. The islands changed hands multiple times between the Spanish, Dutch and French, transplanting crops of tobacco, indigo and sugar for their economic enterprises. The presence of the French on the islands is integral to the development of Carnival. In 1783, the French Christians introduced their Lenten traditions of dinners, balls and masquerade to the islands. Although they shared the same soil, the Afro-Trinidadian enslaved were excluded from all of these celebrations and could only watch with curiosity. The islands were seized by the British in 1797, but the Lenten traditions remained within the fabric of the island's culture.

When Emancipation was formalised in 1834, the symbolic significance of these traditions began to shift and the core essence of Carnival was born. The Afro-Trinidadians, now free, mimicked the elaborate dress and colour of the French, having observed them for decades, throughout the streets. This event in colonial history was termed *canboulay* – evolving from the French term *cannes brûlée* meaning 'burnt cane'. This ritual was common at the end of a plantation harvest to reset the soil and clear unwanted crops. Following abolition, canboulay commonly took place the night before the white elites began their Lenten festivities, purely as a symbol of defiance and ritual commemorating their new-found freedom. With the island now under British rule, and their long-held, uninformed belief that people of African origin were unruly, barbaric and problematic, they began to suppress the annual emancipation celebrations by the free Afro-Trinidadians, placing a ban on masquerading and all African percussion instruments. This led to the Canboulay Riots of 1881, ironically, further solidifying the cultural importance of Carnival across the Caribbean and diaspora to this day.

The transitional chapter between the French and British, simultaneous with the abolition period during the early 1800s, created a labour insecurity for the colonial forces. Although the Emancipation Act of 1834 formally made the enslavement illegal, it did not end immediately, with a clause in the act that stipulated an additional four years of labour by those already on plantations, officially making them free in 1838.

It was during this time the callaloo culture of the twin islands really took form. A new migration of immigrants from the East and beyond shifted the cultural landscape of Trinidad significantly. Between 1834 and 1836, Portuguese migrant labourers and religious refugees from Madeira arrived in Trinidad, eventually dominating the baking and winemaking trades at the time and the century that followed. The communities from China, India and Syria arrived in 1806, 1845 and 1904 respectively. The food scene of Trinidad is so unique and reflects the blend of these communities sharing the same space. The introduction of spices, rice production and dishes such as doubles (see page 99), roti (in all its forms) and gyros, to name a few, are a testament to these people and make the food culture of Trinidad and Tobago truly unique.

ABOVE Palm tree in Trinidad.

DOUBLES

BARAS TOPPED WITH CHICKPEAS & CHUTNEYS

MAKES 12–16

Doubles are wholeheartedly a part of the food landscape of Trinidad and Tobago and loved by all. They were invented in the late 1930s-early 1940s, but by whom is a slight point of contention between Mr. Deen and Mr Ali as both claim the initial idea was theirs. Either way, they are said to have evolved from *chole bhature* and *poori* (chickpeas with fried Indian bread), most popular in the Northern regions of India, then introduced by the communities who arrived in the late 1800s. Doubles' vendors are dotted across the island, setting up at the crack of dawn ready to serve the community until early afternoon – just as the sun reaches its peak. These roadside snacks are, simply, two pieces of *bara* (a yeasted, deep-fried dough), overlapped on a piece of food paper, then ladened with chickpeas and an array of chutneys, from chadon beni to roasted coconut. The freestyling of spoonful after spoonful seems endless when you're waiting patiently by 'de doubles man' for your turn to be served. It almost seems impossible to fit so much in such a small snack, yet, it's done with such precision. Both sides of the paper are flipped and sealed with a twist of the paper then dropped swiftly into a paper bag. The only thing you need to consider when ordering is whether you want yours to be slight, medium or hot with pepper!

Ingredients

Baras

360 g (12½ oz/scant 3 cups) plain (all-purpose) flour
¾ teaspoon baking powder
¼ teaspoon ground turmeric (optional)
3 g (⅛ oz) fast-action dried yeast
1½ teaspoons salt
1 tablespoon golden granulated sugar
250 ml (8 fl oz/1 cup) lukewarm water
6 tablespoons vegetable oil, plus 1 litre (34 fl oz/4¼ cups) for deep-frying

Begin by making the *baras*. Combine the flour, baking powder, turmeric (if using), yeast, salt and sugar in a large bowl, then add the water and lightly mix to form a very soft, slightly sticky dough. Pour over 1 tablespoon of the oil and rub over the top so that it doesn't dry out as it rises. Cover with cling film (plastic wrap) and set aside to prove in a warm place for 2 hours, or until doubled in size. Once risen, add a generous amount of the oil to your fingers, then divide the dough into 12–16 equal-sized pieces and lightly form into balls. Drizzle the remaining oil onto a plate or cutting board, then lightly press out the dough balls on it until they are very thin (about 2 mm/⅛ in thick).

Pour the vegetable oil into a deep saucepan and heat to 200°C (400°F). Carefully lower one of the baras into the oil and cook for a few seconds on each side until golden brown. Immediately remove from the oil using tongs, then place in a container lined with paper towels and cover with a lid to allow it to steam a little. Continue until you have fried all the baras.

Ingredients

Channa Filling

150 g (5½ oz/generous ⅔ cup) dried chickpeas (garbanzos), soaked overnight in 1.5 litres (50¾ fl oz/6⅓ cups) of water (or 2 × 400 g/14 oz tins)

30g (1 oz) yellow split peas or yellow lentils

½ teaspoon bicarbonate of soda (baking soda)

1 tablespoon oil

2–3 garlic cloves, crushed

2 teaspoons ground cumin

2 teaspoons amchar masala

300ml (10 fl oz/1¼ cups) water

1 tablespoon Green Seasoning (see page 299)

2 teaspoons sea salt, or to taste

1 Scotch bonnet, deseeded and finely chopped, or seasoning pepper (pimento/ají dulce), finely chopped

To serve

Cucumber Chutney (see page 301), Chadon Beni Chutney (see page 300), Coconut Chutney (see page 301) or Hot Pepper Sauce (see page 305)

For the channa, place the soaked chickpeas and their water into a large pan and place over a high heat. Once boiling, add the bicarbonate of soda then reduce the heat to medium-high. The water will froth on the surface initially, throughout the cooking you can scoop this off from the surface as the chickpea skins start to break down. Cover and cook the chickpeas for 50 minutes–60 minutes or until the chickpeas are soft and can break easily in between your fingers if pressed together. If using tinned chickpeas skip this step.

Next, heat the oil in a pan and add the garlic, cumin and amchar masala. Cook for a minute to toast the spices, then add the water, chickpeas, split peas, green seasoning, salt and seasoning pepper or Scotch bonnet. Bring to the boil, then reduce to a simmer, cover and cook for 15 minutes. After this time, use a spoon to crush some of the chickpeas, then cook for a further 15 minutes until the crushed chickpeas have thickened the sauce. Place two baras on a plate or sheet of baking parchment overlapping each other, add two–three spoonfuls of the channa, then finish with the toppings of your choice.

TRINI-CHINESE WONTONS & WONTON SOUP

MAKES 32–36 WONTONS

Wontons can be traced back to China's Qing Dynasty 1644. They were a dish reserved for the working classes, however, as the economy grew following the end of their reign in 1840, the taste for wontons spread. Wontons and wonton soup were introduced to Trinidad by the poorer Chinese communities that travelled there, but not straight away. Although the communities existed from the early 1800s, it wasn't until the mid-1900s when migration from China peaked, bringing more ingredients ashore. Now you can find these at Chinese takeaways across the island.

Ingredients

Wontons

200 g (7 oz) raw shelled prawns (shrimp), deveined

125 g (4½ oz) minced (ground) pork

3 garlic cloves, crushed

10 g (½ oz) or 2 thumb-sized pieces fresh ginger root, finely grated

3 spring onions (scallions), finely chopped

a few chives, finely chopped

1 tablespoon toasted sesame oil

1 tablespoon light soy sauce

5 g (⅛ oz) chadon beni (culantro/recao) or coriander (cilantro) leaves, roughly chopped

1 teaspoon sea salt

½ teaspoon ground white pepper

1 teaspoon cornflour (cornstarch)

1 teaspoon golden granulated sugar

1 × 400 g (14 oz) pack wonton wrappers

1 litre (34 fl oz/4¼ cups) vegetable oil

Dipping Sauce

2 tablespoons light soy

2 tablespoons black vinegar

1 tablespoon toasted sesame oil

2 tablespoons water

1 garlic clove, crushed

5 g (⅛ oz) chadon beni (culantro/recao) or coriander (cilantro), finely chopped

1 Scotch bonnet, finely chopped

1 teaspoon golden granulated sugar

Put all the ingredients for the wontons except the wrappers and vegetable oil into a food processor and blend to a rough paste. Place 1–2 teaspoons of the mixture in the centre of a wonton wrapper, brush the edges with a little water. Fold the wrapper over the filling and tightly seal the opposite corners to create a triangle. If you want to, you can then seal the two 'arms' to create a boat shape. With the flat side of the triangle facing you, bring together the left- and right-hand corners of the wrapper and pinch in the middle to seal tightly. Repeat with the remaining filling and wrappers.

Pour the oil into a deep saucepan and heat to 190°C (375°F). Alternatively, you can test the oil by dropping in a piece of bread. If it sizzles straight away and turns gold brown, the oil is ready. Carefully lower the wontons into the oil (in batches if necessary) and deep-fry for a few minutes until golden brown. Turn frequently in the oil to ensure the wontons cook evenly all over, then remove from the oil with a slotted spoon and drain on paper towels.

To prepare the dipping sauce, combine all the ingredients in a bowl and whisk together. Serve the fried wontons with the dipping sauce.

Wonton Soup

1 litre (34 fl oz/4¼ cups) fish stock

2 garlic cloves, crushed

1 thumb-sized piece of fresh ginger root, thinly sliced into short strips

2 teaspoons dark soy sauce

2 teaspoons light soy sauce

15 g (½ oz) chadon beni (cilantro/recao) or coriander (cilantro) leaves, roughly chopped

1½ tablespoons sesame oil

2 spring onions (scallions), thinly sliced

1 Scotch bonnet (split in half if you prefer more heat)

Note

If you are making the wontons for soup, you don't need to fry them first.

Combine all the ingredients for the broth except the spring onion in a saucepan, then bring to a boil. Reduce to a simmer, cover and cook for 15 minutes. Add the wontons to the soup and simmer for a further 5 minutes until the wontons are cooked through. Serve hot, sprinkled with the spring onion.

BULJOL
SALTFISH SALAD

SERVES 4

I've always been curious about the etymology of *buljol*. It is said to have evolved from the French patois term *brule guele*, meaning 'burnt muzzle', referencing the mouth sensation experienced after eating the dish when a lot of hot pepper was added. It now makes sense, as someone describing that hot mouth feel would likely say 'it b'un mi mouth' or 'mi mouth b'un' in our dialect. The term evolved to 'bu'n jaw' and then buljol. Buljol is eaten like this in Trinidad and Tobago and Grenada to name a few. Throughout the islands, some people cook the vegetables in this until softened, whereas others add them in raw. Interestingly, a friend of mine from Carriacou made a very similar preparation of saltfish and called it 'saltfish souse', omitting the tomatoes and adding finely chopped cucumber. I found it fascinating to observe the similarities and differences we share, even if within one dish.

Ingredients

250 g (9 oz) skinless and boneless saltfish or 400 g (14 oz) bone-in saltfish

2 tablespoons rapeseed (canola) or olive oil

1 sweet (bell) pepper, any colour, diced

1 red onion, diced

2 garlic cloves, crushed

1 Scotch bonnet, finely chopped (deseeded if you prefer less heat)

2 tomatoes, diced

juice of ½ lime

3 tablespoons extra virgin olive oil

15 g (½ oz) chadon beni (culantro/recao) or coriander (cilantro) leaves, roughly chopped

To serve

1 avocado, sliced
Sada Roti (see page 240),
Fry Bakes (see page 242) or
Coconut Pot Bake (see page 240)

Put the saltfish into a saucepan, cover with cold water and set aside to soak for a few hours, or overnight. Once soaked, refresh the water, place the pan over a medium heat and boil for 15–20 minutes, slightly covering the pan with a lid to allow the steam to escape. If you're using the skinless and boneless variety, pour off the hot water, rinse in cold water, then set aside. If you're using the bone-in variety, repeat the boiling again with fresh water before draining and rinsing. When the saltfish is cooked, the fish will contract and curl on itself and the water will become cloudy from the salt removed from the fish. Once cooled, flake the fish, removing any skin or bones, then set aside.

Next, heat the oil in a frying pan over a medium heat, then add the sweet pepper, onion, garlic and Scotch bonnet. Cook for a few minutes until starting to soften, then remove from the heat

Put the prepared saltfish into a bowl with the tomatoes and onion mixture. Add the lime juice and extra virgin olive oil, mix well, then finish with the chadon beni or coriander. Serve with freshly sliced avocado and sada roti, fry bake or coconut pot bake.

BAIGAN & TOMATO CHOKAS
ROASTED AUBERGINE & TOMATOES

SERVES 4–6

Roasted over coals or open fire, giving it a smokey flavour until the skin is charred and the middle is soft, tomato and *baigan*, the Hindi word for eggplant or aubergine (also, *melangene, antrouba, belangee*) is turned into a delicious dish of earthy silkiness. Once roasted, the skin is peeled and the fleshy centre is seasoned with salt, topped with freshly crushed garlic and finely sliced onions, before being chunkayed with hot oil. This dish and method of cooking aubergine and sometimes tomatoes in this way is called *choka*. Chokas are made across India, Pakistan and Bangladesh, where it is known by various names and incorporates lots of fresh aromatics. The style common within the Indo-Caribbean communities across the islands evolved from the Bhojpuri speaking regions such as Western Bihar and Uttar Pradesh, originally known as *baingan ka chokha*. Just as it would be in the East, chokas are served with fresh, hot sada roti (plain roti), most commonly for breakfast.

Ingredients

2 aubergines (eggplants) or 8 baby aubergines

4 medium-large tomatoes

½ Scotch bonnet, finely chopped

4 garlic cloves, crushed

2 tablespoons finely chopped coriander (cilantro) or chadon beni (culantro/recao) leaves

2 tablespoons sea salt

4–5 round shallots, thinly sliced

150 ml (5 fl oz/scant ⅔ cup) extra virgin olive oil

To serve

Sada Roti (see page 240)

Put the aubergines and tomatoes onto a baking tray (pan) and grill (broil) under a high heat, turning occasionally until the skin has blackened and blistered all over and the flesh is soft. Once cooked, set aside to cool, then peel off the skin and discard it, retaining the cooked flesh. Put the tomatoes and aubergines into separate bowls, then crush with a spoon or fork to break up the flesh. Add the Scotch bonnet, garlic, coriander or chadon beni and salt to each bowl, mixing well. Divide the shallots between the two bowls, sprinkling them on top.

To chunkay, heat the oil in a small saucepan over a medium heat. Once hot, carefully pour the oil over the shallots on top of the aubergines and tomatoes. It will immediately sizzle and react with the vegetables. To finish, stir in the oil and shallots. Serve with the sada roti.

GEERA PORK

SERVES 4

This pork dish is super simple but full of flavour. It's stewed with fresh green seasoning and lots of freshly ground, roasted geera (cumin) before being fried for a crispy outside, while juicy in the centre. Perfect served with an ice cold Carib – the local beer of Trinidad and Tobago – and pepper sauce, if you like heat.

Ingredients

600 g (1 lb 5 oz) boneless pork leg, diced into medium chunks

1 tablespoon ground cumin

1 teaspoon amchar masala

2 teaspoons sea salt

3–4 garlic cloves, crushed

1 tablespoon Green Seasoning (see page 299)

3 tablespoons rapeseed (canola) or olive oil

1 teaspoon cumin seeds

500 ml (17 fl oz/generous 2 cups) water

To serve

Hot Pepper Sauce (see page 305), to serve

Put the pork into a bowl and add the ground cumin, amchar masala, salt, garlic and green seasoning. Mix well to ensure the meat is well coated, then cover and set aside in the refrigerator to marinate for a few hours, or overnight. When you're ready to cook, heat the oil in a deep frying pan over a medium heat. Add the cumin seeds and toast for 30–60 seconds until they start to colour a little and release their aroma, being careful they don't burn. Next, increase the heat a little and add the pork. Fry for 3–4 minutes until browned all over, then add the water. Once simmering, reduce the heat to medium, cover and cook for 30–40 minutes, or until the water has evaporated and the meat is tender. Serve with a little hot pepper sauce on the side.

CORN SOUP

SERVES 4–6

The cultural symbolism of Carnival that is celebrated widely throughout the region, is the birthplace of the steel pan and calypso music. There are many threads and themes within the lyrics of calypsonians that reference the struggle for equality and independence in a post-colonial land.

Out of pain, this culture was born,
In life's shadowed places, the magic was spawned
Well, the tribe they regrouped again
Fought their wars on a brand new plain
And through this strife their manhood was reborn
And so from all this bacchanal
Life is now a festival
And you can hear the children sing
Dedication, David Rudder, 1987

When I first had corn soup in Trinidad, it was served to my friend and I from a supermarket shopping trolley, inside the pan yard of a band rehearsing for Panorama (the annual steel pan competition). The instrument is special because it is another example of Caribbean culture being created through adversity. Historically, steel pans have been made from disused oil drums which became widely available in Trinidad due to their own oil reserves. As such, pan has become the national instrument of Trinidad and since 2023, August 11th is officially recognised as National Pan Day across the twin islands. This recipe is reflective of the Indo-Caribbean culture of Trinidad as it uses a base of yellow split peas, with the addition of ground provisions, corn when it grows abundantly in season and sometimes cow heel. Especially during Carnival season, you can grab a cup full of it anywhere. When I would arrive at my grandma's house after school, I could sense what was cooking immediately. Now as an adult, I have a different appreciation and it's very much nostalgic.

Ingredients

200 g (7 oz/generous 1 cup) dried yellow split peas or yellow lentils

250 g (9 oz) pumpkin (or butternut squash), peeled and cubed

2 tablespoons Green Seasoning (see page 299)

1 Scotch bonnet (split in half if you prefer more heat)

1 spring onion (scallion), roughly chopped

1½ tablespoons sea salt

2 litres (68 fl oz/8½ cups) water

100 ml (3½ fl oz/scant ½ cup) coconut milk

2 carrots, peeled and diced

2 green (unripe) bananas, peeled and diced

1 large waxy potato, peeled and diced

1 corn cob, cut into 6–8 pieces

Dumplings

100 g (3½ oz/generous ¾ cup) plain (all-purpose) flour

½ teaspoon sea salt

½ tablespoon rapeseed (canola) or olive oil

50 ml (1¾ fl oz/3½ tablespoons) cold water

Put the split peas, pumpkin, green seasoning, Scotch bonnet, spring onion and salt into a large, deep saucepan and pour over 1.5 litres (50¾ fl oz/6⅓ cups) of the water. Bring to the boil, then reduce to a simmer and cook for 40–50 minutes, or until the split peas are soft and break easily if pressed between your finger and thumb.

Meanwhile, prepare the dumplings. Combine the flour and salt in a bowl, mix lightly, then add the oil and gradually pour in the water, stirring as you go. Bring together into a soft dough, knead lightly for a few minutes, then cover and set aside to rest.

Once the split peas are cooked, remove the pan from the heat. Pour in the remaining water, then blend with a hand-held blender until smooth. Place the soup over a low heat, add the coconut milk and bring to a simmer.

Next, finish preparing the dumplings. Divide the dough into four equal-sized pieces, then roll the pieces into thin sausages, about 3 cm (1¼ in) thick. Cut each roll into 8–10 pieces. The dumplings are meant to be small, bite-sized pieces, similar in size to the vegetable chunks. Bring the soup up to the boil, then add the dumplings. Reduce to a simmer and cook for 10 minutes, then add the carrots, green bananas, potato and corn. Cook for a further 10–15 minutes, or until the vegetables are cooked through. Serve hot.

BAKE & 'SHARK'

SERVES 6

When you take the drive up to Maracas beach from Port of Spain, you slowly leave the cosmopolitan metropolis of the urban city and go deeper and deeper into the green, hilly landscapes of the islands. On the other side of the mountains, is the north westerly Atlantic coast where Maracas Bay sits. Sad to say, Trinidad isn't known for its beaches in the same way its sister island of Tobago is, however, this beach is famous for its food. Bake and 'Shark' is the ultimate sandwich, a fried bake (see page 242) filled with deep-fried shark meat, then topped with all of the sauces, chutneys and salads you could imagine. Richard's Bake and Shark is world famous, so if this recipe is anything like his, I'm proud.

Ingredients

500 g (1 lb 2 oz) skinless and boneless white fish fillets, such as pollock or coley, cut in half

5 tablespoons Green Seasoning (see page 299)

1½ tablespoons sea salt

juice of 1 lime

150 g (5½ oz/scant 1¼ cups) plain (all-purpose) flour

50 g (1¾ oz/scant ½ cup) fine cornmeal or semolina

1 litre (34 fl oz/4¼ cups) vegetable oil, for deep-frying

Mayonnaise sauce

150g (5½ oz/scant ⅔ cup) mayonnaise

1 garlic clove, finely crushed

juice of ½ lime

¼ teaspoon sea salt

To serve

Fry Bakes (see page 242)

1 Little Gem lettuce, separated into leaves

1–2 large tomatoes, sliced

1 cucumber, sliced

1 red onion, sliced into rings

fresh pineapple slices

Chadon Beni Chutney (see page 300)

Put the fish fillets into a bowl along with the green seasoning, salt and lime juice. Mix gently but well to ensure the fish is coated, then cover and set aside in the refrigerator to marinate for 1 hour. Mix together the flour and cornmeal in a shallow dish. Once the fish has marinated, place the fillets in the flour mixture, turning to coat them well. Set the coated fillets aside on a plate.

Pour the oil into a deep saucepan and heat to 190°C (375°F). Alternatively, you can test the oil by tearing off a piece of bread and dropping it into the oil. If it sizzles straight away and gradually turns golden brown, the oil is ready. If it turns brown quickly, it is too hot. Carefully lower a few of the coated fillets into the oil and deep-fry for 7–8 minutes until golden and crisp. Remove from the oil with a slotted spoon and drain on paper towels. Continue until you have fried all the fish, set aside until you're ready to serve.

For the mayonnaise sauce, put all of the ingredients into a bowl and mix well.

To serve, slice open one of the fry bakes, spread with 1–2 tablespoons of the mayonnaise sauce, then add a couple of lettuce leaves and a few slices of the tomato, cucumber, red onion and pineapple. Place a couple of pieces of the fried fish on top, then generously drizzle over the chadon beni chutney. Bake and shark is meant to be messy and fun, so expect drips of sauce down the sides of your hands.

CURRY CRAB

SERVES 4

Tobago is the small, sister island of Trinidad, just 52 miles away. The first time I visited, one of the dishes that stood out on that trip was curry crab. Served with cassava dumplings on the side, sitting in a pool of brothy spiced coconut milk, it was so simple and delicious. After snorkelling in the clear waters of the Buccoo Reef, this was the perfect lunch on a hot day with a cold Carib beer. Tobago is home to the world's oldest protected rainforest with an intricate freshwater system that is home to an abundance of seafood. Landcrab are said to have been eaten for centuries, during servitude, as they were easily obtained and did not require deepwater fishing, as colonial powers were not willing to risk any of the enslaved attempting to escape. When the British later introduced indentured workers from East India, the community brought a new influence to cooking on the islands, and curry crab is a homogeneity of this. Blue crab with soft shells are the best to use, as they soak up all of the spices and coconut milk.

Ingredients

2 kg (4 lb 8 oz) small blue crabs, quartered and cleaned (you can ask your fishmonger to do this for you)

1½ teaspoons sea salt

¾ teaspoon freshly ground black pepper

5 tablespoons Green Seasoning (see page 299)

3 tablespoons rapeseed (canola) or olive oil

4 tablespoons Caribbean curry powder, such as Chief or Betapac

1¼ tablespoons ground cumin

3 spring onions (scallions), finely chopped and green and white parts separated

5 garlic cloves, crushed

1 Scotch bonnet, finely chopped (or left whole if you prefer less heat)

200 ml (7 fl oz/scant 1 cup) coconut milk

15 g (½ oz) chadon beni (culantro/recao) or coriander (cilantro) leaves, roughly chopped

Boiled dumplings

250 g (8 oz/2 cups) plain (all-purpose) flour, plus extra for dusting

¼ teaspoon baking powder

1½ teaspoon sea salt

150 ml (5 fl oz/scant ⅔ cup) water

2 tablespoons rapeseed (canola) or olive oil or salted butter

Season the crabs all over with the salt, pepper and green seasoning. Crack the crab shells a little to allow the seasoning to get deep within the crab.

Meanwhile, prepare the dumpling dough. Combine the flour, baking powder and 1 teaspoon of the salt in a large bowl, then gradually add the water and bring together into a dough. Knead in the bowl for 5–6 minutes until you have a smooth dough. If the dough is too dry, add a little water, a tablespoon at a time and knead further. Cover and set aside while you prepare the curry.

Heat the oil in a large saucepan over a medium heat, then add the curry powder and cumin, stirring to cook into the oil. Next, add the white parts of the spring onion, the garlic and Scotch bonnet. Cook for 1–2 minutes, then add the crabs and stir to coat the crab well in the curry mixture. Add the coconut milk, then cover the pan and bring to the boil. Once boiling, add half of the chadon beni or coriander, then reduce to a simmer and cook for 8–10 minutes. Keep an eye on the pan in case the liquid dries – if it does, you can add little water. The crab is cooked when the shells turn a reddish colour. Once cooked, transfer the crabs to a dish, pour over the sauce and finish with the green parts of the spring onion and the remaining chadon beni or coriander.

To cook the dumplings, fill a large saucepan with 1.5 litres (50¾ fl oz/6⅓ cups) of water and add the remaining salt, then bring to the boil. Tip the dough out onto a lightly floured surface, then divide into 8–10 equal-sized pieces. Form each piece into a smooth ball, then place in the palm of your hand and flatten by about half. Press your thumb into the middle to make an indent, but be careful it doesn't become too thin in the centre. As you form each dumpling, place them into the boiling water, then cover and cook for 10–15 minutes, or until they have all floated to the top. Once cooked, serve with the curry crab.

KITCHRI
DHAL COOKED WITH RICE, CUMIN & COCONUT MILK

SERVES 4

Kitchri uses some of the humblest ingredients; rice and lentils, yet this dish has such a long history, starting in the East. It can be cooked in a few different ways, some dry or wet and porridge-like or plain, without spices and vegetables, as it is in Northern India. In some of the poorest communities of South Asia, where many of the Indian communities who travelled to the Caribbean originated, this recipe would be cooked. Ironically, while this dish evolved in the Caribbean to become its own style through imperialism in the West, British colonisation of India in the East resulted in an Anglo-Indian version of the dish called kedgeree – incorporating smoked or salted fish, curry spices and boiled eggs.

Ingredients

110 g (4 oz/½ cup) dried yellow split peas or yellow lentils
100 g (3½ oz/½ cup) jasmine rice
250 ml (8 fl oz/1 cup) water
2 teaspoons sea salt
2 tablespoons rapeseed (canola) or vegetable oil
1 teaspoon cumin seeds
2 garlic cloves, crushed
2 spring onions (scallions), finely chopped and green and white parts separated
1 Scotch bonnet, finely chopped (or left whole if you prefer less heat)
½ teaspoon ground turmeric
1 carrot, grated
200 ml (7 fl oz/scant 1 cup) coconut milk
50 ml (1¾ fl oz/3½ tablespoons) water
½ teaspoon freshly ground black pepper
15 g (½ oz) chadon beni (culantro/recao) or coriander (cilantro) leaves, roughly chopped

To serve (optional)

Smoked Herring (see page 172)
Coconut Chutney (see page 301)

Put the split peas into a saucepan and cover with water. Bring to the boil, then reduce to a simmer and cook for 50–60 minutes, or until the peas are tender and break easily when pressed between your fingers. Once cooked, drain and set aside.

Put the rice and 200 ml (7 fl oz/scant 1 cup) of the water into a saucepan. Bring to the boil, then cover and simmer for 10–12 minutes, or until the rice has absorbed all the liquid. Once the water has been absorbed, remove the pan from the heat and keep covered to allow the steam to continue cooking the rice for a further 10 minutes, then remove from the heat and set aside.

Gently warm the oil and cumin seeds in a saucepan over a medium heat until toasted, then add the garlic, the white parts of the spring onion, the Scotch bonnet and turmeric. Cook in the oil for a minute, then add the carrot, split peas and cooked rice. Stir to mix evenly in the spices, then add the coconut milk, water, salt, pepper, the green parts of the spring onion and chadon beni or coriander. Bring to a low boil, then reduce to a simmer, cover and cook for 15–20 minutes until most of the moisture has been absorbed but it is still wet and rich. Serve by itself or with smoked herring and coconut chutney.

CURRY DUCK

SERVES 4

In Trinidad, whenever I've heard about curry duck it was always in the context of river liming (to hang out and vibe by the river). It wasn't until I visited the island and actually cooked curry duck by the river that I fully appreciated all of the feels. The very essence of cooking outside on a small fire, with a pot nestled between rocks, was something very special. Sitting along the riverbanks, cutting up all the fresh seasonings on a chopping board resting tentatively on my lap was simply the best experience and this dish takes me back every time.

Ingredients

1.5 kg (3 lb 5 oz) duck, cut into pieces

1 tablespoon sea salt

1 teaspoon freshly ground black pepper

6 tablespoons Green Seasoning (see page 299)

2 tablespoons rapeseed (canola) or olive oil

1 tablespoon amchar masala

2 teaspoons ground cumin

4 teaspoons Caribbean curry powder, such as Chief or Betapac

½ tablespoon ground turmeric

500 ml (17 fl oz/generous 2 cups) water

3 garlic cloves, crushed

2 spring onions (scallions), finely sliced

15 g (½ oz) coriander (cilantro) or chadon beni (culantro/recao) leaves, roughly chopped

1 Scotch bonnet, split in half (deseeded if you prefer less heat)

a few sprigs of thyme

5 g (¼ oz) or 1 thumb-sized piece of fresh ginger root, finely grated

250 ml (8 fl oz/1 cup) coconut milk

To serve

Dhal Puri (see page 237)

Curry Mango/Mango Talkari (see page 302)

Chadon Beni Chutney (see page 300)

Put the duck pieces into a bowl and season all over with the salt, pepper and green seasoning. Mix until the duck is well coated, then cover and set aside in the refrigerator to marinate for at least 1 hour, or overnight.

When you're ready to cook, heat the oil in a saucepan over a medium heat, then add the amchar masala, cumin, curry powder and turmeric. Cook out briefly until the spices have absorbed the oil, ensuring it doesn't burn. Add 50 ml (1¾ fl oz/3½ tablespoons) of the water and continue to cook over a low heat for about 10 minutes, or until the oil starts to separate.

Once the oil has separated from the cooked spices, add the duck and any marinade from the bowl. Stir well so that the duck is coated in spices. Next, add the garlic, spring onions, coriander or chadon beni, Scotch bonnet, thyme, ginger and the remaining water, then cover and simmer for 90 minutes, or until the duck is tender and starting to slip away from the bone. If it isn't, cook for a further 20–30 minutes. Finally, add the coconut milk, check for seasoning and cook for a further 30 minutes. The duck is cooked once it is meltingly soft and falling off the bone.

Serve with the dhal puri, mango talkari and chadon beni chutney.

JAMAICA

**XAYMACA
LAND OF WOOD AND WATER**

A common phrase in Jamaican patois '... wi likkle but wi tallawah', is why Charles Town, Moore Town, Accompong Town and Scott's Hall still exist today. The brutality of the slave trade was indescribable. From its inception, there were many uprisings, on trade posts along the West African coast (Mutiny on the Clare near Cape Coast Castle, Gold Coast, 1729), on ships that travelled the middle passage and across plantations by those who refused to be subjugated to a life in bondage. There are countless records of them taking place, but there are a few well-documented ones that must be mentioned: Tacky's Rebellion – Jamaica, (1760), Bussa – Barbados (1816), Prince Klass, Antigua (1736), Demerara Rebellion (Guyana) 1823.

In the Caribbean, those who evaded capture fled to the mountainous areas of the island and were called 'Maroons', from the Spanish word *cimarrones*, meaning 'mountaineers'. From the earliest days of the sugar trade, Maroon communities also established by the Indigenous communities who knew the islands better than the Europeans, existed across the region from Antigua to Barbados to Brazil and Suriname. The Kalinago of St. Vincent joined with those of African descent who fled, forming their own communities. The Afro-Carib who successfully settled St. Vincent, before being expelled to Belize and re-claiming their identity as the Garifuna people, are a group who successfully continued to live on the fringes of coloniality by their own terms.

In Jamaica, these self-governing Maroon communities of the Leeward and Windward maroons are a testament to the continued 'small but mighty' forms of resistance that allowed these people to live freely and on their own terms. Following the seizure of Jamaica from the Spanish in 1655, the British took hold, and many of the enslaved on plantations used this opportunity to escape. These heavy, forest-like areas of St. Ann, Clarendon and Elizabeth, some of the original homes of Jamaican Maroons, made it difficult for escapees to be found. The success of Marronage in Jamaica offered an alternative to plantation life which made it increasingly harder for colonial forces to control. Access to the land and tools for self-sustenance were crucial; as those enslaved were not allowed to live with autonomy, the skills and cultural norms that remained reinforced their self reliance. In 1739, Maroon leaders Quoa and Nanny signed a treaty with the British forces, which called a truce for both groups to operate independently of each other. One of Jamaica's most popular dishes, jerk (page 128) is a testament to this moment in history.

ACKEE & SALTFISH

SERVES 4

Across Ghana (formerly Gold Coast), the land is abundant with its native *ankye* (*anke*). Its utility in cooking and levels of consumption are starkly different to that of Jamaica and the wider Caribbean, where it eventually found itself and became ackee. The name ackee derives directly from *ankye or akye-fufuo*, the Twi term for the fruit. On the Ivory Coast and Mali (also formerly Gold Coast), it is called *kaka*, and *işin*; in Yoruba. On the African continent, ackee is eaten as a fruit once matured, added to sauce to replace sesame or peanuts, or ground dry before being added to sauces to release its oils. Some use the flesh in soup in place of okra or blend into a paste to eat alongside kenkey. The first plant was recorded as arriving in Jamaica in 1778, by whom it is unknown. Although thousands of miles away on the other side of the Atlantic, the fruit grew well in the new environment, becoming a staple in the colonial diet and eventually paired with saltfish to become Jamaica's national dish. Later, upon discovery by the British, the fruit was renamed as 'Blighia sapida' honouring Captain William Bligh of Mutiny on the Bounty, then taken to England and admired by the scientific community at Kew Gardens in 1793. However, testament to Jamaica's resistance, the name it was, and still is most commonly known by in the Caribbean remained connected to its original name, ackee.

Ingredients

250 g (9 oz) skinless and boneless saltfish or 400 g (14 oz) bone-in saltfish

3 tablespoons rapeseed (canola) or olive oil

2 garlic cloves, crushed

1 onion, roughly chopped

½ Scotch bonnet, finely chopped (deseeded if you prefer less heat)

a few sprigs of thyme

2 tomatoes, roughly chopped

1 tablespoon tomato purée

1 spring onion (scallion), sliced

1 × 280 g (10 oz) tin of ackee, drained

Ground Provisions (optional)

1 kg (36 oz) pumpkin, breadfruit, white sweet potato or white yam, peeled and cut into large pieces

1 ½ teaspoon sea salt

To serve

1 avocado, sliced
Fried Dumplings (see page 243)
Boiled Dumplings (see page 114)
Fried Green Plantain (see page 35)

Put the saltfish into a saucepan, cover with cold water and set aside to soak for a few hours, or overnight. Once soaked, refresh the water, then boil over a medium heat for 15–20 minutes, slightly covering the pan with a lid to allow the steam to escape. If you're using the skinless and boneless variety, pour off the hot water, rinse in cold water, then set aside. If you're using the bone-in variety, repeat the boiling again with fresh water before draining and rinsing. When the saltfish is cooked, the fish will contract and curl up on itself and the water will become cloudy from the salt removed from the fish. Once cooled, flake the fish, removing any skin or bones, then set aside.

Place the ground provisions into a large pan with the salt and cover with water. Bring to a boil, then cover and reduce to a simmer. Cook the ground provisions for 20-25 or minutes or until soft, where you can pierce easily with a fork. Drain from the water, then set aside until ready to serve.

Heat the oil in a frying pan over a medium heat, then add the garlic, onion and Scotch bonnet. Cook for a 5-6 minutes until starting to soften, then add the sprigs of thyme, tomatoes and tomato purée. Cook for a few more minutes to soften the tomatoes, then add the prepared saltfish. Continue to cook for a few more minutes, then add the spring onion and drained ackee, folding in carefully and ensuring you don't break the ackee up too much – they are already cooked. Finally, cover and cook for a further 5-6 minutes over a low heat to allow the ackee to warm through and absorb the flavours of the dish. Serve with sliced avocado, fried dumplings, boiled dumplings, ground provisions or fried plantain.

OXTAIL & BUTTER BEANS

SERVES 6

The concept of 'nose to tail' eating has always been standard for me. Oxtail is literally the tail of a cow. The fat that marbles through the meat, all the way down the tail bone makes it extra rich and silky when slowed cooked with the soy sauce and pimento – a nod to the Chinese influence in the islands. Culturally, our food has long been prepared with ingenuity and ingredients used with respect. My mum told me stories of her childhood where my grandad would get a live chicken from the local cattle market in Leicester and butcher it in their back garden. Being immigrants, although British citizens, my grandparents had to cook economically to feed their large families, armed with the ways they knew and learnt back home.

Ingredients

1.5 kg (3 lb 5 oz) oxtail, cut into large pieces

75 ml (2½ fl oz/5 tablespoons) dark soy sauce

75 ml (2½ fl oz/5 tablespoons) light soy sauce

1½ tablespoons sea salt, or to taste

2 teaspoons freshly ground black pepper

1½ tablespoons ground allspice (pimento)

1 garlic bulb, cloves crushed

15 g (½ oz) fresh ginger root, finely grated

a few sprigs of thyme

a few bay leaves

1 large Scotch bonnet, split in half (or left whole if you prefer less heat)

6 spring onions (scallions), thinly sliced

3 tablespoons rapeseed (canola) or olive oil

75 g (2½ oz) dark brown sugar or molasses

1.5 litres (51 fl oz/generous 6 cups) water

8 cloves

1½ tablespoons tomato purée (paste)

1 × 400 g (14 oz) tin of butter (lima) beans, drained

Rice and Peas

200 g (7 oz/scant 1 cup) dried kidney beans, soaked overnight in 1.5 litres (50¾ fl oz/6⅓ cups) water (or 2 × 400 g/14 oz tins of kidney beans, drained, plus 750 ml/25 fl oz/3 cups water)

3–4 sprigs of thyme

a few bay leaves

2½ teaspoons sea salt

2 teaspoons golden granulated sugar

100 ml (3½ fl oz/scant ½ cup) coconut milk

500 g (1 lb 2 oz/2½ cups) long-grain, jasmine or basmati rice, washed

To serve

Fried Green Plantain (see page 35)

Put the oxtail into a large bowl along with both of the soy sauces, the salt, pepper, allspice, garlic, ginger, thyme, bay leaves, Scotch bonnet and spring onions. Cover and set aside in the refrigerator to marinate for at least 3 hours, or overnight.

When you're ready to cook, heat the oil in a large saucepan over a high heat, then add the sugar and allow to caramelise. This will take 3–4 minutes – be careful it doesn't burn. When the sugar has dissolved and is bubbling, add the oxtail pieces and brown all over in the caramelised sugar. Reserve the marinade in the bowl for later. Next, add the water, cloves and tomato purée, then bring to the boil. Reduce to a simmer, cover and cook for 2½–3 hours, or until tender, stirring occasionally.

While the meat is cooking, make the rice and peas. Put the kidney beans and their soaking water into a saucepan and bring to the boil, then reduce to a simmer and cook for 1½ hours, or until the beans are soft and break up easily when pressed between your fingers. Once the beans are cooked, strain them, reserving any remaining cooking liquid. Add extra water to make the liquid up to 750 ml (25 fl oz/3 cups), then return the water, beans and reserved marinade to the pan. If you're using tinned beans, skip this step and combine the beans and water in a saucepan.

Add the thyme, bay leaves, salt, sugar and coconut milk to the pan, place over a medium-high heat and bring up to a low boil. Once boiling, add the rice and stir to mix everything in the pan together well. Increase the heat slightly to bring to the boil again. Once boiling, reduce to a simmer, cover and cook for 25–30 minutes, or until the liquid has been absorbed and the rice is tender. Remove from the heat and set aside. Once the liquid has been absorbed, give the rice a mix to loosen the grains, remove from the heat but keep the lid on to allow the steam to finish softening the rice. If the rice is very soft, leave the lid open to allow the excess steam to escape until you're ready to serve.

Once the meat is tender, add the butter beans and cook for a final 15 minutes. Serve with the rice and peas and fried yellow plantain.

ITAL SIP

STEW PEAS & HARD FOOD

SERVES 4

Rastafarianism is a belief system that encompasses the broader, holistic elements of life from within and how these interactions influence the environment and the foods that are eaten. Health of the body, mind, spirit and connection to the earth are fundamentals of the movement, reminding us of the original ways in which our ancestors used to operate. Although veganism has become a trend in recent years, *ital* eating has long been prominent in Rasta culture across Jamaican and other smaller communities in the region, namely Barbados, St. Lucia and Grenada. In the 1930s, the movement began following a resurgence within the community of seeking re-establishing connections to African ancestry and rejecting the coloniality that had been forced through religion. Ital cooking focuses on nature and plant-based eating from the earth – with respect. No animal products, salt or sugar are used in this way of cooking and being.

Ingredients

150 g (5½ oz/scant ¾ cup) dried kidney beans, soaked overnight in 1 litre (34 fl oz/4¼ cups) water (or 2 × 400 g/14 oz tins)

800 ml (27 fl oz/3⅓ cups) coconut milk

3 garlic cloves, crushed

2 spring onions (scallions), thinly sliced

5 g (¼ oz) fresh ginger root, finely grated

1 Scotch bonnet (split in half if you prefer more heat)

2–3 bay leaves

6–8 allspice (pimento) berries

a few sprigs of thyme

a few sprigs of marjoram

1 chayote (chou chou/christophene), peeled, deseeded and sliced

250 g (9 oz) ground provisions, such as pumpkin, white sweet potato or white yam, peeled and cut into medium pieces

1 carrot, peeled and sliced

Pour the soaked beans and the water they have been soaking in into a saucepan and bring to the boil, then reduce to a simmer, cover and cook for 1 hour, or until the beans are tender and you can crush them easily between your fingers. If using tinned beans, skip this step, and instead put the beans into a saucepan with 400 ml (14 fl oz/generous 1½ cups) water, then continue. Once the beans are cooked, add the coconut milk, garlic, spring onions, ginger, Scotch bonnet, bay leaves, allspice, thyme and marjoram. Bring to the boil, then reduce the heat and simmer for 12–15 minutes to bring everything together and flavour the base. The beans may break up a bit, which will naturally thicken the stew. Next, add the remaining vegetables and cook for a further 20 minutes, or until the vegetables are tender. Serve hot.

Note

The choice of ground provisions in this recipe are just preferences – you could also use taro, eddoes, yellow yam, green banana or plantain to substitute any of the above. There is no salt in this recipe as ital cooking is purely natural and doesn't incorporate it, but you can add to your own taste if you wish.

MACKEREL RUNDOWN
STEWED SALTED MACKEREL IN COCONUT MILK

SERVES 4

The traditional way to enjoy this dish is served in the middle of a table, for everyone to dip their 'bread-kind' (bread type) and enjoy. This communal way of eating roots the dish to the West African or South Indian influences in the culture. The multitude of fascinating names by which it is sometimes known describes this: 'dip and come back', 'dip and fall back', 'dip and shake off', 'assistant', 'breadfruit remedy', 'dip-dip', 'elbow grease', 'pakassa', 'round-de-road' and 'simmer down', to name but a few. The origins of this recipe were very hard to find, however, there was one story that stood out. The Dutch occupation of Indonesia, simultaneous with their colonising of the Caribbean, could have influenced the beginnings of 'Rundown' as Indonesians have a similar dish called 'Rendang'. While the pronunciation is very similar, the key fundamentals of vegetables or meat cooked down in coconut milk until it becomes a thick sauce and splits from the oil, is shared between both.

Ingredients

340 g (12 oz) salted mackerel fillets (usually sold vacuum-packed)

3 tablespoons rapeseed (canola) or olive oil

1 onion, sliced

3 tomatoes, sliced

2 (bell) peppers, any colour, sliced thinly

a few sprigs of thyme

1 Scotch bonnet, thinly sliced (or left whole if you prefer less heat)

2–3 garlic cloves, crushed

5 g (¼ oz) or 1 thumb-sized piece of fresh ginger root, finely grated

3 bay leaves

250 ml (8 fl oz/1 cup) coconut milk or 100 g (3½ oz) creamed coconut, plus 200 ml (7 fl oz/scant 1 cup) water

1 teaspoon sea salt, or to taste

½ teaspoon freshly ground black pepper

To serve

Boiled dumplings (see page 114)
ground provisions (see page 121)

Put the mackerel fillets into a saucepan, cover with water and then bring to the boil. Once boiling, strain the fish, then repeat the process to remove the excess salt. Remove the mackerel and set aside to cool.

Next, heat the oil for the rundown in a deep frying pan over a medium-high heat, then add half the onion, half the tomatoes, a quarter of the peppers and thyme, the Scotch bonnet, garlic, ginger and bay leaves. Fry for a few minutes, then add the creamed coconut and keep stirring and folding as it melts and splits. Skip this step if using coconut milk. It may start to stick to the pan, but that's ok. Once the creamed coconut has fully melted in, add the water or at this stage, the coconut milk, if using, and simmer for 5 minutes. Season with the salt and black pepper, then add the remaining tomatoes, onions, peppers and thyme and fold through gently. Add the cooled mackerel, then gently fold in (not too much, to ensure the fish doesn't break up). Simmer for a further 5–6 minutes, then remove from the heat and serve with dumplings.

Note

To make cassava dumplings, substitute half the flour for the same weight of grated cassava or cassava flour.

JERK CHICKEN & PORK

SERVES 4–6

During Spain's earliest settlements in the Caribbean, they brought with them livestock that wasn't native to the region, as a result, it is said wild pigs roamed the island freely and ultimately became a source of food for the Maroons. This began the origins of jerk. They dug holes in the ground, filled them with wood, buried the meat in the pits, then covered it with greenery and leaves to roast, while hiding any smoke emitted that could attract attention and expose their hiding places.

The wood used within the origins of this dish, and still today is pimento wood – the bark from pimento (allspice) trees named by the Spanish from the word 'piment' (pepper), the seeds of which they mistook for peppercorns. For jerk to be cooked authentically, it must be cooked on pimento wood, giving the meat a smoked and spicy aroma when grilled. As the cooking of jerk has evolved, the meat is often marinated in a dry or wet marinade made from pimento seeds, Scotch bonnet peppers, onions, garlic, thyme and other fresh ingredients.

From a pan on a corner of the roadside to huts along fast roads, with massive grills made of chicken wire and corrugated iron above smoking pimento wood underneath, and the meat sometimes covered with banana leaves while it slowly smokes. Pork is still the most popular meat of choice for jerk, however, chicken is now very common. It's simply served with pepper sauce or ketchup mixed with a little of the spices used in the jerk seasoning and hard dough bread.

Ingredients

1 kg (2 lb 4 oz) chicken legs

500 g (1 lb 2 oz) pork belly, cut into thick slices

Brine

75 g (2½ oz/⅓ cup) golden granulated sugar

45 g (1½ oz/generous ⅓ cup) sea salt

Marinade

30 g (1 oz) fresh ginger root, roughly chopped

2–3 Scotch bonnets

5 spring onions (scallions), roughly chopped

8 garlic cloves

a few sprigs of thyme

2 teaspoons ground allspice (pimento)

2 teaspoons ground cinnamon

2 teaspoons ground nutmeg

juice of 2 limes

100 ml (3½ fl oz/scant ½ cup) light soy sauce

50 ml (1¾ fl oz/3½ tablespoons) dark soy sauce

45 g (1½ oz/¼ cup) dark brown sugar

60 ml (2 fl oz/¼ cup) rapeseed (canola) or olive oil

To serve

Festivals (see page 243)

Start by brining the meat – this step is optional, but ensures the meat is flavoured to the bone. Combine the sugar and salt in a large bowl, then pour over 2 litres (68 fl oz/8½ cups) warm water and whisk until dissolved. Leave the brine solution to cool, then add the meat, ensuring the brine is fully covering it. Cover the bowl with cling film (plastic wrap), then transfer to the refrigerator to brine for 24–48 hours.

Next, prepare the marinade. Put all the ingredients into a food processor and blend until smooth. Scrape into a jar or airtight container and store in the refrigerator. Any remaining marinade can be kept for up to a month.

Strain the meat, discarding the brine, and place it in a clean bowl. Pour over two-thirds of the marinade and rub it all over the meat. You can add a little extra if it isn't covered enough. Cover and set aside in the refrigerator to marinate for a few hours, or overnight.

When you're ready to cook, preheat the oven to 180°C fan (400°F). Place the meat on a baking tray (pan) and roast in the oven for 1 hour, or until browned and cooked through. Serve with the festivals.

Note

This recipe also works well when cooked on the barbecue – simply transfer the marinated meat directly to the hot grill and cook until nicely charred and cooked through, with a core temperature of at least 70°C (158°F).

OKRA, GUINEOS, YAM, ACKEE: FOODS OF THE MIDDLE PASSAGE & BEYOND

The botanical legacies of the African continent in the Caribbean are owed to those who survived the middle passage. The preservation of foodways across this tumultuous journey is a true testament to the power of food culture within communities. Over the 400 years in which the transatlantic trade took place, approximately 30,000 ships left trading posts across the West Coasts of Africa, with at least 11 million lives completing the journey to the unknown, with many lost along the way. Everything about the trade was dictated by profits, and each journey's success heavily determined by the food.

While some supplies came directly from Europe, colonists depended mostly on locally grown, dried cereal grains produced on the continent to facilitate the dietary needs of those on board their vessels. Once captured, they didn't always eat crops familiar to them, as the chaotic journey to the coast displaced many communities. Whether Dutch, French, Spanish, Portuguese or British, the coastal location by which ships were posted on West Africa's shore influenced the edible cargo that was brought on board.

The Upper Guinea Coast (present day Senegal-Liberia) grew millet, sorghum, Bambara groundnut, melegueta pepper (grains of paradise) and African rice. Further south in Lower Guinea (present day Benin-Nigeria) is where African yams, oil palm (for palm oil), black-eyed and pigeon peas were abundant, with African Kola nuts common across both regions. Some plant species such as taro (eddoe) and plantain were originally native to Asia but had been introduced to Africa thousands of years prior and domesticated successfully into the local diet. Traditionally, kola nuts were used for their medicinal properties and ability to enhance plain drinking water. Colonists adopted this practice for water stored aboard ships to ensure it was drinkable for the journey.

The conditions for those aboard the ship were beyond inhumane and almost impossible for us to imagine. At this point in the journey, little remained of their identity, other than the few familiar food items that were stowed on board. As journeys to and from the continent increased, it became apparent to colonists that the more familiar food items were for those held captive, the lower the decreased mortality rates and possibility of onboard mutinies. Those of the Igbo (Nigeria) people preferred yams, while those from the Gold Coast (Ghana) enjoyed rice. These crops originated here, therefore, had connections to the communities. Even with this awareness, colonists made a concoction known as 'slabber sauce' – palm oil, flour, water and pepper, or boiled horse beans to a pulp, rice or yams, which was made cheaply to keep those onboard scarcely nourished.

The establishment of plants native to West Africa in the Americas is not solely as a result of the trade engaged by Europeans or the botanists whose curiosities piqued at fauna unfamiliar to them. The necessity of provisioning trade ships for the journey to the Americas, although inadequately, was primarily to keep the crew and human cargo alive to be sold upon arrival. Indirectly, it served as a vessel that introduced many food staples of West Africa to the Western Hemisphere. The success of these crops is a testament to the ingenuity of those in bondage and gives credence to the importance of the continent's contribution to the foodways that later developed in the Caribbean.

Once docked along coasts of the Caribbean, unmilled grain husks remaining from a ship's voyage would often be discarded. The captain and his crew no longer had use for them. For those who understood these grains and grew up on the soil from where these plants once came, knew there was an abundance of life left in them, subsequently for centuries to come. Thousands of miles away, disoriented and scared, the knowledge of their own crops were retained. Black-eyed peas were said to give good luck, and many wore them as necklaces along the journey, to ensure they had food upon arrival. Rice culture from the African rice-producing communities of the Upper Guinea Coast influenced the cultural significance within the Caribbean. The 'Quilombo oral history of rice' attributes the cultivation of rice in the Americas to African women, where trade ships became vessels for the transferring of the seeds. This 'Maroon rice narrative' (maroon – someone who escaped bondage) celebrates the conscious efforts of African women concealing rice grains in their hair undetected, establishing the continuation of rice and its culture in the Caribbean and Americas. The true development and pioneering of these foodways were largely a testament to the enslaved as plantation owners did not readily adopt these crops any further into their diets as they found them to be unfamiliar.

The environmental and climate similarities of the Caribbean and Africa added another layer of familiarity. Although migration was forced and involuntary, the enslaved taking agency of the parts of their new existence they could control often surfaced through cooking. Group-based traditions such as food preparation, communal gardens and market days were very familiar to that of their homeland Yoruba (Nigeria) traditions. They forged small food plots, which they tended to themselves (provision grounds), with some of the seeds and crops they held from home: black-eyed peas, okra and castor leaves, commonly used for ailments and medicinal purposes.

Sorghum (Guinea corn) and hibiscus (guinea sorrel), among others, although unfamiliar and unrecognisable by Europeans, revolutionised the agriculture and farming systems of the New World. The amalgamation of African and Indigenous techniques is the whisper that informs the Caribbean cooking we know and love today. These 'unidentifiable' crops (to colonists) had no existing names in French, Spanish, Portuguese, Dutch or English. The early names assigned often referenced their original geographical location or a toponym relating to their provenance on the continent. Bananas were originally named *guineos* in the former plantations of Eastern Cuba.

Guinea squash, guinea melon, guinea pepper, guinea yam, and even guinea fowl, were all named after the region (Guinea) where they were first encountered by settlers. Pigeon peas were once termed *pois d'Angole* in French or 'Congo' or 'Angola pea' in English, before later being referred to as *guandu, guandul* or *wando* in Portuguese, Spanish, and Dutch respectively. *Arroz con gandules* (rice with pigeon peas) in Spanish, is an integral part of Puerto Rico's national dish today, illustrating the culinary cultural fusion born out of the colonial period. The colonists' deep-rooted, skewed perception for the communities they captured, reflected how they saw what they ate, often referencing their diet as 'slave food'. It's ironic that those who possessed power within colonies were distrusting of those they enslaved, yet relied on for their labour. The same hands once shackled across the Atlantic who then toiled fields and tended to crops, were too, responsible for stirring pots in kitchens to serve their owners.

The cultivation of their own crops allowed for the continuation of traditional 'memory food' from home and the establishment of creolized, survival food. The long, low and slow cooking of meat into stews common across the African continent remained and became a core cooking method on plantations. Okra, originally named *okuru* by the Igbo (present day Nigeria) would have commonly been used to thicken stews. Prepared in exactly the same way once in the Americas, the Curacao (Dutch Caribbean) dish of *guiambo* (see page 206) is a slow-cooked stew of meat and saltfish with the base made predominantly of okra which thickens the soup. The name evolved from *quingombo*, the Bantu (Ghana) word for okra. Guiambo is often served with *funchi* – turned cornmeal (also *fungee, fungi* – Antigua, Barbuda, British Virgin Islands and beyond) or *cou cou* (Barbados). Cornmeal became the substitute carbohydrate for the pounded starch of plantain or cassava (*fufu*) that would usually accompany a stew of some form or protein in Africa. The true development and pioneering of these foodways were largely a testament to the enslaved as plantation owners did not readily adopt these crops any further into their diets as they found them to be unfamiliar. The middle passage of the Atlantic served as more than just an open, vast, body of water, but a connector of one region, its people and their ingredients to the next.

BARBADOS

**ICHIROUGANAIM
RED LAND/ISLAND WITH WHITE
TEETH (REEFS)**

The origins of rum production in the Caribbean are undisputedly Bajan. In the early seventeenth century, it is said, a small-scale brew, interestingly named 'kill-devil' began to gain attention. The molasses drip jars that sat in the boiling rooms, catching what was once the discarded, undesired by-product of sugar production, had been given a new life. Although not as refined as the spirit we know and love today, its intoxication capabilities gained its popularity among many, and by 1703, the first rum distillery in the Caribbean was opened by Mount Gay, at the top of Mount Gilboa in the parish of Saint Lucy, Barbados.

The beginnings of the name 'rum' is not quite clear, however, the Malay communities of the Indo-Australian archipelago had been fermenting sugar cane for centuries and called it *brum*. Early references to the concoction during the seventeenth century was *rumbullion* of early Barbadian English, used to describe the behaviour of someone after becoming intoxicated, *rhum bouillant* (boiling spirits) referencing the drink by its cooking process, or *eau de vie de cannes* (fire water) describing the burning sensation felt within your chest when drank. 'Fire water', in particular, is still used as a colloquial term for rum today and features in Soca (an evolution of Soul and Calypso music) songs such as the 2020 hit *Stink Behaviour* by Machel Montano and Teddy Rhymez's.

After the brittle canes of sugar were hand cut from the land, the juice had to be extracted within a few days. Iron rollers that continuously turned by windmill or cattle, pressed the fibres, freshly extracting the juice, which was then boiled by the boilerman (or woman) in open kettles in the boiling room. The right amount of lime would be added to form the sugar crystals we are so familiar with, then, once cooled, it was stored in wooden barrels called 'hogsheads'. Every few days, labourers would uncork the barrels to release the thick, dark 'blackstrap' substance left behind – molasses. The molasses was then combined with water and left to ferment, turning it into alcohol before being added to oak barrels to mature, age and flavour further.

Around 1 million gallons of rum was distilled in Barbados by the early eighteenth century, of which 85–90 per cent was consumed on the island. Rum became integral to the daily lives of all on the island as it was cheap to produce. It became a part of daily food rations for those on plantations – numbing the ills of their daily lives. For those at sea, it was included within their budget or payment for the poor conditions in which they worked, often travelling for months in solitude.

The dark side of rum that is important to acknowledge is that it was also used as a trade item across posts along the West African coast. The molasses that was still exported by other islands was sent to the North Atlantic in exchange for saltfish. As a result, during the mid-eighteenth century, Rhode Island became well known for producing rum following the influx of molasses. The 170,000 gallons it exported annually for trade along the trading posts of West Africa became currency for life.

Over time, many islands expanded their own sugar plantations and began fermenting molasses to produce rum. While most islands used molasses, others developed their own methods. The French Caribbean islands of Haiti, Martinique and Guadeloupe developed *clairin* (*kleren*) (meaning clear in Kreyòl) and *rhum agricole*, both made using fresh sugar cane juice, before it is boiled with an array of local aromatics. For clairin (kleren), in particular, the use of fermenting cane juice directly rather than molasses, stemmed from the self-sufficient, small-scale production in Haiti due to its natural biodiversity, along with its political and social instability following the end of the Haitian Revolution, historically, making it more affordable than rum.

The process of making clairin (and rum) has a very similar journey to that of palm wine, where tappers (professional palm wine producers) select trees (coconut, kola nut or palm) to drain their sap, before it is collected to naturally ferment. Since the fields, sugar mills and boiling houses were filled with enslaved labourers from across the West coasts of Africa, centuries old folklore tells us that the rum we know and love today are thanks to these unnamed individuals who continued their age-old practice of creating this treasured drink.

These traditions showed up in its production as well as how we consume the drink. The same way in which palm wine would be used for libations across the regions of present-day Nigeria and beyond, the same continued in the Caribbean. Quietly, under the guise of Obeah and the preserved religious practices, as an offering to their deities, rum was used to connect the living with those who had passed. To pay respects to someone who has passed away, when we commemorate Nine Nights (the days and nights following someone's death), or whenever we open a bottle of alcohol at home, we pour a little on the floor or throw it backwards over one of our shoulders. This ritual is so precious to us culturally as the rum became the vessel used to connect the living with those who have passed.

PUDDING & SOUSE

MEAT BRINED WITH VINEGAR, LIME & FRESH SEASONINGS
& STEAMED SWEET POTATO WITH SPICES

SERVES 4–6

Souse is popular across the Caribbean. Whether chicken feet, pig's tail or cow foot, the fundamentals of this dish are universal throughout the region – the meat is lightly pickled or brined in an acid, such as citrus juice or vinegar – but each island adds its own flair. Pudding with souse is very much a Bajan custom, where Saturday lunchtimes reserved for this dish. The 'souse' is the pickled pork, while the 'pudding' is steamed sweet potato mixed with onions, salt and pepper, often served with breadfruit and cucumbers also marinated in vinegar and/or citrus.

Growing up a part of the Caribbean diaspora in the UK meant certain foods were often eaten 'out of sync' and evolved as new traditions based on accessibility to ingredients and the change in environment. This was souse for me. It was introduced as a festive tradition until I learnt more about it. My Montserratian grandma would make it every Christmas morning as a nostalgic delicacy, for her, mum and grandad, yet, in Montserrat they would eat it all year round. One day, I asked her why she only cooked it at Christmas, and she told me 'A jus so we do it' – meaning, that's just what we do. Through more conversations about her life in the UK, I realised that certain cultural-specific cooking often took a back seat as they acclimated to their new environment, which in turn shaped my identity.

I'd try a little bit sometimes, but it wasn't my favourite thing to eat, as the experience is somewhat acquired – the smell and taste were sweet yet slightly sour from the lime or vinegar, the broth was delicate with a gentle gelatinous texture, a rich taste of pork fat and undertone of fresh thyme and bay. Honestly, exceptionally unique to itself. We'd have it with cucumber on the side, she'd steam hers slightly, whereas others make it into a salad almost.

The story of souse is one of resilience. During servitude, food on plantations was extremely minimal. Plantation owners knew they had to keep their enslaved workforce nourished enough to perform, however, maintained prioritising profits over human rights. The undesired cuts of meat and other unwanted rations from the grand meals served in plantation houses (usually cooked by the enslaved) were often tossed away. It was here the dish of souse was birthed.

RIGHT Pudding and souse stop, Saint Joseph, Barbados.

Ingredients

For Chicken Foot Souse

400 g (14 oz) chickens' feet, trimmed

1 tablespoon sea salt

4 tablespoons Green Seasoning (see page 299)

Pig Foot Souse

800 g (1 lb 12 oz) salted pigs' tails or feet, cut into chunks

1 tablespoon sea salt

2 tablespoons Green Seasoning (see page 299)

a few bay leaves

5 cloves

2 cinnamon sticks

a few sprigs of thyme

a few sprigs of marjoram

Marinade

6 small, round shallots, thinly sliced

8 spring onions (scallions), thinly sliced

1 cucumber, grated or zebra-peeled and diced

2 Scotch bonnets, finely chopped (deseeded if you prefer less heat)

8 garlic cloves, crushed

6 seasoning peppers (pimento/ají dulce), finely chopped (optional)

360 ml (12 fl oz/½ cup) lime juice (about 6 limes)

240ml (8 fl oz/1 cup) apple cider vinegar or white vinegar

400 ml (14 fl oz/generous 1½ cups) water

2½ tablespoons sea salt flakes, or to taste

60 g (2 oz) chadon beni (culantro/recao) coriander (cilantro) leaves, finely chopped

20 g (¾ oz) parsley leaves, finely chopped

Pudding

500 g (1 lb 2 oz) white sweet potato, peeled and grated

a few sprigs of thyme, leaves picked

a few sprigs of fresh marjoram, finely chopped, or ½ teaspoon dried marjoram

2 spring onions (scallions), thinly sliced

1 Scotch bonnet, finely chopped

2 garlic cloves, crushed

1 teaspoon sea salt

3 tablespoons salted butter

Place the pigs' tails and chickens' feet into separate saucepans with their ingredients and cover with about 1.5 litres (50¾ fl oz/6⅓ cups) water in each. Bring to the boil, then simmer for 90 minutes, or until the meat is tender. Strain and set aside to cool separately.

Once cooled, place the chickens' feet into a large bowl and set aside. Break up the pigs' tails into smaller pieces using your hands, removing any bones and excess fat or skin that's undesirable, then transfer to a large bowl.

In a separate bowl, make the marinade. Combine the shallots, spring onions, cucumber, Scotch bonnet, garlic, seasoning peppers, lime juice, vinegar, water and salt, then mix. Finish with the chopped herbs, mix again then divide the marinade equally between the bowls of chickens' feet and pigs' tails. Mix well to ensure the meat is submerged in the marinade, then cover and set aside in the refrigerator to marinate for a few hours before serving.

To make the pudding, combine all the ingredients in a heatproof bowl, mix well, then cover the bowl tightly with foil. Bring a saucepan of water to the boil. Ensure that it is large enough for your bowl to sit on, as the pudding will be steamed. Once boiling, reduce to a simmer, then place the bowl over the boiling water, making sure the bowl isn't touching the water. Steam for 40–50 minutes, or until the sweet potatoes are dark brown, soft and sticky. Serve warm with the souse.

MACARONI PIE

SERVES 6–8

Haitians call this dish *macaroni au gratin*, I grew up hearing this called macaroni and cheese by my grandma and much of the region and diaspora in the UK and US call it macaroni pie, either way it's delicious, especially for Sunday lunch. The first known recording of macaroni pie is said to have been in Barbados in the 1700s. The connection between macaroni cheese and the Caribbean is a really slim one and is likely one that was introduced through the movement of people across the islands to North American colonial lands. As far back as the fourteenth century, one of the oldest Italian medieval cookbooks *Liber de Coquina*, contains a Latin written recipe called *de lasanis*, describing pasta to be cut into squares and sprinkled with cheese, possibly the early beginnings of lasagne. Fast forward 400 years, upon one of his visits to Europe, Thomas Jefferson (the third president of the United States of America) took a liking to this dish. Story has it that his personal chef, James Hemming – 'the ghost of America's kitchen', an enslaved African American – travelled with him and is said to have brought the dish over from France or Italy, further developing the recipe and introducing it to the culinary landscape of the Americas.

Ingredients

1½ tablespoons sea salt

650 g (1 lb 7 oz/7¼ cups) macaroni pasta

60 g (2 oz/4 tablespoons) tomato ketchup

40 g (1½ oz) hot pepper sauce (optional)

2 teaspoons freshly grated nutmeg

1 teaspoon freshly ground black pepper

½ teaspoon ground white pepper

1½ medium onions, finely chopped

1 clove garlic

1½ tablespoons cornflour (cornstarch)

3 medium, free-range eggs

160 g (5¾ oz/⅔ cup) mayonnaise

300 ml (10 fl oz/1¼ cups) evaporated milk

400 g (14 oz) extra mature Cheddar, grated

350 g (12 oz) mozzarella cheese, grated

Preheat the oven to 170°C fan (375°F).

Bring a large saucepan of water to the boil and add 1 teaspoon of the salt, then add the pasta and cook according to the packet instructions. Drain, then rinse with cold water to stop the cooking process.

Mix together the tomato ketchup, hot pepper sauce, nutmeg, remaining salt, pepper, onion, garlic, cornflour, egg, mayonnaise and milk in a large bowl. Whisk until well combined, then stir in 350 g (12 oz) of the mature Cheddar and 250 g (9 oz) of mozzarella cheese. Once everything is well incorporated, add the cooked pasta and mix again. Pour the mixture into a baking dish, then sprinkle with the remaining cheese. Cover with a layer of baking parchment, then foil. Seal tightly and bake in the oven for 40–50 minutes. After this time, carefully remove the foil and parchment, then return to the oven and cook for a further 20–25 minutes, or until set and golden brown on top. Remove from the oven and allow to cool slightly before slicing into blocks.

HONEY HAM

SERVES 8–10

Honey ham or Christmas ham, as the name states, is a big-time Christmas dinner tradition in our family and many others. It used to be my job as grandma's unofficial 'sous chef' and budding cook to prepare it every year until my cousin moved back to England from Barbados and quietly took over. I always wondered how ham became such a big part of our eating culture across the Caribbean. It seems that the cooking and eating of ham during the Christmas period is connected to the medieval German tradition of Yuletide and sacrificing a wild pig during this time. It later found its way into early Pagan and Christian times, then through missionaries, whose role was to 'spread the word of God', it was introduced into the colonial Caribbean. Many islands have a version of this recipe: in Puerto Rico – *jamón al horno con pina* (Baked ham with pineapple), *jambón de Noel* in the French Caribbean or *ham di pasku* in the Dutch Caribbean. The leftovers can be used to make 'cutters' – Bajan sandwiches of salt bread filled with fried fish, cheese or ham. In Trinidad they're called 'ham and hops', with the hops referring to the white bread rolls.

Ingredients

3–4 kg (6 lb 9 oz–8 lb 8 oz) bone-in smoked gammon joint

1½ teaspoons black peppercorns

8 cloves, plus extra for studding the ham

4–5 bay leaves

a few sprigs of thyme

6 star anise

2 tablespoons sea salt

1 Scotch bonnet, split in half

1 cinnamon stick

15 g (½ oz) fresh ginger root, sliced

juice and zest of 1 orange

1 spring onion (scallion), roughly chopped

100 ml (3½ fl oz/scant ½ cup) apple cider vinegar

2 litres (68 fl oz/8½ cups) water

Glaze

3 tablespoons Dijon mustard

6 tablespoons black treacle (molasses)

3 tablespoons Demerara sugar

3 tablespoons rum or orange juice

To garnish (optional)

1 × 432 g (15¼ oz) tin of pineapple rings

12–14 maraschino cherries (optional)

Put the ham into a deep saucepan along with the peppercorns, cloves, bay leaves, thyme, star anise, salt, Scotch bonnet, cinnamon, ginger, orange zest and juice and spring onion. Pour in the vinegar and enough water to just cover the ham. Place the pan over a medium heat and bring to the boil, then reduce the heat to medium–low, cover and simmer for 1 hour, checking intermittently just in case the liquid evaporates (add more water if it does). After 1 hour, remove the pan from the heat and leave it to cool in the liquid. Meanwhile, combine all the ingredients for the glaze in a small bowl.

Preheat the oven to 170°C fan (375°F).

Once the ham has cooled, remove it from the pan (reserving the cooking liquid) and place in a baking dish. Remove the skin from the ham using a sharp knife, being careful not to cut too deep into the fat, then score a criss-cross pattern into the fat, no more than 5 mm (¼ in) deep. Stud the ham with cloves where the horizontal and vertical lines meet, then spoon over two thirds of the glaze, ensuring the entire surface is covered. Any remaining glaze will be used later. Pour some of the cooking liquid into the base of the baking dish until it is just covered – this is to ensure the meat and the dish doesn't dry out. Roast the ham open in the oven for 20–30 minutes until starting to caramelise, then remove from the oven and add the pineapple rings and cherries (if using). Fasten the fruit to the meat using cocktail sticks (toothpicks) and any leftover glaze. Return to the oven and roast for a further 20–25 minutes, or until the glaze has completely caramelised the fat on top. Leave to cool, then slice and serve.

COU COU & FLYING FISH
TURNED CORNMEAL WITH OKRA & FISH IN CREOLE SAUCE

SERVES 4

Barbados is nicknamed 'land of the flying fish' as its waters have been abundant for centuries. Bajans love of the fish is so much so, it features within their national dish. The fish are unique as their fins open out into wings as they swiftly appear from the depths of the sea, allowing them to glide across the top of the ocean's surface. The recent politics with flying fish in the Caribbean is a sensitive one. Global warming and climate changes have had an adverse effect on the fish's natural habitat and they have migrated into the waters of Trinidad and Tobago. The Bajan fishermen followed the shoals into the foreign water, resulting in some friction among the maritime community as Trinbagonians feel they are no longer Bajan – very much an ongoing point of contention.

As part of their national dish, flying fish is served alongside *cou cou* – cornmeal cooked with okra. Cou cou is also referred to as *cou cou pois, fungee or fungi*, the latter preserving its name directly from the original Angolan dish which would use pounded cassava, plantains or cocoyam. The serving of these components together is a continuation of the traditional eating style common across West Africa. Soups and stews are often served with a pounded starch, sometimes referred to as 'swallow', literally describing the action of eating intertwined with its use as a vessel.

Ingredients

6 flying fish fillets (or bream or sea bass)
4 teaspoons sea salt
4–5 tablespoons Green Seasoning (see page 299)
2 tablespoons rapeseed (canola) or olive oil
1 onion, finely chopped
2 garlic cloves, finely chopped
2 teaspoons Caribbean curry powder, such as Chief or Betapac
300 ml (10 fl oz/1¼ cups) fish or shellfish stock
300 g (10½ oz) tinned chopped tomatoes
A few sprigs of thyme
1 teaspoon raw cane sugar
½ teaspoon freshly ground black pepper
2 tablespoon salted butter
1 tablespoon parsley leaves, finely chopped

Cou Cou

300g (10½ oz/2 cups) fine cornmeal
400ml (14 fl oz/generous 1½ cups) cold water + 500ml (17 fl oz/generous 2 cups) hot water
8 okra, finely sliced
2 teaspoons sea salt
2 teaspoons rapeseed (canola) or olive oil, plus extra for greasing

Season the fish with the half the salt and the green seasoning, then set aside to marinate while you prepare the sauce.

Heat the oil in a wide frying pan over a medium–high heat, then add the onion and garlic. Fry for a few minutes, then add the curry powder and fry for another minute or two before adding the stock. Reduce the heat to medium, cover and simmer for 3 minutes. Next, add the tomatoes, thyme, the remaining salt, sugar, pepper and butter. Mix well, then cover and simmer for 5 minutes. Finally, gently place the fish on top of the sauce skin side down, along with any seasonings from the bowl. Cover again and steam for 8–10 minutes, or until tender and cooked through. Finish with parsley.

Meanwhile, make the cou cou. Add the cornmeal to the bowl and whisk in 400ml cold water, until smooth then set aside. In a pan, add 500ml hot water, okra, salt and oil, bring to a boil then simmer for 2–3 minutes or until the okra are soft. Remove from heat and transfer the okra water to a jug and set aside.

Next add 200ml (7 fl oz/scant 1 cup) of the okra water back to the pan, return to a medium–high heat and add the cornmeal and water mix. Ensure the heat isn't too high as the cornmeal won't cook enough and will absorb the liquid too quickly.

Whisk over medium heat, gradually adding the remaining okra water for 15–18 minutes depending on how quickly the cornmeal absorbs the water. The consistency should be smooth, light and thick with no lumps. Using a small bowl add ½ teaspoon of oil to coat, add a quarter of the cooked cornmeal then carefully rotate the bowl swiftly to create a smooth, round dome. Turn out onto a plate then repeat with the remaining cornmeal. Spoon some of the sauce next to the cou cou and place the fish fillets on top.

THE
BAHAMAS

**BAHAMA
LARGE UPPER MIDDLE LAND**

There are over 700 hundred islands within the archipelago of the Bahamas. At the base of their low-lying, shallow waters, abundant with seafood and shellfish, there is one mollusc in particular that is very dear to the food culture. Queen conch *(konk)*, also known as lambi or sea snail, are large molluscs that are beautiful in every single way. The smooth inside of the shell that blends peaches and pinks coils in on itself to create the home of these sea snails. Conch were originally fished by the Lucayans in the Bahamas, and other Indigenous communities throughout the region, their meat used as food and their shells traded as ornaments or horns. As conches later made their way into the colonial diet purely through accessibility, the high consumption by the African communities was likely passed on by the few Indigenous peoples who survived European settlement.

Sourced close to the shoreline, the enslaved were trusted by plantation owners to fish for them without the threat of escaping. Today they're used heavily in cooking throughout the region (St. Lucia, Haiti, Barbuda, to name a few) featuring in dishes such as curried lambi, lambi souse and conch water (see page 188). In the Bahamas, conch fritters and cracked conch (deep-fried with a light dusting of flour) served with rice and pigeon peas is the national dish.

As food traditions in the Caribbean are a creolisation of West Africa, European nations and Indigenous communities' conch shells have evolved to have a special connection to the deity of the sea – *agwe* or *agive* within Vodou, mostly practised in Haiti. Historically, the shells have always been preserved. After the molluscs had been removed, conch shells were used as an instrument to announce uprisings against oppression on plantations. Today, there is a large conch shell graveyard of them in the ocean near the British Virgin Islands that is both serene and historic, commemorating over 800 years of fishing off the local shores.

Across the Caribbean, this sound represents that of liberation. The story of Nèg Mawon (The Unknown Marron) in Haiti, reminds us of the battle cry that is said to have commenced the Haitian Revolution, while, in the Virgin Islands the conch shell signified the end of enslavement and its sound is known as the 'Call to Freedom'.

QUEEN CONCH: CEVICHE SALAD

SERVES 4–6

Conch is my favourite shellfish, probably because of the childhood memories associated with my nana. The ceviche salad is very popular in the Bahamas, beautifully fresh with the citrus vibes when combined with the Scotch bonnet and fragrant culantro or chadon beni. If you are unable to source conch, you can substitute for scallops or another white fish such as sea bass to emulate the firm and juicy texture of conch. Ensure you are sourcing good quality, high-grade fish for this recipe, as some of it will be eaten raw.

Ingredients

400g (14 oz) very fresh conch meat, cleaned or 170 g (6 oz) very fresh scallops, trimmed and cleaned

240 g (8½ oz) very fresh skinless and boneless sea bass or snapper fillet, trimmed and cleaned

juice of ½ lemon

juice of 1 orange

juice of 2 limes

1½ teaspoons sea salt

1 beef tomato, deseeded and diced

½ red onion, finely diced

1 spring onion (scallion), thinly sliced

1 small cucumber, halved, peeled, deseeded and diced

½ red (bell) pepper, diced

1 Scotch bonnet, finely chopped (deseeded if you prefer less heat)

15 g (½ oz) chadon beni (culantro/recao) or coriander (cilantro) leaves, roughly chopped

Place the conch or scallops and fish in a bowl with 500 ml (17 fl oz/generous 2 cups) water and the lemon juice. Leave to sit for a minute, then discard the water, rinse the shellfish and fish and drain. Cut the shellfish and fish into small bite-sized pieces, then transfer to a bowl and add the orange juice, lime juice and salt. Cover and set aside to marinate in the refrigerator for 60 minutes.

Once marinated, add the tomato, onion, spring onion, cucumber, red pepper and Scotch bonnet. Mix well, then set aside to rest for 15 minutes. Finish with the chadon beni or coriander, then serve.

GRENADA, CARRIACOU & PETITE MARTINIQUE

CAMERHOGNE
CONCEPTION ISLAND
KAYRYOUACOU – ISLE OF REEFS

The little specs of freshly grated nutmeg that float on top of a rum punch in between the swirl of aromatic bitters is the sign of a good drink – in my humble opinion (consumed responsibly of course!). There was a time when nutmeg was exclusively grown across the Banda islands of Indonesia and could not be found anywhere else in the world. Now they're a big part of Caribbean foodways. From the sixteenth century, the competition for these tiny seeds and desire for wealth among European nations was in full swing. By the beginning of the seventeenth century, the British and Dutch had both formed their East India Companies independently, opposing each other. Both took over parts of India, Ceylon and Java – where nutmeg, pepper, cloves and cinnamon were native – to monopolise on the crops.

The first nutmeg tree was brought to Grenada and planted on the Belvedere Estate, St. John's by Hon. Frank Gurney in 1843. Soon after, the island's production was large enough to influence world trade. With Grenada once being a volcanic island, the soil's richness and fertility, along with its closer proximity to Europe in comparison to the East, deemed the ideal place for spice production. Quickly, Grenada became known as 'The Spice Isle' as the largest producer of nutmeg and mace in the West. Following centuries-long production of nutmeg, now cinnamon, West Indian bay leaves, pimento (allspice), cloves, ginger, saffron root (turmeric), vanilla, pepper and cocoa are common exports from the island.

Although Grenada is the main producer of spices in the Caribbean, Trinidad, St. Vincent and St. Lucia also have smaller-scale productions of nutmeg, anise and cocoa. As the spices have been a part of the local biodiversity for centuries, they are used throughout cooking, from savoury and sweet dishes such as Grenada's national dish, Oildown (see page 154) to home brewed spiced rum (see page 285) and even tea. The long, green, spiny leaves of fever grass and their subtle lemon balm flavour are extremely comforting and soothing. My grandfather has bushes of it growing in his front garden in Barbuda and there was nothing more joyful than cutting the leaves myself, exactly what I did when I last visited, before steeping them in my cup with a cinnamon stick and sipping on the gallery (front porch), looking out as the sun rose in the morning.

CRAB BACK
STUFFED CRAB SHELLS

SERVES 4

Blue crabs spend most of their life on the land, unless it's mating season, hence their historic uses within Caribbean cooking; where fishing was not possible, landcrabs were easy to utilise as a protein source. The outside shell is a blend of purple, grey and blue with the underbelly commonly white. For the best crab backs, the fresh crabs are boiled, before removing the meat and mixing with fresh green seasoning and topping with breadcrumbs. I used Cornish crab for this recipe, with a mixture of both white and brown crab meat which worked well, however, you can use exclusively white crab meat but that may be a little more pricey.

Ingredients

2 tablespoons rapeseed (canola) or olive oil

1 onion, finely chopped

2 spring onions (scallions), thinly sliced

½ Scotch bonnet, finely chopped (deseeded if you prefer less heat)

1 garlic clove, crushed

a few sprigs of thyme, leaves picked

200 g (7 oz) white crabmeat or a mixture of brown and white) (approx 3–4 Cornish crabs, depending on size)

150 g (5½ oz/scant 2 cups) fresh breadcrumbs

½ teaspoon freshly grated nutmeg

1½ teaspoons sea salt

½ teaspoon freshly ground black pepper

30g (1 oz) salted butter, cut into cubes

Preheat the oven to 180°C fan (400°F).

Heat the oil in a frying pan over a medium heat, then add the onion, spring onions, Scotch bonnet, garlic and thyme and cook for 3–4 minutes until slightly softened. Add the prepared crabmeat (reserving the shells) and 100g (3½ oz/1¼ cups) of the breadcrumbs with the nutmeg and continue to cook for a further 8–10 minutes until the breadcrumbs have softened and absorbed the butter. Season with the salt and pepper, then place in the empty crab shells (or 4–6 ramekins, if you're not using dressed crabs). Top with the remaining breadcrumbs, then cubes of butter. Place on a baking sheet and bake in the oven for 15–20 minutes until golden brown on top. Serve hot or cold.

Note

This recipe can be made using pre-picked crab meat and ramekins only.

PELAU

STEW CHICKEN WITH RICE, PIGEON PEAS, COCONUT MILK & PUMPKIN

SERVES 4–6

Pelau is an Indo-Caribbean creation that has fascinatingly taken influence from so many places. Evolved from pilau of East India, it can be traced back to Persia and other parts of the Middle East – called *pilāw,* which means 'every rice grain is separated' – before it made its way into Asia. From the small number of Muslims who came from North India to the Caribbean, biryani was already a local culinary innovation that combined rice cooked with meat, ghee and nuts, possibly influencing the development of pelau. Across all depictions of pilau or pelau, rice is cooked down in a well flavoured and fragrant broth with fresh aromatics, spices, meat and other vegetables cushioning the rice within the pot. The way in which pilafs have been cooked historically from the Turco-Iranian cultures of West Asia to the Caribbean today, truly reference collectivity, often cooked in a large pot, serving everyone together to celebrate something among a group of people. The creolised Caribbean version of pelau, mostly found where there are Indian communities of previous British colonies, involves meat (chicken, pigtail or oxtail) browned in burnt sugar, before pigeon peas (*pwa kongo* – Haitian Kreyòl), pumpkin, carrots and rice are added and cooked in coconut milk.

Ingredients

1 kg (2 lb 4 oz) skinless and boneless chicken thighs, cut into pieces

4 tablespoons Green Seasoning (see page 299)

1 tablespoon sea salt

1 teaspoon freshly ground black pepper

2 tablespoons dark soy sauce

2 tablespoons light soy sauce

a few sprigs of thyme

2 garlic cloves, crushed

10 g (½ oz) fresh ginger root, finely grated

1 Scotch bonnet (split in half if you prefer less heat)

2 spring onions (scallions), sliced

150 g (5½ oz/generous ⅔ cup) pigeon (gungo) peas, soaked in 1 litre (34 fl oz/4¼ cups) of water (or 1 × 400 g/14 oz tin, plus 600ml (20 fl oz/2½ cups) water)

2 tablespoons rapeseed (canola) or olive oil

30 g (1 oz/2 tablespoons) dark brown soft sugar

250 ml (8 fl oz/1 cup) coconut milk

1 tablespoon tomato ketchup or tomato purée (paste)

1 tablespoon browning (for colour; optional)

75 g (2½ oz) carrot, peeled and diced

75 g (2½ oz) pumpkin or butternut squash, peeled and diced

2 tablespoons chadon beni (culantro/recao) or coriander (cilantro), roughly chopped

500 g (1 lb 2 oz/2½ cups) long-grain rice

Coleslaw

220 g (8 oz) white cabbage, grated

2 carrots (approx 120 g/4½ oz), grated

½ red onion, thinly sliced

¼ teaspoon sea salt

¼ teaspoon ground white pepper

1–2 tablespoons golden granulated sugar

200 g (7 oz/generous ¾ cup) mayonnaise

¼ Scotch bonnet, deseeded and thinly sliced

To serve

sliced avocado

lettuce leaves

sliced tomato

sliced cucumber

Put the chicken into a bowl with the green seasoning, salt, pepper, dark soy sauce, light soy sauce, thyme, garlic, ginger, Scotch bonnet and spring onions. Mix well to ensure the meat is coated, then cover and set aside in the refrigerator to marinate for at least a few hours, or overnight.

Meanwhile, bring a large saucepan of water to the boil and cook the soaked pigeon peas over a medium heat for 40 minutes or until soft, then drain, retaining the cooking liquid and adding extra water to make up to 600 ml (16 fl oz/2½ cups). If using tinned peas, skip this step.

When you're ready to cook, heat the oil in a large saucepan over a high heat, then add the sugar and allow to caramelise. This will take 3–4 minutes – be careful it doesn't burn. When the sugar has dissolved and is bubbling, remove the garlic, onion, ginger and thyme from the marinade and set aside, then add the meat to the pan. Brown the meat all over, then add the cooked pigeon peas, the cooking liquid and the remaining marinade. Bring to the boil, reduce to a simmer, cover and cook for 10 minutes. Next, add the coconut milk, tomato ketchup or tomato purée and browning and bring to a low boil. Once bubbling add the carrot, pumpkin or squash, chadon beni or coriander and rice – the liquid should just cover the contents of the pan. Remove some liquid if there's too much or add a bit more water if there isn't enough. Mix well to ensure everything is evenly distributed throughout the pan. Reduce to a simmer, cover and cook for 35–40 minutes until the rice has absorbed all the liquid. Remove from the heat and gap the lid slightly to allow the steam to escape before serving.

To make the coleslaw, combine all the ingredients in a bowl and mix until well combined with the mayonnaise. Serve the pelau with the coleslaw, avocado, lettuce, tomato and cucumber.

OILDOWN

CHICKEN, SALTED PORK & SALTFISH COOKED WITH GROUND PROVISIONS, CALLALOO & DUMPLINGS IN TURMERIC COCONUT MILK

SERVES 4–6

The blend of colours in oildown celebrate the flag of Grenada and its independence from Britain for the last forty years. The green callaloo, red/orange carrots, and gold, representing the brightness of the turmeric, make them perfect for their national dish. Although one-pot cooking is often associated with plantation life, this celebrates the liberation of the island and is often cooked for large gatherings or parties. A key part of this process is 'packing the pot', everyone has their preferred order and method of layering the ingredients – which some say influences taste and is based on tradition. A selection of ground provisions (breadfruit, yam, sweet potato, pumpkin) are layered alongside salted pork, saltfish and chicken dotted in between, before being topped with dumplings, thick callaloo leaves cooked down in a turmeric and coconut milk until the coconut oil separates from the evaporated milk, hence the name. Oildown has quite a labour intensive preparation, which is worth every moment. The method and finish of oildown is very similar to Guyanese *metemgee*. In Ghanaian Twi, the word metemgee translates to 'and the plantains make it good' – '*metem*' = plantains or bananas; *gye* = to delight. The stew is said to be favoured by men, who think of it as a source of virility and physical strength.

Ingredients

250 g (9 oz) skinless and boneless saltfish or 400 g (14 oz) bone-in saltfish

450 g (1 lb) salted pork, such as pigs' tails, cut into 4 cm (1½ in) pieces

500 g (1 lb 2 oz) chicken legs, cut into pieces

6 tablespoons Green Seasoning (see page 299)

1½ tablespoons Caribbean curry powder, such as Chief or Betapac

2 teaspoons sea salt

2 tablespoons rapeseed (canola) or olive oil

400 g (14 oz) breadfruit, peeled and sliced into wedges

600 g (1 lb 5 oz) ground provisions (your preferred combination of yellow yam, white yam, taro, eddoes or pumpkin), peeled and chopped into large chunks

2 carrots, peeled and chopped into large chunks

2 green (unripe) bananas, peeled and halved

250 g (9 oz) spinach or callaloo leaves

Put the saltfish into a saucepan, cover with cold water and set aside to soak for a few hours, or overnight. Once soaked, refresh the water, place the pan over a medium heat and boil for 15–20 minutes, slightly covering the pan with a lid to allow the steam to escape. If you're using the skinless and boneless variety, pour off the hot water, rinse in cold water, then set aside. If you're using the bone-in variety, repeat the boiling again with fresh water before draining and rinsing. When the saltfish is cooked, the fish will contract and curl up on itself and the water will become cloudy from the salt removed from the fish. Once cooled, flake the fish, removing any skin or bones, then set aside.

Rinse the pigs' tails under cold water, then place in a deep saucepan, cover with water and boil over a medium-high heat for 40 minutes. This will remove the excess salt and begin to tenderise the meat. Once cooked, drain and set aside.

Turmeric Milk

30 g (1 oz) fresh turmeric, finely grated

1 coconut, flesh finely grated

750 ml (25 fl oz/3 cups) warm water

30 g (1 oz) fresh turmeric, finely grated

400 ml (14 fl oz/generous 1½ cups) coconut milk

350 ml (11¾ fl oz/1½ cups) warm water

Dumplings

150 g (5½ oz/1¼ cups) plain (all-purpose) flour

¾ teaspoon sea salt

¾ tablespoon rapeseed (canola) or olive oil

75 ml (2½ fl oz/5 tablespoons) cold water

To serve

1 avocado, sliced

Put the chicken into a bowl and season with the green seasoning, curry powder and salt, then set aside.

Next, prepare the turmeric milk. If using fresh coconut, combine the fresh coconut and turmeric in a bowl with the water. Leave to sit for 1 hour, then strain through a muslin (cheesecloth) and squeeze out as much of the juice as possible. If using tinned coconut milk, combine in a jug with the fresh turmeric and water, stir, then leave to sit for 1 hour before straining as above. Set aside.

To make the dumplings, combine all the ingredients in a bowl and knead to form a soft dough, then cover and set aside for 20–30 minutes so the dough can rest, making it softer to handle. Once rested, divide it into 12–16 pieces and shape into spinners (short log shapes). Place on a plate ready to cook later.

Next, heat the oil in a large saucepan or casserole dish (Dutch oven) over a medium–high heat. Add the marinated chicken and stir for a 3–4 minutes to brown all over, then it's time to pack the pot.

Remove the pan from the heat and push the chicken into the centre, then in a circular, clockwise motion, place pieces of the breadfruit around and on top of the chicken. As you complete a layer, you can stack it up the sides of the pan. Continue this process with the saltfish and salted pork for the next layer, followed by the other ground provisions. Next add the carrots, green banana and dumplings you made earlier on top. You may need to re-roll the spinners in your hands slightly as you add them to the pan to recreate their shape.

Finally, cover everything completely with the spinach or callaloo leaves, then pour over the turmeric milk. Cover and cook over a medium–high heat for 40–50 minutes until the liquid has been absorbed. You won't be able to stir the pan, so keep an eye on it and listen out for any noises that signify it might have caught on the bottom of the pan or for a burning smell. If this does happen, add a little water and continue cooking. Once cooked, remove the pan from the heat and allow to cool a little, then serve. Use a large spoon to scoop out a piece of each layer, being careful not to mash everything together. Serve with the sliced avocado on the side.

DOMINICA

WAI'TUKUBULI
TALL IS HER BODY

My memories of eating cassava bread are early. Sitting at grandma and grandad's kitchen table in Leicester, aged eight or nine, I'm offered a piece with a bright slice of avocado on it. Grandma must have gotten a real nice one at the market that week because I could smell its ripeness at arm's length away from my face, and she was very excited about it. (For context, this was in the 1990s when avocados were still 'exotic' and not as readily available as they are today.) The cassava bread was dry, the avocado was rich, no salt – I couldn't understand what the fuss was about. While it obviously wasn't that traumatic, my younger self speaking still thinks it was! I remember years later I asked her about that day. She laughed and told me how back home it was always made fresh, locally, so buying it from the Caribbean supermarket felt (almost) blasphemous, although a means to an end, even if for nostalgia.

Cassava has long been a primary source of sustenance, equally as important for the Amerindians as it was for the West African communities. Dominica is now home to the largest community of Kalinago (Arawak) descendents throughout the Caribbean today, a community who still process cassava to make cassava bread in the traditional way as it has been for centuries. Sitting in the heart of the French Caribbean (once colonised by the French), north of Martinique and south of Guadeloupe, Dominica was originally inhabited by the Kalinago people and who successfully maintained a strong cultural presence on the island until the present day.

The native ingredient that is cassava is Indigenous throughout Central America and the Caribbean. Of the many ingredients and dishes that are derived from cassava, cassava bread has its own name on almost every island. Whether *casabe* (Dominican Republic, Puerto Rico, Colombia and Venezuela), *bammy* (Jamaica), *kassav or kasave* (Haiti and French Caribbean). *Kassav* is also the name of a popular French Caribbean band formed in Guadeloupe in 1979, specialising in zouk (an evolution of soca and calypso, specifically influenced by the sounds of France in the Caribbean).

In its raw state, cassavas are poisonous. The Kalinago, Taino and countless other Indigenous communities learnt how to process the tuber and create multiple uses for all parts of it. Once harvested from the ground, the thick, dark brown flesh is peeled, revealing a silky white tuber with a slight purple blush. The chalky liquid that it begins to excrete is poisonous.

To safely consume it, the flesh is grated into a pulp (or ground by a mill, which my great-uncle Jerry recalls well from his days growing up in Montserrat). The flesh is then squeezed to extract the poisonous liquid. It is from this liquid that the thick, syrupy cassareep is made, a vital ingredient in pepperpot (see page 86) most common in Guyana and one of their national dishes.

The wet cassava is then dried, before placing over a hot plate and shaped to make cassava breads. As well as making these ancient breads, cassava pulp can be roasted and made into farine. Farine is a very fine grain of cassava, sometimes referred to as cassava flour, traditionally roasted in a large *coppa* – a deep, concaved, metal bowl that sits over a clay oven.

Continuously and patiently, the cassava is stirred gradually with a large paddle, until it is toasted. The necessity of cassava and its by-products such as cassava flour, have stood the test of time, as they became of great importance to food rations on plantations. Of all the items given to the enslaved or traded at Saturday or Sunday market, manioc flour was always in abundance.

KASSAV

CASSAVA BREAD

MAKES 8–10

Cassava bread is an age-old staple made by the Taino, Arawak and Kalinago throughout the Caribbean for centuries prior to colonisation. It was so prominent in the diet of the Tainos, the Spanish referred to it as *pan de indias* (the bread of the indies) upon settling in Hispaniola (present day Haiti and Dominican Republic). Fresh cassava is grated before being dried, then cooked flat over hot coals to roast and form into cassava bread. It is so common within the region it has a multitude of names, *bammy* (Jamaica), *kasave* (French Caribbean) and *casabe* (Spanish Caribbean). For me, cassava truly represents something special when I think of the ancestral past of the Caribbean. This tuber moved through continents, stood the test of time and was so important to the Indigenous people they called the main God in their temple *Yocahu Vagua Maorocoti* meaning 'Our Great Lord of Yuca'.

Ingredients

1 kg (2 lb 4 oz) fresh cassava, peeled and finely grated

1½ teaspoons salt

To serve

a few tablespoons of Mamba (see page 275), to serve

First, dry the cassava. Spread out in a thin layer over a baking tray, then leave uncovered to dry out for a few hours or overnight, depending on where you are and how hot it is. Once dried, you want the cassava to still have a little moisture in it, not totally dry as it won't stick together on the tawa, flat top or frying pan.

Once dried, divide the cassava into 8–10 portions before cooking and place on a baking tray (pan). Heat the tawa, flat top or frying pan on medium–high heat, once hot, place a portion of the cassava into the centre of the tawa and quickly form into a circle around ¼ cm thick. Use a fish slice or spatula, to round the edges and shape. Next, using the fish slice or spatula again, press down the cassava bread across the top to compress the cassava, ensuring it sticks together. As it cooks it will release steam from the remaining moisture. After 1½ minutes, the cassava should feel sturdy enough as it would have lightly set by this stage, carefully turn over and continue to cook on the other side for another minute to 1½ minutes. The cassava bread is cooked once the bread has dried out and has a light brown, speckled colour across both sides. Once cooked, remove from the tawa and place on a tray to cool. Repeat with the remaining cassava.

Once they're all cooled, serve with the mamba. Store the remaining cassava breads in a cool, dry place, in airtight container for 3–4 days.

ACCRA
SALTFISH FRITTERS

MAKES 16–20

Food and religion were intrinsically intertwined throughout communities along the West coast of Africa. For the Lucimi, an Afro-Cuban community who evolved from the Igbo (a group now part of present day Nigeria), corn, beans and rice were prominent in food preparation and integral to worship. Food offerings would be prepared in relation to the deities based on the seasons and harvest. As such, the grains processed from black-eyed peas (*frijol pico negro*) were used in various *'adimu'* (offerings) for the Orisas, such as akara.

Akara are a type of bean cake or fritter made from black-eyed peas by Yoruba communities. To prepare, the black-eyed peas would be soaked in water overnight to remove the skin of the beans, and then ground into a paste. The paste would then be seasoned, then deep-fried in vegetable oil to create a crisp bean fritter. They evolved in the islands to incorporate saltfish, as this became one of the dominant ingredients within the foodways based on its historical accessibility to those on plantations.

Saltfish accra are eaten on almost every island of the Caribbean, each with their own unique style or name. Many islands call them 'fishcakes' (Barbados/Grenada) or 'fritters' (Jamaica), Puerto Ricans refer to them as *'bacalaitos'* and the French Caribbean islands of Guadeloupe and Martinique named them *'acras de morue'*. In Dominica, a tiny, shallow water fish called titire is sometimes used instead of saltfish, while Haitians *akra* use freshly ground malanga root (taro).

The traditional Yoruba preparation of akara is still popularly consumed in Cuba by the Lucumí although referred to as *bollitos de frijoles de carita* (or *bollitos de carita*). In spite of their name, all variations of this are a clear representation of the dishes' origins from akara.

Ingredients

275 g (9¾ oz) skinless and boneless saltfish or 400 g (14 oz) bone-in saltfish

225 g (8 oz/1¾ cups) plain (all-purpose) flour

1 tablespoon baking powder

1 medium egg

220 ml (7½ fl oz/scant 1 cup) cold water

2 garlic cloves, crushed

1 sweet (bell) pepper, any colour, finely chopped

½ Scotch bonnet, finely chopped (deseeded if you prefer less heat)

5 g (¼ oz) chadon beni (culantro/recao) or coriander (cilantro) leaves, finely chopped

5 g (¼ oz) parsley leaves, finely chopped

2 spring onions (scallions), thinly sliced

1 litre (34 fl oz/4¼ cups) vegetable oil, for deep-frying

Note

This recipe makes 16–20, but this is ultimately dependent on the size you fry them.

Put the saltfish into a saucepan, cover with cold water and set aside to soak for a few hours, or overnight. Once soaked, refresh the water, place the pan over a medium heat and boil for 15–20 minutes, slightly covering the pan with a lid to allow the steam to escape. If you're using the skinless and boneless variety, pour off the hot water, rinse in cold water, then set aside. If you're using the bone-in variety, repeat the boiling again with fresh water before draining and rinsing. When the saltfish is cooked, the fish will contract and curl up on itself and the water will become cloudy from the salt removed from the fish. Once cooled, flake the fish, removing any skin or bones, then set aside.

Next, combine the flour and baking powder in a bowl and mix well, then whisk in the egg and water to create a smooth batter. Fold in the prepared saltfish, garlic, chopped pepper, Scotch bonnet, chadon beni or coriander, parsley and spring onions.

Pour the oil into a deep saucepan and heat to 180°C (350°F). Alternatively, you can test the oil by dropping in a piece of batter. If it sizzles straight away and turns gold brown, the oil is ready.

Carefully drop spoonfuls of the mixture into the oil, being careful not to crowd the pan. Deep-fry for 3–4 minutes, turning occasionally, until golden brown all over. Remove from the oil with a slotted spoon and drain on paper towels. Serve while they're hot and crispy.

RED PEAS & SALTED PORK WITH DUMPLINGS

SERVES 4

When it came to finding economical ways of providing food, plantation owners consistently put profit before people and humanity, prioritising land for sugar cane production rather than food for those on plantations. The land that was given was often of poor quality and less forgiving – this is where the term 'ground provisions' originates, one that we still use today. It refers to the 'kitchen gardens' or small pieces of allocated land allowed for the enslaved to grow their own food for sustenance. The beauty of this is, they came with the knowledge and technology to cultivate their own food, although in a foreign place, the similar climate and multitude of native plants made it possible to adapt. Red beans would be an example of this. Red beans or kidney beans are actually native to the Americas, so the heavy presence of them in recipes, particularly as stews, combined with salted meat or fish across the region makes sense.

Ingredients

300 g (10½ oz) salted pigs' tails

160 g (5¾ oz/¾ cup) dried kidney beans, soaked overnight in 1 litre (34 fl oz/4¼ cups) water (or 2 × 400 g/14 oz tins)

4 tablespoons vegetable oil

2 tablespoons Demerara or dark brown sugar

300 ml (10 fl oz/1¼ cups) coconut milk

4 garlic cloves, crushed

10 g (½ oz) or 2 thumb-sized pieces of fresh ginger root, finely grated

a few sprigs of thyme

2–3 bay leaves

2 spring onions (scallions), thinly sliced

1 onion, finely chopped

1 Scotch bonnet, split in half (or left whole if you prefer less heat)

8 allspice (pimento) berries

2 teaspoons sea salt, or to taste

1 teaspoon freshly ground black pepper

Dumplings

100 g (3½ oz/generous ¾ cup) plain (all-purpose) flour

½ teaspoon sea salt

½ tablespoon rapeseed (canola) or olive oil

50 ml (1¾ fl oz/3½ tablespoons) cold water

Rinse the pigs' tails under cold water, then place in a deep saucepan, cover with water and boil over a medium–high heat for 1 hour. This will remove the excess salt and begin to tenderise the meat. Once cooked, drain and set aside.

Meanwhile, transfer the soaked beans and their soaking water to a saucepan and bring to the boil. Once boiling, reduce to a simmer, cover and cook for 1 hour, or until the beans are tender and can be broken easily when pressed between your fingers. If using tinned beans, skip this step.

When you're ready to cook, heat the oil in a large saucepan over a high heat, then add the sugar and allow to caramelise. This will take 3–4 minutes – be careful it doesn't burn. When the sugar has dissolved and is bubbling, pour in the beans and their cooking water (or the drained tinned beans and 400 ml (14 fl oz/ generous 1½ cups water), followed by the coconut milk, garlic, ginger, thyme, bay leaves, spring onions, onion, Scotch bonnet, allspice, salt and pepper. Add the cooked pigs' tails, bring to the boil, then reduce to a simmer, cover and cook for 40–45 minutes until the beans are very soft and the coconut milk has reduced slightly and is a deep red colour.

Meanwhile, put all the ingredients for the dumplings into a bowl, then bring together and knead for a few minutes to form a soft dough. Set aside to rest for 10 minutes, then divide the dough into 16 pieces and roll lightly in the palm of your hands to create small log shapes. After the stew has cooked for 40–45 minutes, add the dumplings to the pan and cook for 5–10 minutes, or until they are firm to touch. Once the dumplings are cooked, the stew is ready to serve.

Note

This recipe can be made plant-based by omitting the pork and substituting with pumpkin or squash.

ST. LUCIA

HEWANORRA
LAND OF THE IGUANA

Bek fwi (fry bakes; see page 242), *lamouwi* (saltfish) and *bouyon* (soup) are examples of foods shared across the Caribbean but uniquely named in St. Lucia. Language and its evolution was once a tool of survival during the colonial period, as such, Haitian Kreyòl, Papiamentu – Dutch Caribbean creole, Jamaican patois (patwa) and St. Lucian creole, to name a few, now exist within the Caribbean. Creole or Kreyòl languages across the region are spoken on at least 29 islands, each being unique to the space and communities that inhabited it. Creoles often have pidgin or jargon in their past, which are a combination of a community's original language and socio-cultural identity, broken through their displacement.

Upon their meeting, at trading posts along the West coasts of Africa, language became an immediate barrier for all. The various dialects that existed throughout the continent meant that there were numerous tongues being spoken, by many who didn't understand one another.

As communities and ethnicities were often mixed while waiting for months at a time along their journey, pidgin languages developed from the numerous African dialects, such as Mandinka and Wolof that formed, Casamance Kriul, when crossed with the Portuguese. When they reached the islands, the languages evolved even further based on who colonised them. St. Lucian creole can be traced back to dialects spoken by the communities of Senegambia (present day Guinea, northern Guinea-Bissau, the Casamance region of Senegal and The Gambia). As the island also sits right in between Martinique (French Caribbean) to its north and St. Vincent and the Grenadines to the south, on the arc of the Eastern Caribbean, much of its colonial activity evolved from that of Martinique, with the French influencing their language for decades, although it was also governed by the British.

The beauty and sadness of creole language is that, along with spirituality, it was used as a form of resistance. The ability to speak in a tongue unknown to colonists, was an ingenious way of survival and protection. As such, the language has always been dismissed, heavily influenced by the cultural superiority of coloniality, therefore never properly recorded or documented. For some, there was a cultural disconnect in speaking creole, especially if it was their mother tongue, because of the historical, painful associations and low socio-economic factors associated with the language.

GREEN FIG SALAD
GREEN BANANA SALAD WITH SALTFISH

SERVES 4

Figs, green bananas or guineos, as they were once termed by the British after importing them from the Guinea coast were transported to the Caribbean as 'plantation food'. Their preference for hot, damp climates, naturalised them into their new environment quickly, affirming them into the local diet. This small fruit later fuelled many British colonies of the Caribbean to independence in the mid-late twentieth century. The exportation of this 'green gold', in St. Lucia, Dominica and St. Vincent, to name a few, fuelled the economy and subsequent political movement, peaking in the mid 1900s. However, trade wars between the US and EU decimated the market, significantly reducing demand for Caribbean banana producers. Green fig salad is very popular in St. Lucia and similar to its national dish of green fig and saltfish. This combination of land and sea has been passed down through generations, and evolved to be what it is today with the addition of mayonnaise. Serve by itself or alongside any meat dish with rice or macaroni pie.

Ingredients

250 g (9 oz) skinless and boneless saltfish or 400 g (14 oz) bone-in saltfish

4 green (unripe) bananas, peeled and quartered

1 small carrot, peeled and diced into small cubes

½ teaspoon sea salt, plus extra as needed

2 tablespoons rapeseed (canola) or olive oil

2 spring onions (scallions), thinly sliced and white and green parts separated

½ Scotch bonnet, finely chopped (deseeded if you prefer less heat)

a few sprigs of thyme, leaves picked

1 red onion, finely chopped

30 g (1 oz) fresh green peas

80 g (2¾ oz/scant ⅓ cup) mayonnaise

¼ teaspoon freshly ground black pepper

To serve
Sliced avocado

Put the saltfish into a saucepan, cover with cold water and set aside to soak for a few hours, or overnight. Once soaked, refresh the water, place the pan over a medium heat and boil for 15–20 minutes, slightly covering the pan with a lid to allow the steam to escape. If you're using the skinless and boneless variety, pour off the hot water, rinse in cold water, then set aside. If you're using the bone-in variety, repeat the boiling again with fresh water before draining and rinsing. When the saltfish is cooked, the fish will contract and curl up on itself and the water will become cloudy from the salt removed from the fish. Once cooled, gently flake the fish, removing any skin or bones. Don't flake it too much as it will break up further when mixed in with the other ingredients. Set aside.

Put the green bananas and carrot into a separate saucepan with the salt and cover with water. Bring to the boil, then reduce to a simmer, cover and cook for 12–15 minutes until the bananas are dense and opaque and the carrots are soft with a little bite. Drain, then set aside to cool.

Next, heat the oil in a frying pan over a medium heat, then add the white parts of the spring onions, Scotch bonnet, thyme, red onion and peas and fry for 4–5 minutes until the vegetables have softened slightly, then remove from the heat.

Once the green bananas have cooled, dice them into small pieces (about 2 cm/¾ in thick), then transfer to a large bowl with the carrots. Add the prepared saltfish, vegetable mixture, mayonnaise, spring onion greens, pepper and salt to taste (it may not need much because of the saltfish) and mix well, then serve with sliced avocado.

DHAL PIE WITH SALTFISH

SERVES 8–10

My mum and I first ate this on our way from Hewanorra airport to Rodney Bay when I first visited St. Lucia. We stopped at a small roadside bakery where they were handmade fresh – it was my first taste on the island and stuck with me. The filling of saltfish and dhal spoke to two chapters of the island's history; migration from the East and trade ingredients from the North Atlantic. The pies are similar to aloo pies in Trinidad and Tobago, which are stuffed with potato and topped with channa or prawns.

Ingredients

Dough

450 g (1 lb/4 cups) plain (all-purpose) flour

1 teaspoon sea salt

4 g (⅛ oz) fast-action dried yeast

10 g (½ oz) raw cane sugar

260 ml (9 fl oz/generous 1 cup) lukewarm water

2 tablespoons vegetable oil

Filling

100 g (3½ oz/scant ½ cup) yellow split peas or yellow lentils

2½ teaspoons sea salt

250 g (9 oz) skinless and boneless saltfish or 400 g (14 oz) bone-in saltfish

2 tablespoons vegetable oil, plus 1 litre (34 fl oz/4¼ cups) for deep-frying

1 tablespoon Green Seasoning (see page 299)

3 spring onions (scallions), thinly sliced

2 garlic cloves, crushed

1 Scotch bonnet, finely chopped (deseeded if you prefer less heat)

2 teaspoons ground turmeric

2 teaspoons ground cumin

To serve

Chadon Beni Chutney (see page 300)

Hot pepper sauce (see page 305)

First, make the dough. Combine the flour and salt in a large bowl. In a separate bowl, combine the yeast and sugar and add 100 ml (3½ fl oz/scant ½ cup) of the water, then mix. Set aside in a warm place for 10–15 minutes to allow the yeast to activate.

Once the yeast mixture is frothy, add it to the flour mixture along with the remaining water and the oil. Bring together into a dough, then tip the dough out onto a clean surface and knead for about 10 minutes until smooth and springy. Return to the bowl, cover and set aside to prove in a warm place for 30–45 minutes to allow the dough to rise.

While the dough is proving, prepare the filling. Put the split peas and 1 teaspoon of the salt into a saucepan, cover with water and boil for 35–40 minutes, or until tender. When ready, they should break easily when pressed between your fingers. Drain, then allow to cool slightly before transferring to a food processor. Pulse to a coarse paste, then set aside.

Meanwhile, put the saltfish into a saucepan, cover with cold water and set aside to soak for a few hours, or overnight. Once soaked, refresh the water, place the pan over a medium heat and boil for 15–20 minutes, slightly covering the pan with a lid to allow the steam to escape. If you're using the skinless and boneless variety, pour off the hot water, rinse in cold water, then set aside. If you're using the bone-in variety, repeat the boiling again with fresh water before draining and rinsing. When the saltfish is cooked, the fish will contract and curl up on itself and the water will become cloudy from the salt removed from the fish. Once cooled, gently flake the fish, removing any skin or bones. Don't flake it too much as it will break up further when mixed in with the other ingredients. Set aside.

In a separate pan, heat the oil over a medium heat. Add the green seasoning, spring onions, garlic, Scotch bonnet, turmeric and cumin. Cook for 5–6 minutes until the onions are soft, then add the puréed split peas. Continue cooking for a few minutes to coat the split peas in the spices. Fold in the saltfish at the last minute, then taste and season with the remaining salt to your preference (the saltfish will have already added some salt). Set aside to cool until you're ready to fill the pies. Once the dough has risen, divide it into 8–10 equal-sized pieces. Place each piece on a tray and keep covered with a damp dish towel to stop the dough from drying out.

To assemble the pies, take a piece of the rested dough and roll it out into a circle, approximately 5 mm (¼ in) thick. Place 2–3 tablespoons of the cooled filling in the centre of one of the circles, brush one edge of the dough with a little water, then fold the dough over to make a half-moon shape. Press down firmly with your fingers to seal. Repeat with the remaining dough, then chill in the refrigerator for 30 minutes, or until you're ready to fry. The dough is quite soft so chilling will allow it to firm up a bit, making them easier to handle.

Pour the oil into a deep saucepan and heat to 180°C (350°F). Alternatively, you can test the oil by dropping in a piece of the dough. If it sizzles straight away and turns gold brown, the oil is ready. Deep-fry the pies in batches for a few minutes on each side until golden brown all over. Serve hot, splitting them open to reveal the filling and spooning in some chadon beni and/or hot pepper sauce.

SMOKED HERRING & CREOLE 'PENNY' BREAD

SERVES 2

Fish is common for breakfast in the islands. Saltfish, herring or even conch (lambi) cooked up with onions, tomatoes, garlic and all the fresh, green seasonings are delicious. Often, they're served with eggs, avocado and ground provisions as well as some type of bread of course. Creole bread is the local name for fresh bread baked daily in bakeries that are shaped like a rounded diamond. They were once called 'penny bread' because they were sold for a penny (½ a penny when stale or leftover) when the currency across the anglophone islands (current Eastern Caribbean islands of St. Lucia, Barbados, Grenada, Montserrat, Dominica to name a few) was the British West Indian Dollar and the islands were still under British rule, prior to their independence.

Ingredients

For the smoked herring

350 g (12 oz) smoked herring

2 tablespoon rapeseed or olive oil

1 onion, diced

2 spring onions (scallions), white and green parts separated, finely sliced

2-3 garlic cloves, crushed

1 Scotch bonnet, diced (seeds removed if you prefer less heat)

2 tomatoes, diced

small handful of fresh chadon beni (culantro) or coriander (cilantro) leaves, roughly chopped

½ tsp ground black pepper

½ tsp salt, to taste (optional)

To serve

Creole 'penny' bread (see page 172)

1 avocado, sliced

Begin by soaking the herring. Cut the whole herring into 3-4 pieces, place in a large bowl then cover with boiling water and leave to soak for approximately 30 minutes. Soaking the fish softens it so you can peel the fish and remove the meat easily. After the herring has soaked, carefully remove the skin and bones, reserving the fish. Once all the meat has been removed, flake up slightly, then set aside. Place a frying pan on a medium-high heat then add the oil.

Once hot, add the onion, white part of the spring onion, garlic and scotch bonnet. Cook for a few minutes, to soften then add the tomatoes. Cook for a few more minutes, then fold through the prepared fish to warm through. After a few minutes, stir through the remaining green parts of the spring onion, fresh chadon beni, then season with the black pepper and sea salt – the herring is quite salty so you can judge this based on your taste preference. Remove from the heat, then serve warm with the creole bread and freshly sliced avocado.

ST. VINCENT & THE GRENADINES

HAIROUNA
LAND OF THE BLESSED

J ust a little way up from the ferry terminal sits Kingstown market in the heart of St. Vincent. The roads are packed with merchants selling absolutely everything: from breadfruits, green bananas and guavas to eddoes, sweet potato and bundles of cinnamon sticks, most likely picked that very morning. No matter where you are in the world, the customs and activities of markets are universal, however, the markets of the Caribbean, particularly embody the spaces that allowed autonomy and self-sufficiency.

During the colonial period, sustenance provided by plantation owners for their labour force meant that food was minimal and never enough for the daily toil of harvesting sugar cane under the hot sun. By the seventeenth century, to ensure the right amounts were provided, laws were put in place to assure adequate food supply across the Eastern Caribbean, including St. Vincent, Montserrat and Grenada. Subsequently, proprietors were required to plant one acre of cassava or sweet potatoes to every two labourers, whether enslaved or indentured.

Provision grounds refer to the patches of land in or near plantations, for the enslaved to grow their own food. Although owners somewhat rejected the idea of giving more freedoms, the idea of labourers growing their own food worked for them.

Kitchen gardens, or house yard gardens, were small patches of cultivated lands in and among the living quarters of the enslaved, used to grow everyday foods such as plantain, yams, eddoes, coconuts and avocado. Often these spaces were also used to raise their livestock and tend to animals. Its proximity to where they rested was purposeful to keep an eye on their harvests. These spaces of plantation grounds designated for the labourers and their daily duties were often generalised and referred to as 'house yard' and it seems the patios term 'back a yard', which is also the title of the 1978 roots reggae album by In Crowd, seems to be a direct evolution of this, now referring to home or place of living.

Provision grounds and mountain grounds were slightly different. Mountain grounds were significantly larger, often on mountain slopes or in deep gullies (ravines), more distant from plantations and commonly utilised the lower quality terrain that plantation owners rejected for cane production. The amounts produced on these lands fed many and surplus was often sold at weekend markets. How well the land performed was very much dependent on the land's own vitality, being that many of it was once volcanic. Time allocated to work provision grounds varied from estate to estate, most commonly Saturdays and Sundays, outside of peak sugar cane season, however it is said on average, only 16 hours per month was allowed on Jamaican plantations.

For those enslaved that eventually acquired their freedom, one cost was the loss of their food rations from plantations, which meant the ground provisions, established on 'no man's land' became of even greater importance. These practices and traditions of kitchen gardens and ground provisions continued to be a part of the wider Caribbean way of life for centuries. Before they moved to England and as long as I've known, my grandparents 'worked ground' or had an allotment, to which I went with them often throughout the year, planting peas, potatoes, sweetcorn and picking blackberries and rhubarb to make crumble for Sunday dinner. *They have Saturdays and Sundays to feed themselves* by Lydia Mihelic Pulsipher exemplifies how centuries of ingenious sustainability and affinity to the land informed many of our rituals around food today.

BELOW When I was growing up, it was always a thing at my grandparents house when cooking, multiple pots on the stove, even if there were only 3 or 4 of us to eat. Why? 'Becasuse yu never know if someone might pass'. Meaning, there's always food left for whom-ever may or may not stop by. If someone did, especially Sundays after church, there was lots to feed everyone. If they didn't, it was leftovers for the next day.

CALLALOO SOUP WITH CRAB

SERVES 4

The identity and use of callaloo in cooking across the region is very diverse. The word callaloo has a vast etymology. In São Tomé e Príncipe and Angola, calulu is a dish made up of stewed leafy greens, dried meat and fish, still cooked today. Some of the early spellings of the word; *calulu*, *colalue* and *calaloe*, (recorded as early as the sixteenth century) show the direct links to West Africa. The mixing of callaloo leaves with okra stems to make a stew is an ingenious replication of *palava* (palaver) or kontomire, a green stew commonly eaten across (present day) Ghana, Liberia, Nigeria and Sierra Leone. From the early 1900s, Jamaica's longest running newspaper, the *Gleaner* founded at the abolition of enslavement, recorded callaloo as being cooked in a stew or broth with *ochro* (okra) and landcrab or served alongside agouti or manicou (large rodent-like mammal) among the islands of Trinidad and Grenada, showing its heavy presence in the foodways at that time.

Ingredients

1 kg (2 lb 4 oz) blue crabs, halved and cleaned
1 tablespoon sea salt, or to taste
4 tablespoons Green Seasoning (see page 299)
400 g (14 oz) salted pigs' tails (optional)
1 litre (34 fl oz/4¼ cups) water
2 tablespoons rapeseed (canola) or olive oil
1 onion, finely chopped
3 spring onions (scallions), finely chopped
2 seasoning peppers (pimento/ají dulce), roughly chopped (optional)
3 garlic cloves, crushed
a few sprigs of thyme
7–8 okra, trimmed and sliced
400 g (14 oz) pumpkin, peeled and cubed
15 g (½ oz) chadon beni (culantro/recao) or coriander (cilantro)
600 g (1 lb 5 oz) callaloo or spinach leaves
1 Scotch bonnet (split in half if you prefer more heat)
500 ml (17 fl oz/generous 2 cups) coconut milk
1½ teaspoons freshly ground black pepper

Put the crabs into a bowl along with the salt and green seasoning. Mix well, then cover and set aside in the refrigerator to marinate while you prepare everything else.

Put the pigs' tails (if using), in a pan and cover with 1 litre (34 fl oz/4¼ cups) water. Place over a medium–high heat, bring to a boil, then reduce to a simmer, cover and cook for 40–50 minutes to remove excess salt from the pork and tenderise the meat. Once cooked, remove from the heat, drain then set aside. If you are not using pigs' tails, skip this step.

In a separate pan, heat the oil over a medium heat. Once hot, add the onion, spring onions, pimento peppers (if using), garlic, thyme, okra and pumpkin. Cook for a few minutes before adding the callaloo, Scotch bonnet, chadon beni or coriander, coconut milk and black pepper.

Bring to the boil, reduce to a simmer, then cover and cook for 25–30 minutes, stirring occasionally.

Once the callaloo is cooked, remove from the heat then carefully remove the Scotch bonnet and any thyme stalks that haven't broken down. Pulse using a hand-held blender or traditional swizzle stick to create the soup base – it should be a coarse liquid texture, not fully smooth. Return the pan to a medium heat, then add the seasoned crabs, all the seasonings from the bowl and the cooked pigs' tails (if using). Cover and cook for a further 12–15 minutes until the crabs have turned orange and are cooked through. Check for seasoning and add more salt if needed, then serve hot.

FRIED JACKFISH WITH ROASTED BREADFRUIT

SERVES 6

A national dish often mirrors the popularity of local ingredients or wider tastes of a community, reflecting the multiple cultures that subsequently share them, even if their identities conflict. This is somewhat the case with this recipe. Jackfish is a species of fish abundant in the waters surrounding the islands, as far north as the Gulf of Mexico. Fish in the colonial diet was more common among the enslaved, as the British often had apprehensions eating species unrecognisable to them and their palates. Breadfruit native to Polynesia, was brought to the region specifically as 'plantation fuel' or 'food for the enslaved'. The natural versatility of breadfruit was astonishing to the Europeans who first encountered it in the Indo-Malay – starchy, yet soft, velvety and wonderfully smokey once roasted. Its fast-growing trees and high yielding fruit deemed it suitable for their purposes. Although initially, it was not well received, breadfruit has become a much-loved ingredient as an integral piece of the Caribbeans' culinary fabric ever since. Fried fish cooked like this is common across the Caribbean for example *pescado frito* in the Dominican Republic and Puerto Rico, which is simply served with lime wedges and *banann peze* or *tostones*.

Ingredients

1 breadfruit, peeled and sliced into 12–16 wedges (left whole if roasting in the oven, see note below)

6 jackfish (Northern Pike), cleaned and gutted (or small snapper)

2 tablespoons sea salt

4 tablespoons Green Seasoning, (see page 299)

150 g (5½ oz/scant 1¼ cups) plain (all-purpose) flour

50 g (1¾ oz/scant ½ cup) fine cornmeal

2 limes, cut into wedges

1 litre (34 fl oz/4¼ cups) vegetable oil, for deep-frying

To serve

salad

1 avocado, sliced

Note

If you don't have access to a barbecue, you can also cook the breadfruit in the oven. Mark a cross on the rounded end of the breadfruit, about ¼ cm deep. Roast in a preheated oven on 230°C (450°F) for 80–90 minutes. You know when the breadfruit is done when the cross opens up and if you insert a knife into the cross it comes out dry. Leave to cool before peeling. Once cooled, peel the outside, split into quarters to remove the core. Then slice quarters in half again.

Prepare a barbecue, then place the breadfruit slices directly onto the hot coals and roast for 25–30 minutes, turning occasionally, until charred. Remove from the coals and set aside until the fish is ready.

To prepare the fish, carefully score the fish diagonally a few times on both sides using a sharp knife. Then, season the fish with the salt, green seasoning and lime juice, rubbing it into the incisions and inside the cavity, then set aside.

Combine the flour and cornmeal in a dish, then add the fish and coat generously in the flour. Dust off the excess, then place on a clean dish.

Pour the oil into a deep saucepan until it reaches 180°C (350°F), then carefully add the fish one or two at a time, depending on the size of your pan. Fry for 7–9 minutes or until golden brown and crispy all over. Remove from the oil with tongs or a slotted spoon and drain on paper towels. Serve with the roasted breadfruit, salad and avocado.

CURRY GOAT

SERVES 4

The word 'curry' originates from the term *kari* – an evolution of the Portuguese word 'Caril' meaning spiced sauce. Pluralised, it became 'carie' or 'curee', which eventually became 'curry' through the British. Following the imperialist force of the British East India Company during the seventeenth century, their use of the term 'curry' conflated a multitude of dishes and spice mixes they became familiar with, from various castes, creeds and communities that had their own nuance and complex identities.

Following the abolition of enslavement and the large North and East Indian population of indentured workers that populated the Caribbean in the mid- late 1800s, curry was subsequently introduced to the Caribbean en masse. Depending on where you are or the diaspora will determine how this dish is served. Commonly in Jamaica you can expect rice and peas, whereas in Indo-Caribbean communities across Martinique, Grenada, Trinidad or Guyana, it will be served with roti.

Ingredients

4 tablespoons rapeseed (canola) or olive oil

2 tablespoons Caribbean curry powder, such as Chief or Betapac

2 teaspoons ground cumin

2 teaspoons ground turmeric

1 teaspoon ground coriander

1 litre (34 fl oz/4¼ cups) water

4 garlic cloves, crushed

3 bay leaves

3 sprigs of thyme

2 spring onions (scallions), thinly sliced

1 Scotch bonnet, split in half (or left whole if you prefer less heat)

2 teaspoons sea salt

2 teaspoons raw cane or golden granulated sugar

1 kg (2 lb 4 oz) bone-in goat shoulder or leg (or a mixture of both)

50 g (1¾ oz) creamed coconut or 100 g (3½ oz) coconut milk

To serve

Rice and Peas (see page 123)
Dhal Puri (see page 237)
Paratha (see page 238)
Fried Yellow Plantain (see page 46)

Heat the oil in a large saucepan over a medium heat, then add the curry powder, cumin, turmeric and coriander and cook for 1–2 minutes, then add 100 ml (3½ fl oz/scant ½ cup) of the water and stir to create a paste. Keep stirring to cook the spices, then add the remaining water along with the garlic, bay leaves, thyme, spring onions, Scotch bonnet, salt and sugar. Bring to the boil, then add the meat. Stir to ensure the meat is well submerged, topping up with a little extra water if needed. Reduce to a simmer, cover and cook for about 2 hours, stirring occasionally, until the meat is tender. Once the meat is cooked, add the creamed coconut or coconut milk, stir and continue cooking for a further 5–10 minutes until the coconut dissolves into the liquid. Serve with rice and peas, dhal puri, paratha or fried yellow plantain.

ANTIGUA & BARBUDA

**CAMERHOGNE
CONCEPTION ISLAND**

It's funny, whenever I get asked 'where are you from?' and the conversation takes a direction in which I name the islands, I'm often corrected. 'Did you mean Barbados? Or Bermuda?' Nope! Barbuda. It's such a small island with an even smaller community, it's relatively unknown, to a degree, but that's what makes it special.

Twinned together with Antigua since gaining independence from the British in 1981, Barbuda is one of my home nations (along with Montserrat). Thirty-nine miles across the Caribbean sea sits the flat, low and somewhat dry land of Barbuda. The landscape speaks to centuries-old resilience and self-sustenance, which still remains within the pride of the people. Unlike neighbouring islands, Barbuda was used slightly differently during the colonial period, which has had a direct effect on how the descendants, including my family, are now connected.

My paternal grandparents migrated to Leicester in late 1961, quite late into the mass immigration of Caribbeans following World War II. My nana was 23 when she made the spontaneous decision to travel on her sister's ticket to the 'Mother Country'. When she left Barbuda, my eldest aunt (who was already born) was left to be raised by my great-grandparents. These first born children, sometimes referred to as 'Barrel Children', were commonly left behind during this period, while their parents made the journey abroad for a better life, before sending for them. Pregnant with my dad when she left, my nana made the journey to England alone. My grandfather had travelled ahead of her, joining many other friends and relatives from Barbuda that had found the path to Leicester. I always wondered why they ended up in Leicester? Coming from the Caribbean how would they have heard of it? I imagine the first place that would spring to mind when thinking of England would be London, or maybe Birmingham, but during this time, you went where there was community and jobs to give yourself the best chance at this 'opportunity'. This forged a very tight-knit Barbudan community, unique to Leicester, and a section of the wider Caribbean that I grew up in.

As you arrive at Barbuda's ferry port from Antigua, there are the remnants of a lone sugar mill's base that still stands tall, in and among the prickly bush and wilderness that covers it. The rugged terrain, shallow soil, and often lack of rainwater, refused to support sugar production as no plantations thrived.

Instead, the people brought to the island were mostly used to produce food and raise livestock to supply the multiple estates owned by the Codrington family across Antigua and Barbados. Cocoplum, pumpkin and pigeon peas, common across the Eastern Caribbean, grew well in the dry climate of Barbuda, with the latter a key component in our beloved fungee (see page 206), would be sent across the waters to feed plantations. Even prior to colonisation, Barbuda was never inhabited, simply used by a variety of Indigenous communities to fish the abundance of seafood, lobster and conch living in the waters.

When Codrington leased the island from the King of England in 1685, the payment was 'one fat sheep' every year. Once servitude was abolished and the Codrington family left, although relatively underdeveloped, Barbuda remained with the people and went on to govern itself. As the people had always used the land collectively, they continued to operate with this communal system, eventually formalising a customary system of land tenure which gives every Barbudan and descendants equal rights to the land. An issue that has unfortunately become more and more contentious in today's capitalist world.

LEFT Old Sugar Mill, Richmond Hill, Montserrat.
ABOVE 'Duke' the dog sitting outside of his kennel, All Saints, Antigua.
RIGHT Grilling freshly caught lobster on Princess Diana Beach, Barbuda.

QUEEN CONCH: CONCH WATER

SERVES 4

I grew up seeing conch shells as ornaments in my nana's house, having no idea of their historical value or cultural significance. On one of the few trips my nana made 'back home' to Barbuda from England, her suitcase was often stocked with items that brought her nostalgia – conch being one of them. Or, when she didn't go back to Barbuda, anyone who flew in would be given a clear directive to bring back conch, wild fever grass tea and cornfish. The value they held was so much that conch often went 'missing' from her freezer when back in Leicester.

Their spiral-shaped shells, blushed with shades of pink and orange, looked so beautiful displayed as ornaments in her pristine front room – the one no one would sit in, other than Church people and other visitors. My admiration for them was mostly through the gaze of it connecting me to the place I was 'from, from' yet, I never knew the details of their deeper cultural significance.

This conch water recipe is another way to enjoy it. It's like a light soup or broth with a bit more depth from the fresh seasonings, rich base and juicy conch. Simply serve as it is with some fresh bread.

Ingredients

1 kg (2 lb 4 oz) raw fresh conch, cleaned

3 litres (101½ fl oz/12⅔ cups) water

3 tablespoons Green Seasoning (see page 299)

2 spring onions (scallions), roughly chopped

1 Scotch bonnet (split in half if you prefer more heat)

2 seasoning peppers (pimento/ají dulce), finely chopped

10 g (½ oz) chadon beni (culantro/recao) or coriander (cilantro), roughly chopped

a few sprigs of thyme

1 tablespoon sea salt, or to taste

1 teaspoon freshly ground black pepper

15 g (½ oz) salted butter

15 g (½ oz) plain (all-purpose) flour

To serve

Plait Bread (see page 241), Creole Bread (see page 241) or any fresh bread

Put the conch and 1.5 litres (50¾ fl oz/6⅓ cups) of the water into a pan. Bring to the boil, then reduce slightly to a high simmer and cook for 90 minutes to tenderise the conch. The conch will stiffen slightly when it first enters the water but will soften once cooked. Drain the conch and set aside to cool a little, then cut into medium pieces.

Pour the remaining water into a large saucepan over a medium heat and add the conch. Bring to the boil, then add the green seasoning, spring onions, Scotch bonnet, seasoning peppers, chadon beni or coriander, thyme, salt and pepper. Reduce to a simmer, cover and cook for 20–25 minutes until the broth is well-flavoured, the liquid has reduced slightly and is green from the seasonings.

Meanwhile, combine the butter and flour in a bowl and mix to a smooth paste. Once the conch is cooked, add a few spoonfuls of the broth to the butter and flour mixture to achieve a smooth batter-like consistency, then add this to the pan and mix well until fully incorporated. Continue to simmer for a further 5–10 minutes to cook out the flour. The conch water will change to a slightly cloudier colour. Serve hot as it is, with a little hot pepper sauce (see page 305) or with freshly baked bread.

PUDDIN'

'BLOOD' PUDDING WITH RICE AND SPICES

SERVES 6–8

Puddin', a shortened version of black pudding when said in local dialect throughout Anglophone islands, is essentially a blood sausage, made from rice soaked in rum, pig's blood and spices then steamed in pork intestines. In the days when the slaughter of a whole animal was common, cooking nose to tail was everyday practice, as refrigeration didn't exist and ingredients were unable to be stored easily. Blood sausage is also known as black pudding, *morcilla* in the Spanish Caribbean islands and *sanger yean* in the Dutch Caribbean. There is a similar recipe for blood sausage made in Louisiana, linked by the French and Haitian populations that resided there following the Haitian Revolution in 1804. The difference is a key ingredient that sets them apart – *graine de bois d'inde* (seed of wood from India) now found commonly across the islands. *Boudin*, in the French Caribbean islands, is similar, using bread soaked in water, instead of rice. *Boudin* comes from the Anglo-Saxon word for sausage and is said to have been first recorded by an Ancient Greek cook called, Aphtonite. *Boudin blanc Antillais* (West Indian white pudding) is made slightly differently, omitting the pig's blood in exchange for milk with the addition of ham or chicken. Although traditionally, this is made using pig's blood, it can be quite difficult to find. Using gravy browning instead works well as it recreates the colour even though it alters the taste slightly.

Ingredients

4.6 metres (15 feet)/100–150 g (3½–5½ oz) pork intestines, cleaned
100 g (3½ oz/generous ½ cup) long-grain rice
350 ml (11½ fl oz/1½ cups) water
1½ tablespoons browning
1½ teaspoons sea salt
1 teaspoon freshly ground black pepper
1 tablespoon coriander (cilantro) or chadon beni (culantro) leaves, finely chopped
½ Scotch bonnet, finely chopped (deseeded if you prefer less heat)
2 seasoning peppers (pimento/ají dulce), roughly chopped
1–2 garlic cloves, crushed

Poaching liquid

a few sprigs of thyme
a few bay leaves
5 cloves
6 allspice (pimento) berries
a few blades of mace
1 tablespoon browning

Put the intestines into a bowl and cover with cold water, then set aside.

Next, combine the rice and 250 ml (8 fl oz/1 cup) of the water in a saucepan and bring to the boil, then reduce to medium–low and cook for 15–18 minutes, or until the water has been absorbed and the rice is soft. If the water dries out too quickly, add a little more. Remove from the heat and set aside.

Pour the remaining 100 ml (3½ fl oz/scant ½ cup) water into a bowl along with the browning, salt, pepper, coriander or chadon beni, Scotch bonnet, seasoning peppers and garlic and mix well. Add the rice and mix again. To assemble, carefully tie one end of the intestine with cooking string, then place a funnel in the open end. Pour the rice mixture into the casing carefully to gradually fill it up. Gently push the rice down as it fills to fill any air pockets, but not too tightly as the casing may split. You'll see if there are any holes as it will seep out. If you do find a hole, carefully make a break in the pudding length by squeezing the rice on either side within the casing, then twist it on itself to seal and create a link in the sausage. Carefully remove the funnel and tie the end, then set aside.

Combine all the ingredients for the poaching liquid in a saucepan with 1 litre (34 fl oz/4¼ cups) water and bring to the boil, then reduce to a simmer and add the pudding. Ensure the water doesn't boil as it can break the pudding as it cooks. Cover and cook for 35–40 minutes until it has turned a darker colour and is firm to the touch. Carefully remove from the poaching liquid, then slice and serve.

GRILLED LOBSTER

SERVES 6

The bright, crystal clear waters of Barbuda wash up against its striking pink sand. Barbuda is very distinct, with is flat landscape and abundance of prickly bush making it quite different from what most would imagine in their minds when they think of the Caribbean in an often-stereotypical way. The masses of limestone and natural dry climate meant the island was unsuitable for sugar enslavement. Instead, it has long been self managed by the community that populated it and used as a space to grow fresh produce and rear livestock for the other estates owned by the Codrington family on the neighbouring islands of Antigua and Barbados. As a result, the population of Barbuda has always remained low in comparison to other islands, which has also meant the access to the natural resources have not suffered overfishing or over-exploitation. Lobster (as well as conch) are readily available and taste even better when you know they were fished out of the sea moments before being cooked – exactly what my cousin did for me when I visited.

Ingredients

3 lobsters, split in half down the middle

Garlic Butter

90 g (3¼ oz) salted butter, softened

2 tablespoons rapeseed (canola) or olive oil

4–5 garlic cloves, crushed

a few sprigs of thyme, leaves picked (optional)

a few leaves of broad leaf thyme, Spanish thyme, Mexican mint, Cuban oregano or any other oregano, leaves picked, finely chopped (optional)

1 small Scotch bonnet, finely chopped (optional)

lime wedges, to serve

First, make the garlic butter. Put the butter into a bowl and whip lightly, then add the remaining ingredients and mix well until incorporated. Place in the refrigerator to chill for 20–30 minutes.

Preheat the grill (broiler) to medium–high. Place the lobsters cut side up on a baking tray (pan). Place 1–2 tablespoons of the chilled garlic butter onto each lobster half. Cook under the grill for 10–12 minutes, or until the butter has melted and the lobster meat is opaque and has turned golden brown on top. Serve immediately with the lime wedges.

Note

You can also grill the lobsters on a hot barbecue for 5–6 minutes on each side. Once cooked, remove from the grill, then spoon on the garlic butter before serving.

NANA'S SALTFISH WITH CHOP-UP
STEWED SALTFISH WITH AUBERGINE, OKRA & SPINACH

SERVES 4

This recipe is an ode to my nana. The Barbudan in her never left, and she dedicated mealtimes to eating food from 'back home'. She was adamant that 'English food nuh av' nuh tase (taste)'. As a second-generation Barbudan, I too inherited this. Through her commitment to making meal times culturally relevant, I was able to stay rooted in my origins. She was blind, so watching her use every other sense when cooking taught me a lot. Feeling how much salt in the palm of her hand or even tasting the tiniest 'tetch' (as she would say), of marinade on the end of her tongue to make sure it was just right, was so beautiful to watch. On the days I saw my dad, he took me to her house, and saltfish was often cooked, usually alongside chop up, and maybe fried or boiled dumplings – depending on how she felt. This recipe is exactly how she would make it and is perfect for brunch.

Ingredients

250 g (9 oz) saltfish (skinless and boneless) or 400g (14 oz) bone-in saltfish

5 tablespoons rapeseed (canola) or olive oil

1 onion, roughly chopped

½ sweet (bell) pepper, any colour, thinly sliced into short strips

2 garlic cloves, crushed

½ Scotch bonnet, finely chopped (deseeded if you prefer less heat)

2 seasoning peppers (pimento/ají dulce), finely chopped

1 tablespoon tomato purée (paste)

2 tomatoes, roughly chopped

a few sprigs of thyme, leaves picked

2 spring onions (scallions), sliced

Chop-up

3 tablespoons rapeseed (canola) or olive oil

1 onion, roughly chopped

½ Scotch bonnet, finely chopped

2 aubergines (eggplants), partly peeled and cut into chunks

6 okra, trimmed and sliced

180 g (6¼ oz) spinach leaves

2 teaspoons sea salt, plus extra as needed

320 ml (11 fl oz/1⅓ cups) water

1 tablespoon extra virgin olive oil (optional)

To serve

Conkie/Ducana (see page 198)
Boiled or fried dumplings (see page 114)
Ground Provisions (see page 121)
Fried yellow plantain (see page 48)

Put the saltfish into a saucepan, cover with cold water and set aside to soak for a few hours, or overnight. Once soaked, refresh the water, place the pan over a medium heat and boil for 15–20 minutes, slightly covering the pan with a lid to allow the steam to escape. If you're using the skinless and boneless variety, pour off the hot water, rinse in cold water, then set aside. If you're using the bone-in variety, repeat the boiling again with fresh water before draining and rinsing. When the saltfish is cooked, the fish will contract and curl up on itself and the water will become cloudy from the salt removed from the fish. Once cooled, gently flake, removing any skin or bones. Set aside.

Next, heat the oil in a frying pan over a medium–high heat, then add the onion, sweet pepper, garlic, Scotch bonnet and seasoning peppers. Fry for 3–4 minutes to soften slightly. Add the tomato purée and cook into the oil for a minute or two, then fold in the fresh tomatoes and thyme leaves and cook for a further 2–3 minutes before folding in the saltfish. If the ingredients start to stick to the pan, add 2 tablespoons of water. Finally, fold in the spring onions and cook for a minute more, then remove from the heat and set aside.

Next, make the chop-up. Heat the oil in a frying pan over a medium-high heat, then add the onion and Scotch bonnet. Cook for a few minutes to start softening the onions, then add the aubergines, okra and spinach. Cook for a few more minutes to coat the vegetables in the oil, then season with the salt and add the water. Reduce the heat slightly, then continue to cook for 20–25 minutes until the aubergine and okra are soft. By this time, a good amount of the water should have been absorbed. If it hasn't, drain the excess. Next, remove from the heat and crush the mixture with a fork or potato masher. The texture should be like that of wet scrambled eggs. Finally, stir in the extra virgin olive oil (if using) and more salt to taste.

Serve with the saltfish and ducana or boiling dumplings, fried dumplings, ground provisions or fried yellow plantain.

THE SWEETNESS
OF SALTFISH

SALTFISH

BIG MONEY DOES RUN BEHIND IT
SALTFISH
MAN DOES LICK DOWN MAN TO FIND IT
SALTFISH
IT'S SWEETER THAN MEAT
WHEN YOU WANT TO EAT
ALL SALTFISH SWEET.

(Excerpt of lyrics from 'Saltfish' by Mighty Sparrow)
The Mighty Sparrow, was born on July 9, 1935 in Grand Roy,
Grenada and migrated to Trinidad with his family when
he was one year old.

Dinner time at my grandparents' was important. I was always a curious child and I loved to eat. When grandad and I pulled up outside the house from the school run, I'd rush to the steps as he stretched over my head to put the key in the front door – I was excited! As soon as the door opened, the assessment of dinner began. I knew we were having saltfish to eat before I saw it on my plate. The condensation on the windows and the intense, earthy smell of saltwater greeted you abruptly. Although the stench was foul, there was great anticipation as I knew what was coming.

If we were having saltfish, that meant hard food (all of the ground provisions): sweet potato, yam, cassava, fried plantain and, of course, dumplings – boiled or fried depending on her mood. Oh the JOY! This was one of the many moments when we closed the front door and left England outside. Inside, they took me back home, to Montserrat.

It was never a last-minute meal as the preparation, now centuries old, required planning, time and commitment, which I respect so greatly.

My great, great, great grandparents were born into bondage; these methods had been passed on from them. My mum didn't have the time or patience to cook this mid-week after full-time work, so I looked forward to eating at my grandparents' house. As with everything, it started in the market.

The fishmongers that catered to the many cultures who now resided in Leicester city by the mid 1990s, had what we needed. The piles of salted fish sat right next to the usual fresh salmon, prepared Cornish crab and jellied eel. In its original form, a whole side of it could stand as tall as my three-year-old self. They were huge and their size really demonstrated how cooking saltfish was a great labour of love. This crisp, dried, sea creature would eventually become delicate flakes of 'back home' on my plate.

Saltfish has been integral to cooking across the region since the seventeenth century and its context within our food culture has evolved continuously. What was once disregarded simply as 'food for negroes', evolved to become a traditional pantry staple and now a culinary commodity, yet today is slowly becoming financially inaccessible to the communities who redefined it through their ingenuity in the kitchen.

While it is so dear to us and eaten with pride, it was once used as a tool for control and a substandard attempt at feeding masses purely for survival. The wider, socio-political connotations saltfish carried, fully contextualised my place within our cultural history which I've learnt more and more about writing this book.

My grandmothers, along with many other Caribbeans who had migrated to the 'Mother Country' (Britain) during the early 1950s, valued cooking as a means to stay connected to the colonies they'd travelled from. They'd inspect the fish they were about to buy with great detail – prodding, poking and peeling the fish, just a small part, to 'mek sure it good'. I was always fascinated by this attention to detail from start to finish. When we took it home, the overnight soaking began. A large pan of cold water filled high to the brim, submerged the salt-crusted fish. The next morning, the water would be refreshed and the pan placed on the hob to begin cooking. As the water boiled, it would, without fail, spill over and stain the stove top, leaving these second-hand salt cakes that would need to be scoured off. The water would be changed a few times to reduce the sodium while the fresh seasonings would be prepared. Garlic, spring onions (scallions), Scotch bonnet, fresh tomatoes and (bell) peppers were sliced and diced awaiting the next stages of the cooking.

The sole purpose of the European's seizure of the Americas and creation of the 'New World' was economic power. The potential for capitalist fortune seemed limitless and colonists became extremely austere when allocating land for crop production. The Caribbean was abundant with its own Indigenous plants, the Tainos, Caribs and Sibohney had lived off it for centuries prior, however, much of this had been destroyed to make way for trade crops of sugar, indigo and tobacco, diminishing the biodiversity of the region. The captured islands produced virtually no food for the enslaved, as traders refused to dedicate land they deemed valuable to feed or nourish the thousands of humans they had acquired. Some plantations dedicated space for growing food, but it was usually land that was hard to cultivate or infertile. In Nevis, a 1755 plan of an old plantation shows an area marked as 'Negro Grounds'. Initially, salt beef was imported, along with dried staples such as rice and a variety of beans (black-eyed or cowpeas) from the West African coast travelling the middle passage. However, this wasn't sufficient to endure the toil of cane cutting from sunrise to sunset. With permission, some held their own, small vegetable gardens, called 'provision grounds' (a term still used today) to sustain themselves, but this wasn't available to all.

Even though the islands were surrounded by water, seafood and local fish played a minimal role in the diets of the enslaved. The British found themselves at odds, being outside of their usual environment, as much of the local fauna on the new land they settled was unrecognisable. The precarity of their colonial position fed their lack of trust when eating Indigenous foods, which meant the importation of commodities was key.

The icy waters of the North Atlantic were brimming with sea-life, in particular, cod. These large water mammals were easy to fish, lean and meaty. By the seventeenth century, hundreds of tons of salted fish left the shores of Nova Scotia and beyond, destined for the Caribbean. Compressed in tightly sealed wooden barrels with salt produced in the Americas, it quickly established itself as a crucial cog in the system of commerce that criss-crossed the Atlantic for centuries to come. As the demand grew, and sugar production rose, copious amounts of molasses and rum headed north in exchange for the saltfish that returned south.

Codrington, Barbuda – the village my paternal grandparents were born in, named after the family who once owned plantations across Antigua, Barbuda and Barbados, kept a series of detailed records from 1700–1869 relating to their estates across the three islands – 'The Codrington Papers'. These documents hold the precise inventories of all imported and rationed foods, giving a glimpse into plantation life. Between 1793–1861, 34,652 lb (15,718 kg) of codfish were ordered and imported for the Codrington estates in Antigua. Although, its primary purpose was to nourish cheaply, saltfish quickly became a tool to maintain, legitimise and deconstruct power. The increased production of saltfish naturally influenced the palates of Europe with some shipments of the 'best quality cod' heading East. Of all the grades, the lowest was termed 'West India' or 'Refuse fish' – simply put, for the market it was reserved for or the European markets who denied it. It was drier and yellowish with the lowest meat to skin ratio compared to its superior. It wasn't considered food, but served its purpose as edible. The better cuts were whiter, had less skin and a thicker flesh. The way I learnt to discern a piece 'good' from 'bad' – too much bone, little flesh or discoloration, replicated that of my ancestors from centuries prior when premium cuts were reserved as a reward to enforce class and hierarchy. There's something to be said about how food can transcend us, as even with that history, one of my favourite foods to eat is saltfish.

ST. KITTS & NEVIS

**CAMERHOGNE
CONCEPTION ISLAND**

The Georgian-style buildings that still stand across the capital of Basseterre, capture a part of St. Kitts' past. Pottery played an important role inside and outside people's kitchens during the colonial period. Unlike language, which was forcibly removed, food and the means to prepare it became the space that enabled those on plantations to hold onto their culture as best they could. When cooking, it was only natural to repeat practices that were already learnt, even if utilising new or different cooking techniques for survival.

St. Kitts and Nevis has a long history of traditional pottery making. The natural clay stores, limestone reserves, black sand and other earthly materials across Nevis, created the perfect environment to create such wares, often made by those free and enslaved to be used in plantation kitchens or sold at market.

Brimstone Hill, an old fortress, now a national park once used as a military base during one of the many conflicts between the British and French, sits on the north-western side of St. Kitts. Over the years, remnants of pottery have been discovered throughout its grounds, giving an insight to the foods that were cooked and how. 'Monkey jugs' – a cylindrical vessel with a constricted neck, a strap handle and spout, commonly used for catching water or yabba – typically used for cooking over fire. Some items discovered were understood to be native to other places based on the materials they were made from, however, the discoveries did paint a broader picture of inter-island trade and how this was common practice among those that were 'free' before abolition. Many of the ceramic remnants discovered were often bowl-like in shape and design giving us an idea of what type of meals were cooked.

The village of Juffure, conveniently located on the Gambia River emerged at the heart of the Atlantic trade and commercial presence. They too produced ceramic wares made from sand, clay and broken oyster shells, which they often traded for New World ingredients. It was most likely low, slow, liquid-based cooking, such as soups or baobab leaf stew, that would have taken place; evolved once in the Caribbean. Not only is it a reflection of the preserved foodways, but it was also an efficient way to use limited ingredients or feed a larger group of people without having to stand over a stove if there were, likely, many other responsibilities or limited time. When I think back to the small rationales that existed when my grandparents were cooking, this sentiment still is ever present in the cooking today – 'Always cook a lil' extra just in case someone pass'. You never cooked just enough, and the food sat on the stove for hours for whomever to be fed.

CONKIE/DUCANA
CORNMEAL, SWEET POTATO & COCONUT STEAMED IN BANANA LEAVES

SERVES 4–6

The method of wrapping, then steaming or boiling ingredients in banana leaves is an ancient method used by communities across the world. *Kenkey* is a dish made from fermented corn, then cooked in corn husks or banana leaves by the Ga people of Southern Ghana. It is also known as *komi* (Ga), *dokono* (Twi), *dokon/dokono* (Fante), and *tim* (Ewe) across other regions of Ghana, *moi moi* in Nigeria and *olele* in Sierra Leone. The cooking technique was retained, evolving the ingredients to incorporate dried cornmeal or sweet potato, pumpkin and coconut instead of beans or fermented corn. The term *dokono* by the Fante of Ghana, bears great similarity to the first recorded use of a 'pudding dressed in banana leaf' in Jamaica in 1740. Now, almost every island and parts of South America have their own name for this dish: Haiti – *doukounou*, Jamaica – blue draws, Barbados & Guyana, St. Kitts – *conkie*, Puerto Rico – *pasteles*, Antigua and Barbuda – *ducana*, Trinidad and Tobago – *paime* (sweet) and *pastelle* (savoury), Cuba – *tamales*, Aruba, Bonaire and Curaçao – *ayaka*, Dominican Republic – p*asteles en hoja*.

Ingredients

30 g (1 oz) salted butter

60 g (2 oz/⅓ cup) dark brown soft sugar

120 g (4¼ oz) white sweet potato, finely grated

100 g (3½ oz) dry coconut (copra), finely grated (or desiccated/dried shredded coconut)

2 teaspoons ground cinnamon

1 teaspoon freshly grated nutmeg

1 teaspoon vanilla extract or vanilla bean paste

150 g (5½ oz/1 cup) fine cornmeal

100 g (3½ oz/generous ¾ cup) plain (all-purpose) flour

50 g (1¾ oz/scant ½ cup) raisins or sultanas (golden raisins)

120 ml (4 fl oz/½ cup) water

1–2 tablespoons rapeseed (canola) or vegetable oil

banana leaves or greaseproof paper, for wrapping, cut to 15 × 20 cm (6 × 8 in)

To serve

Saltfish and Chop-up (see page 191)

Put the butter and sugar into a bowl and beat until soft and fluffy. Add the grated sweet potato and coconut, then mix until combined. Add the spices, vanilla, cornmeal, flour, raisins or sultanas, then mix again. Slowly add the water and bring together to form a soft, sticky dough.

Place 3–4 tablespoons of the dough into the centre of each banana leaf (alternatively, you can use greaseproof paper). Rub a little oil onto your fingertips and form the dough into a rectangle shape, then fold the long edges of the leaf into the centre. Next, fold the top and bottom end into the middle to completely encase the filling. Finally, use a piece of cooking string or twine to fasten the closed parcel. Repeat with the remaining parcels, then place them in a steamer. Steam for 30–40 minutes, or until the dough is solid and no longer sticky. Carefully remove from the steamer and serve.

STEW SALTFISH & COCONUT DUMPLINGS

SERVES 4–6

Stew saltfish and coconut dumplings is the national dish of St. Kitts and Nevis. The main ingredient of saltfish became common throughout the British West Indies during the colonial period. Thousands of miles north in Newfoundland, the region was sought out to be utilised for its marine capabilities. Most fish caught in this area was produced for export, and top destinations were the British colonies in the Caribbean, as well as Spain and Portugal. The fishery in Newfoundland produced a variety of grades of saltfish to meet the different market demands. Spain and Portugal requested higher grades of fish, whereas the British colonies demanded poorer quality and cheaper cures, so much so, it was labelled 'West India', specifically for plantations. Salting is an ancient technique for preservation that can be dated back as far as the Egyptians. While saltfish became a cheap and easy commodity to feed those on plantations from Newfoundland in the North Atlantic, the salt needed to come from somewhere. The Dutch led the way on salt mining across Aruba, Bonaire, Curaçao and Sint Maarten – their colonies in the Caribbean – exporting it as a vital component in the transatlantic trade of commodities during this time. The ability to preserve and store fish allowed it to become a mainstay in the diet of the region, which it is still to this day.

Ingredients

250 g (9 oz) skinless and boneless saltfish or 400 g (14 oz) bone-in saltfish
2 tablespoons rapeseed (canola) or olive oil
1 onion, roughly chopped
3 garlic cloves, crushed
1 Scotch bonnet, diced (deseeded if you prefer less heat)
1–2 (bell) peppers, any colour, finely chopped
2 seasoning peppers (pimento/ají dulce), roughly chopped
2 tomatoes, roughly chopped
175 ml (6 fl oz/¾ cup) coconut milk
1 teaspoon freshly ground black pepper
2 spring onions (scallions), sliced
2 tablespoons chadon beni (culantro/recao) or coriander (cilantro), finely chopped

Coconut Dumplings

50 g (1¾ oz) shredded fresh coconut or desiccated (dried shredded) coconut
160 g (5¾ oz/generous 1¼ cups) plain (all-purpose) flour
2 teaspoons sea salt
¼ teaspoon baking powder
1 tablespoon rapeseed (canola) or olive oil
75 ml (2½ fl oz/5 tablespoons) coconut milk

First, prepare the dough for the coconut dumplings. Combine the coconut, flour, 1 teaspoon of the salt, the baking powder, oil and coconut milk in a bowl and mix together to form a soft dough. Lightly knead, then cover and set aside to rest for 30 minutes.

Meanwhile, prepare the saltfish. Put the saltfish into a saucepan, cover with cold water and set aside to soak for a few hours, or overnight. Once soaked, refresh the water, place the pan over a medium heat and boil for 15–20 minutes, slightly covering the pan with a lid to allow the steam to escape. If you're using the skinless and boneless variety, pour off the hot water, rinse in cold water, then set aside. If you're using the bone-in variety, repeat the boiling again with fresh water before draining and rinsing. When the saltfish is cooked, the fish will contract and curl up on itself and the water will become cloudy from the salt removed from the fish. Once cooled, gently flake the fish, removing any skin or bones. Don't flake it too much as it will break up further when mixed in with the other ingredients. Set aside.

Once the dumpling dough has rested, bring a large saucepan of water to the boil and add the remaining teaspoon of salt. Divide the dough into 8–10 pieces and roll into balls. Add them to the boiling water, pressing them in the middle to flatten them slightly as you do so. Reduce to a simmer, then cover and cook for 15–20 minutes, or until they rise to the top of the water and become firm.

While the dumplings are cooking, finish making the saltfish. Heat the oil in a frying pan over a medium heat, then add the onion, garlic, Scotch bonnet, peppers and seasoning peppers. Fry for a few minutes until they have softened a little, then add the tomatoes and saltfish. Cook for a few minutes more, then add the coconut milk and black pepper. Mix carefully to bring everything together then cover and cook for 10 minutes. Finish with the chadon beni and spring onions, then serve with the coconut dumplings.

THE DUTCH
CARIBBEAN:
ARUBA,
BONAIRE
& CURAÇAO

OUBAO
SHELL ISLAND
BONAY
LOW COUNTRY

Most of us are familiar with the mass sugar production across the Caribbean and Americas, but there's another crucial commodity that we couldn't imagine our lives without today. Before refrigeration was invented, the crystallised fragments of evaporated sea water was the only mineral that could preserve fresh meat or fish. 'Salu' is the Papiamento word for salt, an industry of which the Dutch dominated across the region from the seventeenth century. Papiamento (or Papiamentu) is a Creole language spoken across the Dutch Caribbean combining the Dutch, Afro-Portuguese pidgin – a language developed and used between the enslaved and colonisers of Portuguese – and Gbe, Bantu languages from the Congo-Angola region of West Africa) and, the Judeo-Spanish spoken by the Sephardic Jewish community who fled persecution to Brazil before finally settling in Dutch ruled Curaçao after being expelled in 1651.

The landscapes of the ABC (Aruba, Bonaire and Curaçao) islands, sitting just off the northern coasts of Venezuela are not what you'd typically expect when thinking of the Caribbean, in a sense. While visiting Aruba a few years back, I was so surprised to see the terrain is dry, somewhat dusty and the greenery is thick with cacti and prickly bush instead of lush palm trees bearing coconuts.

Across all three islands, the Indigenous communities such as the Caquetio (a group who travelled to the islands from Venezuela), had already been utilising the naturally occurring salt pans that sat just off the low-lying southern coasts of Bonaire. Much to the disappointment of the Spanish who arrived in the early sixteenth century, the land wasn't considered of 'value'. They continued to collect the naturally occurring salt deposits used to prepare salt beef, until the arrival of the Dutch who expelled them. The Dutch were in search of alternative sources of salt – other than Portugal – with whom they were at war with over the commodity – for their prized Baltic herring catches. At this time, Spain dominated salt pans across the Mediterranean and production globally.

Seizing the opportunity, they established salt mining at an industrial level across the ABC islands as well as, Saba, Sint Eustatius and Sint Maarten (the southern part of the island of Saint Martin which The French and the Dutch signed the 'Treaty of Concordia' or 'Partition Treaty', on March 23rd, 1648, acknowledging the split of the island between France and Holland). This very salt went on to be exported across the Americas, in particular to the North Atlantic to produce the salt fish that would return in barrels to feed the people that once harvested that same salt to preserve it.

SOPI DI PISKA
ANTILLEAN FISH STEW

SERVES 4–6

Sopi means soup in the local dialect of Papiamentu, found across the islands of the Dutch Caribbean. Papiamentu is considered the mother tongue of the Dutch Caribbean and evolved from Dutch and Portuguese pidgin. With the Aruba, Bonaire and Curaçao being so close to the Northern coasts of South America, there is a large Venezuelan and Colombian influence in the cuisine. This seafood stew is one I tasted when visiting Aruba, and it was absolutely delicious, very similar to *cazuela de mariscos*, a Colombian seafood soup made with coconut milk and a mixture of seafood.

Ingredients

200 g (7 oz) fresh conch (or substitute for more prawns, squid or snapper)

2 tablespoons rapeseed (canola) or olive oil

30 g (1 oz) salted butter

3 garlic cloves, crushed

140 g (5 oz) carrots, peeled and diced

400 g (14 oz) pumpkin, peeled and diced

1 onion, finely chopped

1 green (bell) pepper, finely chopped

1 tablespoon tomato purée (paste)

3 spring onions (scallions), finely sliced

2 tablespoons chadon beni (culantro/recao) or coriander (cilantro), roughly chopped

1.4 litres (47⅓ fl oz/6 cups) fish stock

400 ml (14 fl oz/generous 1½ cups) coconut milk

250 g (9 oz) mussels, cleaned

250 g (9 oz) clams, cleaned

¼ teaspoon freshly ground black pepper

1 tablespoon sea salt, or to taste

200 g (7 oz) squid, cut into strips and scored

150 g (5½ oz) raw shelled prawns (shrimp)

1 snapper, filleted and cut into medium-large chunks

To serve

Hot Pepper Sauce (see page 305)

Put the conch into a saucepan with 1.5 litres (50¾ fl oz/6⅓ cups) water. Bring to the boil, then reduce slightly to a high simmer and cook for 90 minutes to tenderise the conch. The conch will stiffen slightly when it first enters the water but will soften once cooked. Drain the conch, then set aside to cool a little before cutting into medium pieces.

Heat the oil and butter in a large saucepan over a medium-high heat, then add the garlic, half the carrots and pumpkin, onion, green pepper, tomato purée, half of the spring onions and half the chadon beni or coriander.

Stir and cook the vegetables for a few minutes, then add the fish stock and coconut milk. Reduce the heat slightly, cover and simmer for 15–20 minutes, or until the pumpkin is soft. Next, remove the pan from the heat and blend the soup with a hand-held blender until smooth, then set aside.

Put the mussels and clams into a large saucepan, cover with boiling water, then cover and simmer for 2 minutes, or until the shells have opened. Strain the shellfish and discard any that haven't opened.

Return the soup base to the heat, then add the black pepper and salt, the remaining carrots and pumpkin and the squid, conch and shrimp. Cook for 5 minutes, then add the snapper and cook for a further 5 minutes. Finally, add the mussels and clams, cook for a further 2–3 minutes to heat through, then serve hot, finished with the remaining spring onions, chadon beni and a dash of hot pepper sauce.

GUIAMBO & FUNGEE
OKRA STEW WITH SALTED PORK & FISH & TURNED CORNMEAL

SERVES 4

The beauty of okra is that the etymology of its native name has somehow remained in the dishes it's prominent in, keeping it forever connected to its origins. Guiambo, just like Louisiana gumbo, derives from the Bantu word *ki'ngombo*, which translates to 'okra'. Originally used as a thickener for traditional dishes across the West coast of Africa, such as okro soup or stew in present day Nigeria or Ghana, the style in which it was used in cooking was beautifully preserved, incorporating the limiting provisions of salted pork or fish as the main protein and flavour of the dish. Similarly, guiambo is served with fungi (*fungee/cou cou/cou cou pois*) on the side, just as okro soup would be served with *fufu* (pounded cassava, plantain or yam).

Ingredients

500 g (1 lb 2 oz) salted beef or pigs' tails cut into medium chunks

1.2 litres (40 fl oz/5 cups) fish stock

300 g (10½ oz) okra, finely sliced

a few bay leaves

a few sprigs of thyme

3 spring onions, finely sliced

1 Scotch bonnet, left whole (split in half if you prefer more heat)

½ teaspoon freshly ground white pepper

¼ teaspoon black pepper

1 medium snapper, sea bream or sea bass, cleaned and scaled, then sliced into 6–8 steaks

1 teaspoon sea salt (optional, to taste)

Fungee

300g (10½ oz) fine cornmeal

400 ml (14 fl oz/generous 1½ cups) cold water + 500 ml (17 fl oz/generous 2 cups) hot water

2 teaspoons sea salt

2 teaspoons rapeseed (canola) or olive oil

Put the salted meat into a saucepan and cover with 1.2 litres (40 fl oz/5 cups) of cold water. Bring to the boil, then reduce to a simmer and cook for 25–30 minutes. Remove from heat and strain, then set the meat aside.

Pour the fish stock into another large pan over a medium–high heat. Add the okra, bay leaves, thyme, spring onion, Scotch bonnet, both peppers and bring to a boil. Once boiling, return the meats to the pan. Boil for a few minutes then reduce the heat slightly to a low boil/high simmer. Cover and cook for 20 minutes. At this stage, add the fish then continue to cook the guiambo for a further 15–20 minutes or until the okra has broken up and the soup becomes thick. Check again for seasoning and salt to taste and set aside.

Meanwhile, make the fungee. Add the cornmeal to the bowl and whisk in 400ml cold water, until smooth then set aside.

Next add 200ml (7 fl oz/scant 1 cup) of the hot water to a pan with the salt and oil over a medium–high heat and add the cornmeal and water mix. Ensure the heat isn't too high as the cornmeal won't cook enough and will absorb the liquid too quickly.

Whisk over medium heat, gradually adding the remaining hot water for 15–18 minutes depending on how quick the cornmeal absorbs the water and how hot the pan is. The consistency should be smooth, light and thick with no lumps. It shouldn't feel grainy but smooth when tasted. If it feels dry or stiff, add extra water 1 tablespoon at a time.

Once the right consistency has been achieved, remove the pan from the heat and shape the cornmeal. Using a small bowl add ½ teaspoon of oil to coat, add a quarter of the cooked cornmeal then carefully rotate the bowl swiftly to create a smooth, round dome. Turn out onto a plate then repeat with the remaining cornmeal. To serve, place a ball of the fungee in a wide bowl or deep plate and serve alongside the guiambo.

THE FRENCH CARIBBEAN: GUADELOUPE & MARTINIQUE

**KARUKERA
ISLAND OF GUMTREES
JOUANACAEIRA
LAND OF IGUANA**

The he French joined the colonial race in the West during the mid-seventeenth century. Originally named (*Karukera* – 'Island of Beautiful Waters' and *Iouanacaera* – 'Land of Iguana'), Guadeloupe, Martinique and the neighbouring islands within the archipelago, which were named Les Saintes, Marie-Galante and La Desirade, were captured from Spain. The northern half of Saint Martin – in 1648 – and St. Domingue (the west side of Santo Domingo, present day Haiti) – in 1697 – also became part of the colony.

The French began establishing masses of indigo plantations across its colonies and some of the smaller islands it held momentarily in the Lesser Antilles (such as Dominica, St. Lucia and briefly Montserrat) as well as cotton, coffee and sometimes tobacco due to its success in the Southern states of America. The Spanish had already dispelled the majority of the Tainos and Caribs upon landing in the region in the early fifteenth century. The major shift to a sugar monoculture occurred during the eighteenth century with communities from across Africa, Bantu (Southeast and West Central Africa), Senegambia, Sierra Leone, Bight of Benin and Biafra, Congo-Angola, Hausa and Gbari of Northen Nigeria, Igo, Ewe-For and Yoruba of Southern Nigeria used as free labour.

Unique to the French Caribbean colonies, especially that of Martinique and Guadeloupe, was the *Code Noir* (Black Code) – a charter established to regulate the French colonial system, with the intent of protecting those enslaved from the late seventeenth century. It mandated a standardised dietary minimum across all estates:

'… *each week planters would provide: "two pots and a half, Paris measure, cassava flour, or three cassava, each weighing 2 and ½ pounds at least, or the equivalent, with 2 pounds of corned beef, 3 pounds of fish or other things in proportion."*'

The subsistence provided for them was never enough, with many suffering from malnutrition and other diet-related diseases. The actual foods provisioned varied from estate to estate but were mostly a combination of the creolised foodways evolving in the region, carbohydrate-based with little protein. For example: manioc (cassava), potatoes (imported, then propagated), green bananas, proteins – salted beef (eventually imported from Puerto Rico), fresh fish, or turtle – and mostly manioc flour. It was hard for governments to implement the *Code Noir* on plantations, as owners mostly operated under their own terms across their claimed lands. As a result of the continued lack of sustenance, the self-provisioning by the enslaved across the French Caribbean islands increased over time. Plantation owners encouraged the growing and rearing of their own produce as it relieved them of the burden.

The enslaved communities created their own unique system of foodways and self-sufficiency to survive, which has informed the basis of French Caribbean cooking today. They reared cattle, sheep, goats, pigs (often slaughtered for special occasions or to be sold at market) and chickens (for meat and eggs) – all of which were brought to the islands from Europe – and also caught native opossum, agouti, and mongoose (introduced in the second half of the nineteenth century).

Fish varieties found in the swampy mangroves or reefs of low-lying coastal waters were also utilised for shellfish, sea turtle, land crab, sea urchin, and numerous marine and mangrove shellfish. Snapper, grouper, balao, barracuda and herrings, still consumed today within the French Caribbean diet, featuring in dishes such as *crab matété* (see page 213) or *blaff* – similar to fish broth (see page 227).

Fish is a big part of Caribbean food culture, from as early as the indigenous communities that inhabited the land before it was taken over by European colonists. Access has always been easy due to the fact the islands are surrounded by the Atlantic Ocean on the eastern coasts and Caribbean sea towards the west-both of which have an abundance of glorious sea life.

RIGHT Cleaning fish at the fish market, Pointe-à-Pitre, Guadeloupe.
BELOW Boats on Heywoods Beach, Saint Lucy, Barbados.

MATOUTOU/MATÉTÉ
LANDCRAB & RICE

SERVES 4

Landcrabs have been eaten for centuries in the Caribbean, initially by the Indigenous communities, then African populations. During the colonial period, colonists saw crab as 'poor food' and valued the meat of land mammals such as goat, ox and chicken, hence it wasn't something they consumed often. The forced conversion of the enslaved from their own belief systems to Christianity, meant they had to participate in all of the religious occasions. During the lenten period, they were forbidden from eating fatty meats, instead only allowed to consume fish and shellfish. On Easter Sunday, at the end of the fasts, the enslaved were said to meet in the *rue cases-Nègres* (streets between the houses of the enslaved), to finish the large quantities of crab that remained, knowing they could consume meat again the next day. Over time, to assimilate into society, the consumption of crab on Easter Sunday was rejected by some, as they wanted to eat meat like the 'upper classes' once did. Since then, as a way of preserving the past, the dish is now eaten on Easter Monday.

Ingredients

4 blue crabs, cut in half (or 8 large crab claws, such as brown crab)
juice of 2 limes
2 tablespoons sea salt
3–4 garlic cloves, crushed
3 spring onions (scallions), thinly sliced
1 Scotch bonnet, finely chopped (or left whole if you prefer less heat)
3 tablespoons rapeseed (canola) or olive oil
1 onion, finely chopped
200 g (7 oz) smoked ham or bacon, diced
3 tablespoons Colombo Spice Mix (see page 214)
6 cloves
6 allspice (pimento) berries
4 tomatoes, finely chopped
500 ml (17 fl oz/generous 2 cups) water or fish stock
300 g (10½ oz/1½ cups) jasmine or basmati rice
a few sprigs of thyme
a few bay leaves
3 tablespoons roughly chopped parsley leaves

Put the crabs into a bowl with the lime juice, salt, garlic, spring onions and Scotch bonnet. Mix well, then set aside to marinate.

Heat the oil in a large saucepan over a medium-high heat, then add the onion and ham or bacon and cook a few minutes before adding the colombo spice mix, cloves and allspice berries to cook out briefly. Next, stir in the tomatoes and cook for a few minutes, then add the crab and the marinade from the bowl. Mix well to coat the crab in the pan's contents. Keep stirring for a few minutes, then add the water or fish stock. Bring to the boil, reduce to a simmer, cover and cook for 5–6 minutes. Add the rice, thyme and bay leaves and mix well so that the crab is evenly distributed throughout the rice, then cover and cook for 15–20 minutes, or until all of the liquid has been absorbed by the rice. Once cooked, remove from the heat, open the lid to allow the steam to escape and ensure the rice doesn't over cook. If the rice is still a little firm, keep the lid on and allow it to steam for a further 5 minutes or until ready to serve. Finish with the parsley, then serve.

COLOMBO
MARTINIQUE/GUADELOUPE CURRY

SERVES 4

Indo-Martiniquans and Indo-Guadeloupeans make up approximately 10 per cent of the population on the island, mostly descended from the indentured labourers that arrived during the 1800s. A recipe introduced to the island by this community is colombo. It is said to have derived from the Tamil word *kulambu*, which references curry. The recipe has a unique addition of roasted, uncooked rice added to the whole spices before being ground, making the sauce thicker and richer. On my travels, I tried colombo from a small, casual eating place in Guadeloupe. It was lightly spiced, and the sauce was thick with a strong citrusy flavour from the added lime juice. Sometimes courgette and aubergine are added to the sauce; the one I had was made without. Definitely unique.

Ingredients

1 kg (2 lb 4 oz) chicken thighs and drumsticks

juice of 2 limes

a few sprigs of thyme

3–4 garlic cloves, crushed

1 Scotch bonnet, split in half
(or left whole if you prefer less heat)

2 teaspoons sea salt, or to taste

2–3 tablespoons rapeseed (canola) or olive oil

100 ml (3½ fl oz/scant ½ cup) water

1 onion, finely chopped

400 ml (14 fl oz/generous 1½ cups) coconut milk

1 aubergine (eggplant), courgette (zucchini)
or 1 chayote (chou chou/christophene), diced
into medium chunks diced (optional)

Colombo Spice Mix

30 g (1 oz/scant ¼ cup) white rice, any variety

15 g (½ oz) cumin seeds

15 g (½ oz) coriander seeds

½ tablespoon black mustard seeds

½ tablespoon black peppercorns

½ tablespoon fenugreek seeds

1 teaspoon fennel seeds

½ teaspoon whole cloves

½ teaspoon allspice (pimento) berries

30 g (1 oz) ground turmeric

To serve

White Rice (see page 34)

First, make the spice mix. Heat a dry frying pan over a medium heat, then add all the ingredients except the turmeric. Toast in the pan for no more than a minute to ensure they don't burn. The pan will smoke a little and you will be able to smell the spices toasting. Remove from the heat and transfer to a spice grinder or pestle and mortar along with the turmeric, then grind to a fine powder.

Next, put the chicken into a bowl along with the lime juice, thyme, garlic, Scotch bonnet, salt and 3 tablespoons of the spice mix. Mix well to ensure everything is coated, then cover and set aside in the refrigerator to marinate for a few hours, or overnight.

When you're ready to cook, remove the marinated meat from the refrigerator and set aside for 30 minutes to allow to come to room temperature.

Heat the oil in a saucepan over a medium-high heat, then add 3 tablespoons of the colombo spice mix and cook in the oil for a few minutes. Pour in the water, add the onions then simmer for 3–4 minutes before adding the chicken. Mix the chicken into the spices, then reduce the heat slightly and cook for a few minutes, allowing the meat to release its juices. Next, add the coconut milk, increase the heat slightly and bring to a low boil. Once bubbling, add the aubergine, courgette or chayote (if using), reduce to a simmer, cover and cook for 40–50 minutes, or until the meat is tender. Serve with white rice.

CHATROU FRICASSÉE

STEWED BABY OCTOPUS WITH TOMATO AND CLOVES

SERVES 4

Chatrou fricasée literally translates to octopus stew in French. The baby octopus are cooked down slowly with tomatoes, thyme and really good fish stock, making it extra rich once finished. The addition of whole cloves and lime juice add a lovely subtle spice and acidity to the dish. It's perfect served with white rice.

Ingredients

700–750 g (1 lb 9 oz–1 lb 10 oz) whole baby octopus (or whole baby squids)

juice of 2 limes

1 tablespoon sea salt

2 garlic cloves, crushed

2 spring onions (scallions), finely chopped

a few sprigs of thyme

4 tablespoons rapeseed (canola) or olive oil

1 onion, finely chopped

40 g (1½ oz) tomato purée (paste)

200 g (7 oz) tinned chopped tomatoes

1 bay leaf

5 cloves

400 ml (14 fl oz/generous 1½ cups) fish or shellfish stock

1 Scotch bonnet split in half if you prefer more heat)

2 tablespoons roughly chopped parsley leaves

To serve

White Rice (see page 34)

Put the octopus into a bowl along with the lime juice, salt, garlic, spring onions and thyme. Mix well to coat the octopus, then cover and set aside to marinate in the refrigerator for 1 hour, or overnight.

Heat the oil in a large saucepan over a medium–high heat, then add the onion and fry for a few minutes until starting to soften. Add the octopus and the marinade from the bowl and cook for a few minutes until the octopus starts to change to turn pink and opaque. Next, add the tomato purée, chopped tomatoes, bay leaf and cloves. Cook for a few minutes, then add the stock and whole Scotch bonnet, cover and simmer for 45–50 minutes, or until the liquid has reduced by half, the oil has separated and the octopus are tender. Finish with the parsley and serve with rice.

POULET BOUCANE

GRILLED CHICKEN WITH SAUCE CHIEN (DOG SAUCE)

SERVES 4

Poulet boucane, literally translates to 'smoked chicken' in French Creole. The words *barbakot* and *boukan* are said to be Carib (Kalinago) for 'stick framework, grill'. Prior to the colonisation of Europe, the Taino, Carib and Guanahatabey in Hispaniola (present day Haiti and Dominican Republic) used wooden structures to roast meat over fire. This was their way of cooking and preserving meat. The term became known as *barbacoa* and is said to be the origins of the modern day barbecue.

Today, the many plumes of smoke you'll find across the island is an indication of how popular this dish is. It's not something you'll find on the tables of eating establishments or restaurants, only on roadsides, by those who are known to do it best. Martinicans are particularly loyal to their *poulet boucane* griller, even though the flavour profiles of lime, garlic and olive oil in the marinade are common. Naturally, each cook has their own unique taste, and their recipe is often guarded with great secrecy. Grilled chicken is common to most, but what makes this dish special is the caramelised flavours that encases the chicken from roasting the sugar cane. Some even toss discarded coconut shells into the coals, for extra flavour and burning fuel.

Ingredients

1.5–2 kg (3 lb 5 oz–4 lb 8 oz) chicken, spatchcocked (or chicken legs)

Brine

60 g (2 oz/scant ½ cup) sea salt

100 g (3½ oz/scant ½ cup) raw cane sugar

1 litre (34 fl oz/4¼ cups) water

Marinade

4–5 spring onions (scallions), finely sliced

8 garlic cloves, crushed

2 Scotch bonnets, finely chopped

4 sprigs of thyme, leaves picked

juice of 3 limes

2 tablespoons apple cider vinegar

2 teaspoons freshly ground black pepper

Sauce Chien

15 g (½ oz) parsley leaves, finely chopped

2 garlic cloves, crushed

3 spring onions (scallions), finely sliced

1 round shallot, finely chopped

2 Scotch bonnets, finely chopped (deseeded if you prefer less heat)

juice of 2 limes

100 ml (3½ fl oz/scant ½ cup) extra virgin olive oil

60 ml (2 fl oz/¼ cup) warm water

1 teaspoon sea salt, or to taste

½ teaspoon freshly ground black pepper

The brine in this recipe is optional and not traditional, but I find it makes the meat extra juicy when being barbecued. To make the brine, combine all the ingredients in a large bowl and stir to dissolve, then add the chicken and top up with water so that it just covers the meat. Cover, then set aside in the refrigerator for 24 hours. Once brined, remove the chicken and place it in a clean bowl, discarding the brine. Combine all the ingredients for the marinade in a food processor and blend to a paste. Rub the marinade all over the chicken, cover and set aside in the refrigerator to marinate for a few hours, or overnight.

When you're ready to cook, prepare a barbecue. When the coals are white, place the chicken on the grill. Cook for 1¼–1½ hours, turning regularly, until the core temperature reaches at least 75°C (165°F), or the juices run clear when poked with a knife.

Meanwhile prepare the sauce chien. Combine the parsley, garlic, spring onions, shallot, Scotch bonnet, lime juice and oil in a bowl. Slowly pour in the warm water, mixing until well incorporated. Finish with the salt and pepper, then mix again. Once the chicken is cooked, place it on a large platter or board and slice into pieces. Spoon the sauce over the meat or serve on the side.

Note

If you don't have access to a barbecue, you can cook the chicken in the oven. Preheat the oven to 180°C fan (400°F), then place the chicken on a baking tray (pan) and roast in the oven for 1 hour 20 minutes, or until the juices run clear.

THE BRITISH CARIBBEAN: MONTSERRAT, THE CAYMAN ISLANDS & ANGUILLA

ALLIOUAGANA
LAND OF THE PRICKLY BUSH
LAGARTOS
LARGE LIZARD
MALLIOUHANA
ARROW-SHAPED SEA SERPENT

uring the mid 1900s following the end of World War II, a political opportunity opened across the Caribbean, through which many sought to gain independence from their European powers. The islands that didn't – Anguilla, The Cayman Islands, The British Virgin Islands and Montserrat – still operate under the British Crown, classed as British Overseas Territories.

There's a special place in Montserrat that says, 'If you drink the water from this turn, you shall return'. I did the first time I went to Montserrat at 14 and again at 31. This very waterway, Runaway Ghaut (a deep ravine that carries rainwater), was named as such following a French attack on the island in 1712, after being used as an escape route. The trail, which my family and I trekked, along the waterway and deep into the mountainous bush, is still there today. Along the route were fruit trees bearing their greatness; soursop, fresh almonds and bay leaves. Tamarind trees flourished as their pods hung over the roadside, young coconuts filled with water were in abundance and cinnamon bark that peeled off the tree stump like a roll of wallpaper.

The mountainous landscapes of the island, one being the dormant Soufriere volcano, reminded Columbus of the Jesuit Monastery on the outskirts of Barcelona, to which he renamed the island *Santa Maria de Montserrate* when he sighted them on November 10th, 1493.

One thing unique about Montserrat, or 'The Emerald Isle' as it is also known, is that it is the only place outside of Ireland that celebrates St. Patrick's Day as a national holiday. I always wondered why this was and had no idea how poignant the Irish ancestry on the island was. Although a festival and celebration now, St. Patrick's in Montserrat historically commemorates the largest rebellion by the enslaved on March 17th, 1768.

The Irish later settled around 1632, as Montserrat became a haven and political, religious refuge for Irish Catholics fleeing persecution in Virginia, North America, and oppression by the English Oliver Cromwell, who set out to capture parts of the Caribbean from Spain. Many planters of the white elite and indentured workers, who had been exiled from neighbouring St. Kitts and Nevis, continued their sugar slavery endeavours, and for the first time, unlike other islands, the white middle class was predominantly Irish. They followed the same plantation system on neighbouring islands that they were once subjugated by, instead, bringing free labour from the West Coasts of Africa.

Story has it that, on one particular St. Patrick's day, the enslaved planned an uprising to free themselves, as they knew the plantation owners would be distracted by the festivities. Unwittingly, their plans were overheard and abruptly quelled. To make an example of those involved, Cudjoe's head, the perceived leader, was hung in a tree for all to see. I remember hearing my grandparents' reference *Cudjoehead* in conversation, a place that not only marks a poignant time in history, but an area they frequented at a time in their life. After the sugar industry started to decline, Montserrat thrived in Sea Island cotton, arrowroot and lime production especially, which helped the island survive from the mid 1800s to the early 1900s.

The legacy of my family and countless other Montserratians was forever changed in the summer of 1995. For the first time in approximately four hundred years, the dormant Soufrière Hills Volcano erupted, completely destroying anything in its path, burying the capital city of Plymouth (now termed 'the buried city') and neighbouring villages of Bethel, Bramble Village and Long Ground, to name a few. Many others within the vicinity, such as Harris's, Gages and Dyers – where my grandparents were born and raised – were evacuated and still remain uninhabited. Overgrown with thick bush and greenery, the roofs of buildings are now at ground level, never to be recovered. I will never be able to see or touch the lands they once called home. The closest I got this year was standing at the top of Garibaldi Hill, on the South Western coast, high enough to look down into the valley that abruptly turns from a bright, blushed green to a dusty brown, where the pyroclastic flow ran down into the Caribbean Sea. The southernmost two-thirds of the island have been covered in deep layers of thick ash and mud for over twenty years. Possibly in future decades to come, the earth will renew but as it stands, Montserrat will never be the place it once was.

GOAT WATER

SERVES 6

The national dish of one of my home nations, Montserrat, is goat water. One you will not find on any other island. Its unique subtle spiced flavour is in between a stew and a broth that has this slight silky texture from the goat's bone marrow. We call it goat water because of the layers of pimento, mace and fresh herbs that make this so flavourful. Some add a touch of rum for a little extra fire, which I love. Goat water is widely believed to have originated as an adaptation of traditional Irish and West African stews, indicative of the presence of both communities on the island. When I visited Montserrat aged 14, I tasted goat water for the first time, and it was euphoric. There was only one man who sold it on the entire island from the boot of his truck every Friday. Then in 2023, I returned again as an adult and the feeling of being 'back home' connected differently. After playing J'ouvert for St. Patrick's Day, covered in green paint, my cousins and I had a fresh batch, right on the waterfront by Little Bay. Both times, it was served simply with a freshly baked roll from the bakery in a white polystyrene cup, it was just perfect.

Ingredients

1.5 kg (3 lb 5 oz) bone-in goat leg and shoulder, cubed

1½ tablespoons sea salt, or to taste

4–5 tablespoons Green Seasoning (see page 299)

3 tablespoons rapeseed (canola) or olive oil

2½ tablespoons dark muscovado sugar

1.5 litres (50¾ fl oz/6⅓ cups) water

8 cloves

15 allspice (pimento) berries

6–8 blades of mace

a few bay leaves

a few sprigs of thyme

3 spring onions (scallions), roughly chopped

2–3 teaspoons browning

6–7 garlic cloves, crushed

1–2 Scotch bonnet (split in half if you prefer more heat, use 1 if you prefer less heat)

2 teaspoons freshly ground black pepper

1 tablespoon cornflour (cornstarch) mixed with 4 tablespoons water

3 tablespoons dark rum

Serve with

Plait Bread (see page 241),
Creole Bread (see page 241) or
other fresh bread of your choice

Put the meat into a bowl along with the salt and green seasoning and rub the seasonings into the meat. Cover and set aside in the refrigerator to marinate for a few hours, or overnight.

When you're ready to cook, heat the oil in a large saucepan over a high heat, then add the sugar and cook for 3–4 minutes or until it bubbles into a caramel. Ensure it doesn't become too dark as it can burn very quickly and become bitter. Once the caramel is bubbling, reduce the heat slightly, then add the meat and coat well in the sugar to brown, then add the water and bring to a boil. Once boiling, add the cloves, allspice berries, mace, bay leaves, thyme and spring onions, browning, garlic and Scotch bonnet. Continue to boil for a minute or so then reduce to a low boil/high simmer, cover and cook for 2–2½ hours or until the meat is very tender. Once the meat has cooked, stir in the cornflour and water mixture and rum. Simmer for a further 10 minutes until the liquid has thickened slightly, then serve with fresh bread.

UNCLE JERRY'S FISH TEA

SERVES 4

My grandma's 99-year-old brother who migrated from Montserrat to East London, via France still makes this to this day, so when I wrote this recipe, I had to consult with him. Although the fundamentals are mostly the same, I love that this dish has so many names, and I can well imagine how it came to be named so. Through the transitions of language and dialect or in the way (culturally) we often name things with literal descriptions – fish tea, fish water, fish broth, fish broff or braff is exactly that. Fish tea is essentially a light fish soup made by boiling fresh fish, sometimes just the heads, seasoned with lots of fresh aromatics and seasonings, then finished with a little 'food' – as Uncle Jerry instructed me. Food meaning, ground provisions such as yam, dasheen or sweet potato. Only a little is added for substance and texture because this dish is all about the broth. That's where the focus of the flavour is, with little bits of the fish breaking off into the liquid as you sip.

Ingredients

4 snapper, cleaned and gutted, then sliced into 3–4 steaks

3–4 tablespoons Green Seasoning (see page299)

2 limes, 1 juiced and 1 sliced for garnish

2 teaspoons sea salt, or to taste

1 teaspoon freshly ground black pepper

2 litres (68 fl oz/8½ cups) water

2 spring onions (scallions), thinly sliced

2 garlic cloves, crushed

5 g (¼ oz) fresh ginger root, finely grated

1 Scotch bonnet (split in half if you prefer more heat)

10 g (½ oz) chadon beni (culantro/recao or coriander (cilantro), finely chopped

2 tomatoes, finely chopped (optional)

a few sprigs of thyme

250 g (9 oz) yam (white or yellow), peeled and cubed

1 carrot, peeled and thickly sliced

2 green (unripe) bananas, peeled and cut into chunks

6–8 okra, trimmed, then cut in half widthways

2 tablespoons salted butter

Put the fish into a bowl along with the green seasoning, lime juice, 2 teaspoons of the salt and the pepper. Mix well to ensure the fish is coated, then cover and set aside in the refrigerator to marinate.

Pour the water into a deep saucepan and bring to the boil. Add the spring onions, garlic, ginger, Scotch bonnet, coriander or chadon beni, tomatoes (if using) and thyme. Reduce to a simmer, then cook for 8–10 minutes to allow the fresh seasonings to infuse the soup base. Add the yam, carrot and green banana, turn up the heat slightly and low boil for a further 8–10 minutes to start cooking the ground provisions, then add the fish and the marinade from the bowl. Simmer for 5 more minutes, then finally add the okra and butter. Simmer for a further 5–8 minutes until the okra is tender but not too soft and the ground provisions and fish are cooked through. Serve hot with the sliced lime.

Note

You can use any combination of ground provisions for this dish, including eddoes, potatoes or sweet potatoes. I chose a selection, but there are no rules.

WHITE GOLD: THE BITTER SWEET TRUTH OF SUGAR

At the heart and soul of the seventeenth century Caribbean is sugar cane – distinctly different to the touristic paradise it's often presented as. Sugar is abundant in today's society. It's in many of the foods we eat. You can buy a bag of it for less than £1 and it seems almost infinite to some of us. For me, growing up, sugar always presented itself in two ways. There was the granulated stuff that sat in a jar for when someone visited our house and wanted to sweeten their tea and the bags of it Grandma would unpack when we baked together. Then there were these large canes that looked like extra thick bamboo at Leicester Carnival or that I'd seen fields of when visiting the islands. Taller than me when I was six or seven, hardy, dense and streaked with myriad of green and purple shades. The ultimate treat would be to get a few sticks to suck on while we walked the parade route. It was Carnival after all.

Piled in a cart or laid across a trestle table, the stall holders would take a cutlass (large knife) and slash ever so precisely, yet freely, against the grain of the cane, removing the hard outer skin and revealing this fibrous, stringy flesh that almost immediately leaked its sap. This clear, wholesome liquid was sugar cane juice in all its glory. Sweet, rich, fresh and full of nutrients. Unrefined and at its best, it put the granulated kind to shame. They sliced it up and put it in a clear, plastic bag for me. While walking alongside the floats and steel bands, holding my mum's hand on one side, I held these sticky batons in the other, chewing away silently.

It was only when I visited Barbados for the first time that I saw a fully grown sugar cane field up close. At the peak of the sun's sweltering heat, they towered over me, twice. I felt like my seven-year-old self at Leicester Carnival again, but this time felt less nostalgic. My perception changed and the reality of this basic, cheap commodity in England shifted. Sugar was no longer reduced to Tate & Lyle and Billington's brands who essentially built their businesses off the back of my ancestors' servitude. It was a commodity that was once the epicentre of capitalism and the economic development of the Western world. But deeper than that, sugar meant brutality, hardship and resistance – it was then I learnt the truth about sugar.

Sugar cane can be traced back to the Pacific island of New Guinea over 10,000 years ago. It then made its way to ancient India in 350 B.C. where sugar was locally consumed occasionally as it was and very labour-intensive. For many, it was simply an exotic spice, medicinal glaze or sweetener for elite palettes. Following its successful establishment in the Azores and Canary Islands, during his second voyage across the Atlantic in 1493, Christopher Columbus brought back a few stalks of this new crop that came to his attention – sugar cane. In Europe, refined sugar was a luxury product. The backbreaking toil and dangerous labour required meant it was never mass-produced in its native environments, and would have likely remained so if it weren't for the establishment of an enormous market in enslaved African labourers who were forced into this treacherous work.

Originally, gold was the primary resource being mined on the island by the Indigenous Taino communities. Their harsh working conditions quickly declined the Taino population by 80 per cent, and accelerated the desire for a new commodity. In 1510, as the mining of gold ceased to meet the expected demand, King Ferdinand of Spain officially proclaimed the 'Indies' open to the trade of people from Africa as indentured servants to carry out the labour, simultaneously proclaiming sugar production as the new capitalist venture. Settlers from the Canary Islands established the first sugar mill by 1516 and the importation of labour from the East grew at an exponential rate. As the Spanish continued to develop plantations in the neighbouring islands of Jamaica, Cuba and Puerto Rico, the Portuguese focused heavily on the South American mainland.

This invasive imperialism was not without contest. In 1521, the Wolof, a Muslim ethnic group taken from Senegambia, contested the colonial forces by joining with the Bahoruco maroons – a community of Taino and Africans who had already evaded the Spanish – living incognito on the island. By the mid-sixteenth century, the sugar economy was extremely profitable and replicated throughout the region, simultaneously forming a colonial elite. Raids and attacks from other European nations began, with the hope of taking over the established Spanish colonies. France gained control of Martinique and Guadeloupe in 1635 and 1674 respectively, while Britain overtook Barbados first in 1627, followed by Montserrat, Antigua, St. Kitts and Nevis and Grenada.

The introduction of sugar slavery in the 'New World' changed the way we cook and eat today, establishing the beginning of Europe's amassed economic empire. However, this success came at a price. Working in sugar was especially harsh, and the life expectancy of the enslaved was as low as 19 years. The toughest work of planting, manuring, and cane-cutting was reserved for the strongest and healthiest, usually men. Britain's largest sugar-producing colony, Jamaica, recorded the arrival of 335,000 enslaved West Africans between 1748 and 1788 across 1,200 ships voyages. Yet in 1788 a Jamaican census recorded only 226,432 enslaved men, women and children were alive on the island.

What originally started as indentured labour quickly evolved into brutal enslavement. As more tales regarding the conditions aboard ships and the treatment of those on plantations spread, awareness of the realities of the colonies became apparent. So far away in people's minds, literally and figuratively, it took the first hand testimonies of witnesses, such as Alexander Falonbridge – a surgeon who travelled aboard trade ships and published the first piece of abolitionist 'propaganda' – among others, to demonstrate the dark side of the trade. Simultaneously, revolts among the enslaved across the middle passage and plantations was very common. Day-to-day resistance was anything from refusal to adopt colonial language and continuing to speak in native tongue (i.e. Yoruba or Twi) or pretending to be ill, in order to do less work. With Africans making up approximately 80 per cent of the population in Nevis, Jamaica and British Guiana by the eighteenth century, larger-scaled mutinies were of great threat to plantation owners. Cudjoe (Montserrat), Tacky (Jamaica) and Bussa (Barbados) to name a few, all led widespread mutinies, without knowing what freedom looked like. Ultimately, anything was better than sugar slavery.

The sugar trade finally began to crumble following the start of the Haitian Revolution and the introduction of the first parliamentary bill condemning enslavement in 1791. Without human labour, the production of sugar was no longer feasible to be produced at such high yields, making the colonies financially unviable. The success of the Haitian Revolution achieved the first African-led republic in the Western hemisphere, marking the start of the end of servitude in the Caribbean. The movement shifted the consciousness of those in bondage and the reality of emancipation throughout the region. Plantations across the islands began to follow suit, and by 1807, the abolition bill was finally agreed to by the British parliament. For the first time in over 200 years, human rights superseded profit and sugar ceased to prevail over the liberty of the communities of the Caribbean.

ROTI, DUMPLING & BAKES

My Barbudan nana would say 'bread kind' when referring to the various types of bread, and I've adopted it for this. There are some many styles and methods of bread making across the Caribbean that speak to the entire globe.

Bread is communal. Almost every culture across the planet has some form of it, which is often central to communities. While you'll find bakeries across the islands making fresh bread as the sun rises daily, hard dough seems to have created an identity that is unique to Jamaica. Just like patties and jerk, it is a global point of culinary reference, which beautifully displays the reach of its culture. It is said this sweet loaf bread was first produced in Jamaica during the early 1900s by Chinese migrant Chin Bwang, when mass Chinese migration came to the islands from the 1830s following abolition. Hundreds of bakeries across the island bake and sell fresh loaves daily. My favourite way to eat it is simply with a good slather of butter or alongside jerk (see page 126), just as you'd find in Jamaica.

Roti (rotee), meaning bread in Hindi, evolved massively in the Caribbean from what it was across Northern India. Originally, it used whole wheat flour, was made a lot smaller then roasted on a tawa, before being burned directly on an open flame, making it puff slightly. In the Caribbean, rotis increased in size by 4–5 times as it is believed labourers were not given enough time to prepare them so instead, made larger versions to share with family at mealtimes. Dhal puri or puri roti, a light, soft dough stuffed with a paste made from finely ground yellow split peas, before being roasted on a tawa, is also still cooked across India, predominantly in Bihar, as well as Mauritius, and was usually reserved for weddings and special occasions. The consumption of them daily is said to be an exclusively Caribbean practice due to their laboriousness, with the addition of curried meat, vegetables and other fillings, then wrapping as a complete meal is said to have evolved from the Western influences on the food and the way it is consumed.

Paratha has also been preserved with time. Most popular among the Muslim communities before being accepted among the wider food culture in India, it was not something eaten daily. Using refined wheat flour (white flour) before being layered with copious amounts of oil or ghee, the flaky, soft layers that reveal themselves once roasted on a tawa, gave it its unique name in Trinidad – 'buss up shot' or 'buss up', referring to its resemblance of an unironed or creased shirt (buss up shirt). The roti shops across the islands are a testament to the preservation of Indian cooking in the region. Fried dumplings across most of the anglophone islands, fry bakes or 'bek fwi' in Lucian (St. Lucia) creole, are all names used to reference 'journey' or 'johnny cakes'. They're savoury fried breads made from a dough of white flour eaten as a starch to accompany vegetables or protein such as saltfish. It's not quite clear which name came first or whether the name evolved with the evolution of language and local dialect. It is said that English speaking Caribbeans of African descent introduced johnny cakes to the Dominican Republic in the nineteenth century, which eventually evolved through local culture to become *yaniqueque*, commonly found along the beach and served with rice, beans and chicken.

RIGHT & BELOW Lovely lady rolling and roasting fresh dhal puri roti, Georgetown, Guyana.

DHAL PURI

ROTI STUFFED WITH YELLOW SPLIT PEAS

MAKES 8

Ingredients

Dough

460 g (18 oz/3⅔ cups) plain (all-purpose) flour
1 tablespoon baking powder
1 tablespoon sea salt
1½ tablespoons golden granulated sugar
1 tablespoon vegetable oil, plus extra for greasing and brushing
200 ml (7 fl oz/⅔ cup) water

Filling

250 g (9 oz/scant 1¼ cups) yellow split peas or yellow lentils
2 teaspoons ground cumin
1 teaspoon sea salt
1 tablespoon Green Seasoning (see page 299)
2 garlic cloves
1 Scotch bonnet
15 g (½ oz) chadon beni (culantro/recao) or coriander (cilantro)

To serve

Curry Duck (see page 116)
Curry Goat (see page 182)

First, make the dough. Combine the flour, baking powder, salt and sugar in a bowl. Add the oil, then slowly add the water and bring together into a dough. Tip the dough out onto a clean surface and knead for 10 minutes until smooth and elastic, then cover and set aside to rest for at least 1 hour.

Meanwhile, prepare the filling. Put the split peas, cumin, salt, green seasoning, garlic cloves and whole Scotch bonnet into a saucepan. Cover with 750 ml (25 fl oz/3 cups) water, cover and bring to the boil, then reduce to a high simmer and cook for 35–40 minutes or until the split peas are tender but not overcooked. They should break easily when pressed between your fingers. Drain the split peas of any remaining water, then transfer to a food processor along with the garlic cloves, Scotch bonnet and chadon beni or coriander, then blend to a fine crumb. Be careful not to blend the split peas too much as they can turn into a paste.

Once the dough has rested, divide it into 8 equal-sized balls, place on a tray and cover with a damp dish towel. Take one of the balls and place it in the palm of your hand. Rub a little flour on your fingers, then press into the centre of the ball to create a dent. Sprinkle a little more flour into the dent – this space will hold the split pea mixture. Fill the dough with 3–4 tablespoons of the split pea mixture. Press down carefully to pack it tightly and keep it in the centre. To close, bring the edges of the dough towards the middle then pinch together to seal the split peas inside the dough. Turn the dough over and shape into a ball again, then rub with a little oil and place back the tray under the damp dish towel. Repeat with the remaining dough and filling. Once all of the loyas have been filled, transfer to the refrigerator to chill for 1 hour before cooking.

To roast (cook) the rotis, heat a tawa or heavy-based wide frying pan over a medium heat. Roll out the rotis to 2.5 mm (⅛ in) thick, keeping them as round as possible. Gently place a roti on the hot tawa or pan. Cook on each side for a minute or so – once the surface bubbles, brush it with oil, then turn over. Repeat this process for about 6 minutes until the roti cooks through – the dough will become more translucent and you'll be able to see the yellow peas come through a little. Once cooked, place on a plate covered with a dish towel to keep warm, then repeat with the remaining rotis. Serve hot.

BUSS UP SHOT

PARATHA/OIL ROTI – ROTI ROLLED WITH BUTTER AND OIL

MAKES 8

Ingredients

700 g (1 lb 9 oz/5⅔ cups) plain (all-purpose) flour, plus extra for dusting

4 teaspoons sea salt

2 teaspoons raw cane sugar

2 teaspoon baking powder

2 tablespoons oil, plus extra for brushing

380 ml (12¾ fl oz/generous 1⅔ cups) water

150 g (5½ oz) salted butter (or vegetable shortening)

To serve

Curry Duck (see page 116)
Curry Goat (see page 182)

Combine the flour, salt, sugar and baking powder in a large bowl. Add the oil, then slowly add the water and bring together into a dough. Tip the dough out onto a clean surface and knead for 5–10 minutes until smooth and elastic, then cover and set aside to rest for 1 hour.

Once rested, divide the dough into ten equal-sized pieces. Roll out each dough ball into a circle 2.5 mm (⅛ in) thick, then spread with 1 tablespoon of the butter. Sprinkle with a little flour, then make a cut from the centre of the circle to the edge at a 45-degree angle. Lift the cut edge, then roll it over itself in an anticlockwise direction to form a cone shape. Once you have reached the end, stand the cone upright, pull the loose edge of the dough from the bottom and tuck into the top of the cone, pushing the tip down and inside itself. Repeat with the remaining dough balls, place on a tray and cover with cling film (plastic wrap), then set aside in the refrigerator to chill for 1 hour before cooking.

When you're ready to cook the parathas, heat a roti tawa or heavy-based wide frying pan over a medium–high heat. One at a time, roll out the parathas to 2.5 mm (⅛ in) thick and gently place in the hot tawa or pan. Cook for 1 minute, then brush lightly with oil and turn. Keep turning and brushing with oil until the roti is fully cooked – this should take 5–6 minutes in total. As the roti cooks, it may puff up and gather hot air on the inside so be careful. Remove from the pan and rest in a clean dish lined with a dish towel that can also cover them on top – the steam will soften them a little. Repeat until all the parathas are cooked.

Note

What makes parathas unique are their buttery layers. Some people clap the parathas in between their hands to break up and expose the layers, but you need good, strong hands for this. An alternative method is to place them in a clean dish towel and clap them to break them up a bit. It creates the same effect and saves your hands!

SADA ROTI
PLAIN ROTI

MAKES 10

Ingredients

500 g (1 lb 2 oz/4 cups) plain (all-purpose) flour
10 g (½ oz) baking powder
5 g (¼ oz) sea salt
1 tablespoon rapeseed (canola) or vegetable oil
300 ml (10 fl oz/1¼ cups) water

To serve

Baigan and Tomato Choka (see page 107) or Buljol (see page 104)

Combine the flour, baking powder and salt in a bowl. Add the oil, then slowly add the water and bring together into a together. Tip the dough out onto a clean surface and knead for 5–10 minutes until smooth and elastic, cover then set aside to rest
for 1 hour.

Once rested, divide the dough into ten equal-sized pieces. Heat a roti tawa or heavy-based wide frying pan over a medium–high heat. Then, one at a time, roll out the rotis to 2.5 mm (⅛ in) thick and gently place in the hot tawa or pan. Cook for about 1 minute on each side, then continue cooking, turning regularly, for a total of 4–5 minutes. As the roti cooks, it will blister a little, creating dark spots as the air bubbles expand. It may puff up and gather hot air on the inside, so be careful. Remove from the pan and rest
in a clean dish towel – the steam will soften them
a little. Repeat until all the rotis are cooked.

COCONUT POT BAKE
ROASTED COCONUT BREAD

SERVES 8–10

Ingredients

45 g (1½ oz/3 tablespoons) golden granulated sugar
15 g (½ oz) fast-action dried yeast
160 ml (5½ fl oz/⅔ cup) lukewarm water
800 g (1 lb 12 oz/scant 6½ cups) strong white bread flour, plus extra for dusting
10 g (½ oz) sea salt
50 g (1¾ oz/generous ½ cup) desiccated (dried shredded) coconut or 100 g (3½ oz) fresh coconut, grated
90 g (3¼ oz) salted butter, melted
240 ml (8 fl oz/1 cup) coconut milk
vegetable oil, for greasing

To serve

butter, cheese or Buljol (see page 104)

Put the sugar and yeast into a bowl with half the water, then mix well and set aside in a warm place
for 15–20 minutes to allow the yeast to activate.

Meanwhile, combine the flour, salt and coconut (if using) in a large bowl. Once the yeast mixture starts to bubble and froth, it's ready. Add the yeast mixture to the flour mixture along with the melted butter, coconut milk and remaining water. Mix well until all the liquid has been absorbed by the flour and a loose dough starts to form. Tip the dough out onto a clean surface and knead for 8–10 minutes until the dough is soft, smooth and springs back when pressed lightly. Alternatively, knead in a stand mixer fitted
with the dough hook.

Shape the dough into a large round, then place in a lightly greased casserole dish (Dutch oven), cover and set aside to prove in a warm place for 1 hour, or until doubled in size.

Preheat the oven to 200°C fan (425°F). Transfer the dish with the bread to the oven and bake on the middle shelf for 50–60 minutes, or until evenly brown all over and hollow-sounding when tapped underneath.

PLAIT BREAD
BUTTERY GUYANESE LOAF BREAD

SERVES 8–10

Ingredients

45 g (1½ oz/3 tablespoons) golden granulated sugar
15 g (½ oz) fast-action dried yeast
160 ml (5½ fl oz/⅔ cup) lukewarm water
800 g (1 lb 12 oz/scant 6½ cups) strong white bread flour, plus extra for dusting
10 g (½ oz) sea salt
240 ml (8 fl oz/1 cup) whole (full-fat) milk
110 g (4 oz) salted butter, melted, plus extra to serve

To serve

Pepperpot (see page 86)

Put the sugar and yeast into a bowl with the water, then mix and set aside in a warm place for 10–15 minutes to allow the yeast to activate. Meanwhile, combine the flour and salt in a large bowl. Once the yeast mixture starts to bubble and froth, it is ready. Add the yeast mixture to the flour along with the milk and 90 g (3¼ oz) of the melted butter. Mix well to form a dough, then tip out onto a clean surface and knead for 8–10 minutes until smooth, soft and a little springy when pressed. Alternatively, knead in a stand mixer fitted with the dough hook. Cover and set aside to prove in a warm place for 1 hour, or until doubled in size.

Once risen, divide the dough into three pieces. Roll each piece into a long sausage shape, then form into a braid. Place the bread onto a baking sheet lined with baking parchment, then cover with a damp dish towel and set aside to prove again for 1 hour, or until doubled in size.

Preheat the oven to 180°C fan (400°F).

Bake the bread in the oven for 45–50 minutes, or until golden brown on top and hollow-sounding when tapped underneath. Remove from the oven and brush the top with the remaining melted butter to glaze, then slice and serve with butter.

CREOLE 'PENNY' BREAD
PENNY BREAD

MAKES 10

Ingredients

250ml (8 fl oz/1 cup) warm water
4g (⅛ oz) yeast
1 tablespoon golden granulated sugar
500g (1lb 2 oz/4 cups) strong white bread flour, plus extra for dusting
3 tablespoons vegetable oil
2 teaspoons salt

Meanwhile, combine the flour and salt in a large bowl. Once the yeast mixture starts to bubble and froth, it is ready. Add the yeast mixture to the flour along with the vegetable oil. Mix well to form a dough, then tip out onto a clean surface and knead for 8–10 minutes until smooth, soft and a little springy when pressed. Alternatively, knead in a stand mixer fitted with the dough hook. Cover and set aside to prove in a warm place for 1 hour, or until doubled in size.

Once risen, knock the dough back then divide into 10 pieces. Roll each piece into a long sausage shape, approximately 10cm long. Then make into oval shapes, focus the rolling on the ends to make them stretch and the centre of the bread stay fuller forming a soft, long diamond shape.

Place the breads onto a baking sheet lined with baking parchment, then cover with a damp dish towel and set aside to prove again for 45 minutes-1 hour, or until doubled in size. Preheat the oven to 190°C fan (380°F). Bake the bread in the oven for 25–30 minutes, or until golden brown on top and hollow-sounding when tapped underneath. Remove from the oven and and serve warm with butter, cheese or smoked herring (see page 172).

FRY BAKES
FLOAT BAKES/BOKIT

MAKES 8

These light, airy bakes are deep fried and eaten as they are with cocoa tea in St. Lucia (see page 291), filled with saltfish, cheese or eggs to make bokit, a popular street food you'll find across the streets of Guadeloupe or used to make the Trinidadian favourite bake and 'shark' (see page 110).

Ingredients

30 g (1 oz/2 tablespoons) golden granulated sugar

4 g (⅛ oz) fast-action dried yeast

200 ml (7 fl oz/scant 1 cup) lukewarm water

400 g (14 oz/3¼ cups) plain (all-purpose) flour

½ teaspoon sea salt

1 teaspoon baking powder

2 tablespoons rapeseed (canola) or olive oil

1 litre (34 fl oz/4¼ cups) vegetable oil, for greasing and deep-frying

To serve

Buljol (see page 104)
Bake and Shark (see page 112)
Cocoa Tea (see page 293)

Put the sugar and yeast into a bowl and add half the water, then mix well and set aside in a warm place for 10–15 minutes to allow the yeast to activate. Meanwhile, combine the flour, salt and baking powder in a bowl. Once the yeast mixture starts to bubble and froth, it is ready. Add it to the dry ingredients, followed by the oil and remaining water. Mix well and bring together into a dough, then knead in the bowl for 5–10 minutes until soft and smooth. Cover and set aside to prove in a warm place for 1 hour.

Once the dough has risen, divide it into eight equal-sized pieces. Form each piece into a ball, then place on a lightly oiled baking tray (pan), cover with a clean, damp dish towel and set aside to prove again for 1 hour.

Once the dough has proved for the second time, the bakes are ready to fry. Drizzle a little oil onto a plate or clean work surface. Pour the oil into a deep saucepan and heat to 190°C (375°F). Alternatively, you can test the oil by tearing off a piece of the dough and dropping it into the oil. If it sizzles straight away and turns brown, the oil is ready.

Take one of the dough balls and place it on the greased plate, then grease your fingers and gently press out the bake to flatten it slightly. Carefully lower the bake into the oil. It should immediately react with the oil and may begin to puff up. Cook on each side for 1 minute until puffy and golden brown all over. Remove from the oil using tongs or a slotted spoon and drain on paper towels. Continue until you have fried all the bakes, then serve warm with the buljol.

FESTIVALS & FRIED DUMPLINGS

MAKES 8–10

Fried dumplings always remind me of my Barbudan nana as these were a staple in her house. Whenever I entered the house I could smell the hot oil that bubbled in the seasoned dutch pot from the front door and there would be a bowl of them on the kitchen table right next to the bread and biscuit jars. Sometimes she made stew saltfish (see page 119) to go with them or we ate them just as they were – hot and crispy on the outside and soft and fluffy on the inside. Festivals are very much Jamaican, a slightly different shape with the addition of sugar and spices.

Ingredients

360 g (12½ oz/1½ cups) plain (all-purpose) flour, plus extra for dusting

50 g (1¾ oz/scant ½ cup) fine cornmeal

1½ teaspoons sea salt

1 teaspoon baking powder

60 g (2 oz/4 tablespoons) golden granulated sugar

1 teaspoon ground mixed spice (optional)

30 g (1 oz) salted butter or vegetable fat

2 teaspoons vanilla extract (optional)

200 ml (7 fl oz/scant 1 cup) water

1 litre (34 fl oz/4¼ cups) vegetable oil, for deep-frying

Combine the flour, cornmeal, salt, baking powder, sugar and mixed spice (if using) in a bowl. Add the butter or vegetable fat and vanilla and use your fingers to rub it into the dry ingredients, then gradually pour in the water and bring together into a dough. Knead the dough in the bowl for 5 minutes, then cover and set aside to rest at room temperature for 30 minutes.

Once the dough has rested, divide it into 8–10 equal-sized pieces, then shape each piece into a ball.

Pour the oil into a deep saucepan and heat to 160°C (325°F). Alternatively, you can test the oil by tearing off a piece of bread and dropping it into the oil. If it sizzles straight away and gradually turns golden brown, the oil is ready. If it turns brown quickly, it is too hot.

Take each dough ball and gently roll it in your hands to create a log shape, then carefully lower a few into the oil, ensuring you don't overcrowd the pan. Deep-fry for 6–7 minutes until golden brown all over and the dough is cooked through, soft and fluffy in the centre. Remove from the oil using tongs or a slotted spoon and drain on paper towels. Continue until you have fried all the festivals.

Note

To make fried dumplings, follow the recipe as above, using half the sugar and omitting the vanilla and mixed spice. Fry the dough as balls rather than in log shapes.

PASTRIES IN THE CARIBBEAN

PÂTE KODÉ, PATTIES & EMPANADAS

t seems many cultures across the globe have their own version of savoury pastries. In the Caribbean alone, there is an abundance of varieties, with each island having its own, unique version. Whether baked or deep-fried, these staples are filled with myriad of ingredients, reflective of the environment and communities they belong to. They are often made popular by those from lower socio-economic groups and its ability to make a delicious snack affordable for all.

Probably the most iconic from its appearance – the golden, turmeric-laced Jamaican patties, eaten on their own or stuffed inside a fresh coco bread – evolved from the Cornish pasty. In the seventeenth century, during the peak of Britain's involvement in the Trans-Atlantic trade, many vessels from the coast of Cornwall began their journey to the West coast of Africa, headed for the Caribbean. As Jamaica was Britain's largest colony, it became heavily influenced by elements of its culture. Cornish pasties were common among Cornish coal and tin miners as the shape made them easy to eat on the go as a meal in one. Cornish sailors also travelled with them at sea, bringing them into the Americas where they evolved further.

The Spanish Caribbean islands of Cuba, the Dominican Republic and Puerto Rico utilise cassava flour as well as wheat flour for their outer pastry casings – empanadas are an example of this. The journey of empanadas can be traced back to the Middle East, and are said to have evolved from Arabic meat pies called 'sfeehas'. The first record of sfeehas has been acknowledged to be in a 1520 Spanish cookbook, *Libre del Coch*, by Ruperto de Nola, suggesting they made their way from the Middle East to the Iberian Peninsula alongside the Moors sometime before their expulsion by the Spanish in 1609. Between the conquering of the Iberian Peninsula and the Americas, sfeehas eventually became empanadas, literally translating to 'wrapped in bread'. Upon invasion of the Americas, the Spanish and Portuguese introduced empanadas to the 'New World'. It is said during this transition the pies reduced from a larger, single pie to the smaller sized ones they are today and their variety across the region is due to climate and cultural nuances.

In the French Caribbean pâte are the most common – deep-fried using a thick, crisp pastry dough, they are a common snack found in Haiti as well as those with French influences: Guadeloupe, Martinique and Dominica. When visiting Aruba in 2022, I tasted my first *pâté kode*. The pastries can be filled with cheese or saltfish but mine was stuffed to the brim with a filling of sautéed onions, smoked herring, a little tomato surprise and a hard-boiled egg.

CALLALOO PATTIES

MAKES 4

Ingredients

Pastry

480 g (17 oz/scant 4 cups) plain (all-purpose) flour, plus extra for dusting

20 g (¾ oz) turmeric

2 teaspoons sea salt

150 ml (5 fl oz/scant ⅔ cup) cold whole (full-fat) milk (or a plant-based alternative)

100 ml (3½ fl oz/scant ½ cup) cold water

300 g (10½ oz) butter or vegetable fat, at room temperature

Filling

2 tablespoons rapeseed (canola) or vegetable oil

1 onion, finely chopped

2 garlic cloves, crushed

2 (bell) peppers, any colour, finely chopped

½ Scotch bonnet, finely chopped (deseeded if you prefer less heat)

a few sprigs of thyme, leaves picked

240 g (8½ oz) fresh callaloo (or spinach), finely sliced

1 tablespoon sea salt

½ teaspoon pepper

First, make the pastry. Combine the flour, turmeric and salt in a large bowl. Pour in the milk and water and bring together into a dough. Knead lightly to form a ball, then wrap in cling film (plastic wrap) and chill in the refrigerator for 30 minutes.

Meanwhile, place the butter between two sheets of baking parchment and roll out into a rectangle about 2 cm (¾ in) thick, then transfer to the refrigerator to chill.

Once the dough has chilled, place it on a lightly floured surface and mark a cross lightly in the centre (do not cut through the dough). Next, gently push out each corner of the dough to create a large cross, ensuring the centre is thicker than the sides. Place the butter in the centre and fold the dough corners over the butter – first the top, then the bottom, then the left and finally the right. You should end up with the butter encased by the dough. Seal the edges to ensure there are no gaps. Roll out the dough lengthways to create a rectangle, then give it a quarter turn and fold it into three like a letter – fold the top third down and then the bottom third after that. Repeat this process three times, pressing a finger mark in the dough to count the turns. Refrigerate the dough for 1 hour, then repeat again so you have turned and rolled the dough a total of six times. Refrigerate once more while you make the filling.

For the filling, heat the oil in a frying pan over a medium heat, then add the onion, garlic, peppers, Scotch bonnet and thyme. Fry for 3–4 minutes, then add the callaloo, season with the salt and pepper and cook everything together for a few more minutes until its soft and cooked through. Remove from the heat and set aside to cool.

Preheat the oven to 190°C fan (400°F) and line a baking sheet with baking parchment.

Roll out the chilled pastry on a lightly floured surface to 5 mm (¼ in) thick, then cut out circles to your desired size using a glass, bowl or pastry cutter. You can reuse the offcuts of the pastry, but they may not rise as well. Place a few tablespoons of the filling in the centre of each of the pastry discs, then brush the edges with a little water and fold over to create a semi-circle. Seal the edges together using a fork, poke a small hole in the top to allow any steam to escape, then place on the prepared baking sheet. Bake in the oven for 30–35 minutes, or until puffed up and golden.

EMPANADILLAS DE CARNE

BEEF & OLIVE EMPANADAS

MAKES 8

Ingredients

Pastry

500 g (1 lb 2 oz/4 cups) plain (all-purpose) flour
1 teaspoon sea salt
1½ tablespoons golden granulated sugar
½ teaspoon baking powder
60 g (2 oz) cold lard
1½ teaspoons distilled white vinegar
160 ml (5½ fl oz/⅔ cup) cold water
1 medium egg white

Filling

2 tablespoons rapeseed (canola) or olive oil, plus extra for frying
500 g (1 lb 2 oz) lean minced (ground) beef (no more than 10 per cent fat)
1 onion, finely chopped
2–3 garlic cloves, crushed
2 tablespoons Sofrito (see page 299)
½ Scotch bonnet, finely chopped (deseeded if you prefer less heat)
2 tablespoons tomato purée (paste)
2 teaspoons sea salt
¼ teaspoon ground pepper
70 g (2½ oz) pitted green olives, sliced
1 litre vegetable oil, for deep-frying

First, make the pastry. Combine the flour, salt, sugar and baking powder in a large bowl, then add the lard and use your fingers to rub it into the flour until the mixture resembles breadcrumbs. Combine the vinegar with the water in a jug (pitcher) or bowl. Add the egg white to the flour mixture, then slowly pour in the vinegar and water mixture and bring together to form a dough. Wrap tightly in cling film (plastic wrap), then transfer to the refrigerator to chill for 1–2 hours.

While the dough is chilling, make the filling. Heat the oil in a saucepan over a medium heat, then add the beef, onion, garlic, sofrito and Scotch bonnet. Fry for 8–10 minutes, or until the meat is almost cooked through, then add the tomato purée, salt and pepper and cook for a few more minutes. Finally stir through the olives, then remove from the heat and set aside to cool.

Once the pastry has rested, place it on a lightly floured work surface, then divide it into eight equal pieces. Roll out each piece into a 5 mm (¼ in) thick circle. Spoon 2–3 tablespoons of the filling onto one side of each of the pastry circles, leaving a border, then brush the edges of the pastry with a little water and fold the pastry over the filling to create a semi-circle. Using a fork, seal the edges tightly. Place the empanadas on a baking sheet or plate and chill in the refrigerator for 1 hour.

When you're ready to fry, pour the oil into a deep saucepan and heat to 175°C (350°F). Alternatively, you can test the oil by tearing off a piece of bread and dropping it into the oil. If it sizzles straight away and gradually turns gold brown, the oil is ready. If it turns brown quickly, it is too hot. Remove the patties from the refrigerator and carefully lower a few into the oil. Deep-fry for 6–8 minutes until golden brown all over, turning them occasionally. Remove from the oil with a slotted spoon and drain on paper towels. Continue until you have fried all the patties, then serve warm.

PÂTÉ KODE
SMOKED HERRING & EGG PATTIES

MAKES 12

Ingredients

Filling

1 whole smoked herring (about 350 g/12 oz), cut into 3–4 pieces

2 tablespoons rapeseed (canola) or olive oil

1 onion, finely chopped

1 (bell) pepper, any colour, thinly sliced into short strips

100 g (3½ oz) white cabbage, thinly sliced

2–3 garlic cloves, crushed

1 Scotch bonnet, finely chopped (deseeded if you prefer less heat)

1 tablespoon tomato purée (paste)

½ teaspoon ground black pepper

4 medium eggs, hard-boiled, peeled and cut into thick rounds

1 litre (34 fl oz/4¼ cups) vegetable oil, for deep-frying

Pastry

500 g (1 lb 2 oz/4 cups) plain (all-purpose) flour

2 teaspoons sea salt

60 g (2 oz) cold lard (or vegetable shortening), cubed

20 ml (1½ tablespoons) distilled white vinegar

150 ml (5 fl oz/scant ⅔ cup) cold water

2 medium eggs

To serve

Pikliz (see page 305)

Put the herring pieces into a large bowl and cover with boiling water, then set aside to soak for about 30 minutes. Soaking the fish softens it so you can peel off the skin and remove the meat easily.

Meanwhile, prepare the pastry. Combine the flour and salt in a bowl, then add the lard and use your fingers to rub it into the flour until the mixture resembles breadcrumbs. Next, combine the vinegar with the water in a jug (pitcher) or bowl. Add the eggs to the flour mixture, then slowly pour in the vinegar and water mixture and bring together to form a dough. Wrap in cling film (plastic wrap), then transfer to the refrigerator to chill for 1 hour while you prepare the filling.

Carefully remove the skin and bones from the soaked herring, reserving the meat. Heat the oil in a frying pan over a medium heat, then add the onion, pepper, cabbage, garlic and Scotch bonnet. Fry for a few minutes, then add the tomato purée and black pepper. Add the prepared herring and cook for a few minutes more until the vegetables have softened a little – they don't need to be fully cooked as the filling will steam inside the pastry when frying. Remove the filling mixture from the heat and set aside to cool.

Once the pastry has rested, roll it out on a lightly floured surface into a large rectangle, about 5 mm (¼ in) thick. Using a sharp knife, divide the rectangle into 12 equal-sized rectangles, then separate them slightly on the surface to ensure the cuts are clean. Place 1–2 tablespoons of the herring mixture onto one half of each pastry rectangle, leaving a 1 cm (½ in) border around the edge. Top each one with a piece of the boiled egg, then brush the edges of the pastry with a little water. Fold the pastry over the filling and lightly press around the edges to seal, then place on a baking sheet or plate and chill in the refrigerator for at least 30 minutes.

When you're ready to fry, pour the oil into a deep saucepan and heat to 175°C (350°F). Alternatively, you can test the oil by tearing off a piece of bread and dropping it into the oil. If it sizzles straight away and gradually turns gold brown, the oil is ready. If it turns brown quickly, it is too hot. Remove the patties from the refrigerator and carefully lower a few into the oil. Deep-fry for about 8 minutes until golden brown all over, turning them occasionally. Remove from the oil with a slotted spoon and drain on paper towels. Continue until you have fried all the patties. Serve warm with the pikliz.

SWEET

BAKED AND FRIED
SET
HOT
COLD

rowing up, even through baking, my grandparents kept our culture alive. My Montserratian Grandma often shared stories of her own childhood and how baking was such an integral part of it. Although her time with her mother was short before she made the journey to England aged 27, the precious moments they shared throughout her younger years stayed with her. They baked bread together every morning, at the small bakery next to her home in Dyers village, hand shaping loaves of bread and cakes using local sugar, cassava and coconut. The oven was shared with the village, so if others in the community needed to bake, they could, as it was always on.

The ingredients that form the beautiful foundation of sweets, cakes and desserts in the islands take influence from the various parts of its past. Firstly, the abundance of native fresh fruits and nuts across the islands such as pineapple, guava, mango, all spice (pimento), annatto, almonds, custard apple, soursop and figs (bananas), raw cocoa, sea moss, maiz (corn), sweet potato, coconut and cassava are grown freely in abundance. Whenever something is in season, it's everywhere! Cinnamon, nutmeg, clove, bois bande (a bark used like cinnamon), tamarind and sugar cane, all from Asia and the East are now cemented within the foodways. This, combined with cooking styles from across the globe, have filled bakeries and households with classics. As such, when I was growing up, no Christmas would be the same without a black cake at its centre.

GRANDMA'S PLATE TART

SERVES 8

This recipe is an ode to my grandma. She grew up making these with her mother in the village bakery where they worked back in Montserrat when she was small. Then she taught me. I can't count how many times we've made coconut tarts together and the irony is, I can't remember how she made them because she never wrote the recipe down (and nor did I)! Every time the measurements were slightly different, but they always came out the same. And whenever I asked it was '... ahh, just a likkle dis' and a likkle dat.' Not helpful when you're writing a cookbook. She's no longer here with us, so this recipe is mine through her. Purely based on memory, taste, texture, look and feel, I developed this recipe. The irony again is, that's how she cooked, how she remembered what her mother taught her after all those years and how we always have cooked culturally. We were once denied the opportunity to read and write, so conversation and storytelling have been crucial to allow us to preserve vital pieces of our culture. Maybe I was never meant to know the exact measurements for this, and it was always meant to be shared through spirit.

Ingredients

Pastry

250 g (9 oz/2 cups) plain (all-purpose) flour, plus extra for dusting

160 g (5¾ oz) cold salted butter, cubed, plus extra for greasing

2 medium eggs

2–3 tablespoons water

1 tablespoon Demerara sugar, for sprinkling

Filling

150 g (5½ oz/generous ⅔ cup) Demerara or golden granulated sugar

250 ml (8 fl oz/1 cup) water

200 g (7 oz) dried coconut, freshly grated or desiccated (dried shredded)

¼ teaspoon freshly grated nutmeg

½ teaspoon ground cinnamon

1 teaspoon vanilla extract or bean paste

3 g (⅛ oz) or 1 small thumb-sized piece of fresh ginger root, finely grated

Preheat the oven to 170°C fan (375°F) and grease a 20 cm (8 in) tart tin (pan) or pie dish.

First, make the pastry. Put the flour and butter into a bowl, then use your fingers to rub the butter into the flour until the mixture resembles breadcrumbs. Next, add one of the eggs and enough water to bring it together into a soft dough. Wrap in cling film (plastic wrap), then transfer to the refrigerator to chill for at least 30 minutes.

Meanwhile, make the filling. Put the sugar and water into a saucepan and whisk until the sugar has dissolved, then bring to a low boil. Add the remaining ingredients to the pan, then reduce to a simmer, cover and cook for 8–10 minutes, stirring continuously, until the moisture has been absorbed by the coconut and the mixture becomes rich and sticky. Remove from the heat and set aside to cool.

Remove the pastry from the refrigerator and roll out on a lightly floured surface to 5 mm (¼ in) thick. Place the pastry into the prepared tin or dish and press it in lightly. Slice off the excess pastry, reserving the offcuts and leaving 5 mm (¼ in) overhanging to allow for shrinkage when baking. Press a few fork marks into the base of the pastry to allow steam to escape, then add the coconut filling. Smooth the top with a spatula, ensuring there are no gaps. Re-roll the pastry offcuts, then slice into even strips. Brush the edge of the tart with water, then create a lattice by placing a row of pastry strips in one direction, then weaving in another in the opposite direction. Press the edges down lightly, then trim again. Finally, beat the remaining egg and brush it over the top of the pastry, then sprinkle with the sugar and bake in the oven for 45–55 minutes until golden brown. Allow to cool, then slice and serve.

PAIN DE MAIS

HAITIAN CORNBREAD WITH BANANA AND RUM

SERVES 8–10

Pain de mais is a cake-like, sweet cornbread, made with maize, coconut and banana. Its texture is a cross between banana bread and cornbread with a hint of coconut, and is typically eaten after a meal with the family. Rural farming is still common in Haiti, and corn is a native ingredient to the island, so it is grown and eaten there a lot to this day.

Maize (*maiz*) is Indigenous to the Americas. Across the region, from the northern mainland to the islands of the Caribbean, there are a variety of grains and species that were used prominently by the Tainos who first inhabited Haiti. When Columbus arrived in Haiti on his first expedition, he found that the Indigenous people were very experienced in corn cultivation and that it was done to a very high standard. Their process was ritualistic, which spoke to their great awareness of the environment and respect for the earth. Planting always took place twice per year on the hillsides. The ash burned from the forests was used as fertiliser and this process always commenced after a new moon appeared following rainfall. In Haiti, the native grain is known as Haitian yellow. Historians have found that these communities would grind and pressure damage the starch kernels of maize (with a pestle and mortar type instrument) to produce the fine ground grains we see today, which were then baked and consumed as bread. This cornbread/cake style was made by the Tainos for centuries and has evolved over time with the introduction of sugar into the region, a product of the empire.

Ingredients

240 g (8½ oz) salted butter, plus extra for greasing

150 g (5½ oz/generous ¾ cup) dark brown soft sugar

150 g (5½ oz/scant ⅔ cup) caster (superfine) sugar

1 medium egg

400 ml (14 fl oz/generous 1½ cups) coconut milk

1 × 410 g (14½ oz/1⅓ cups) tin of evaporated milk

2 teaspoons vanilla extract or bean paste

2 tablespoons spiced or dark rum (optional)

90 g (3¼ oz/¾ cup) plain (all-purpose) flour

1 teaspoon baking powder

¼ teaspoon salt

50 g (1¾ oz/generous ½ cup) desiccated (dried shredded) coconut

300 g (10½ oz/2 cups) fine cornmeal

2 bananas, peeled and mashed

10 g (½ oz) fresh ginger root, grated

Preheat the oven to 160°C fan (350°F) and grease a baking dish or line with baking parchment.

Put the butter and sugars into a bowl and beat until light and fluffy. Whisk in the egg, coconut milk, evaporated milk, vanilla and rum (if using), then fold in the flour, baking powder, salt, coconut and cornmeal until well incorporated. Fold in the mashed banana and ginger, then pour into the prepared baking dish and bake in the oven for 50 minutes, or until brown on top and a skewer inserted into the centre comes out clean. Serve warm or cold.

BONBON SIWO

HAITIAN GINGERBREAD WITH MOLASSES & SPICES

SERVES 8–10

Bonbon siwo are deliciously spiced Haitian gingerbreads. Coincidentally they have beautiful buildings by the same name with an interesting story. Scattered throughout Port-au-Prince, Turgeau, Pacot, Bois Verna, and beyond, gingerbread houses in Haiti are a protected part of their infrastructure and tell us so much about the island's history. Once housing some of the island's elite class, they are unique to Haiti and famous for their steep roofs, ornate details and bright contrasting colours. They're particularly special because they are a relic of Haiti's past and many of them have managed to withstand the many natural disasters. These cakes are an ode to this infrastructure that celebrates Haiti's national pride.

Ingredients

160 g (5¾ oz) salted butter

100 g (3⅓ oz/generous ½ cup) dark brown soft sugar

2 medium eggs

2 teaspoons vanilla extract or vanilla bean paste

2 teaspoons almond extract

150 ml (5 fl oz/scant ⅔ cup) whole (full-fat) milk or coconut milk

400 g (14 oz/scant 3¼ cups) plain (all-purpose) flour

½ teaspoon ground cinnamon

¼ teaspoon ground cloves

¼ teaspoon ground nutmeg

½ teaspoon sea salt

1 teaspoon baking powder

1 teaspoon bicarbonate of soda (baking soda)

200 g (7 oz/generous ½ cup) black treacle (molasses)

1 tablespoon grated fresh ginger root

Preheat the oven to 180°C fan (400°F) and line a 900 g (2 lb) loaf tin (pan) with baking parchment.

Put the butter and sugar into a large bowl and beat until light and fluffy. Add the eggs, vanilla extract and almond extract. Beat until well combined, then gradually add the milk. Sift in the flour, cinnamon, cloves, nutmeg, salt, baking powder and bicarbonate of soda. Fold in gently using a metal spoon or spatula, then gently mix in the molasses and ginger, being careful not to knock the air out.

Pour the batter into the prepared tin, then bake in the oven for 50–60 minutes, or until a skewer inserted into the centre comes out clean. Remove from the oven and leave to cool in the tin before slicing to serve.

BLACK CAKE

SERVES 8–10

Making black cake used to be one of the baking moments I looked forward to with my grandmother. Every year, around late October, sherry, glacé (candied) cherries and dried fruit mix would be added to the Saturday shopping list, which meant only one thing. It was time to soak the fruit for Christmas cake. Upon returning, we'd spend the afternoon, dowsing and blitzing the dried fruits and sherry, ready to be packed away until December. Although laborious, it was necessary for the density, richness and luxuriousness that are key to a good black cake. Originally the cake was called 'The Empire Christmas Pudding', as the sweet evolved from the British plum pudding and utilised ingredients, such as sugar, molasses and spices, from the places Britain had proudly colonised and now claimed as their own. Its presence in the anglophone islands (Montserrat, Barbados, Trinidad and Guyana), connects the British introduction of Christianity and the observation of new religious holidays.

Ingredients

60 g (2 oz/½ cup) sultanas (golden raisins)

100 g (3½ oz/generous ¾ cup) raisins

40 g (1½ oz/scant ¼ cup) mixed candied peel

20 g (¾) glacé (candied) cherries

50 g (1¾ oz/scant ¼ cup) pitted prunes

150 ml (5 fl oz/scant ⅔ cup) dark rum, plus extra for feeding the cake

270 g (9½ oz) unsalted butter, plus extra for greasing

270 g (9½ oz/scant 1½ cups) dark muscovado sugar

6 medium eggs

2 teaspoons vanilla extract or vanilla bean paste

1½ teaspoons almond extract

180 g (6⅓ oz/scant 1½ cups) plain (all-purpose) flour

1½ teaspoons baking powder

1 teaspoon ground cinnamon

1 teaspoon ground nutmeg

½ teaspoon ground cloves

zest of 1 orange

Browning

60 g (2 oz) black treacle (molasses)

60 ml (2 fl oz/¼ cup) dark rum

First, soak the fruit. Put the sultanas, raisins, mixed candied peel, glacé cherries and prunes into a bowl or container and then pour over the rum. Mix well, then cover set aside to soak. The longer the fruit soaks the better – anything from overnight to 1 year is good. Some people start soaking the fruit for their black cake for the next Christmas during the current Christmas period.

When you're ready to bake, transfer the fruit to a food processor and blend to a rough purée with some chunky pieces, then set aside.

Put the butter and sugar into a bowl and beat until light and fluffy, then add the eggs one at a time, followed by the vanilla and almond extracts. Next, sift in the flour and baking powder, then fold in slowly to ensure you don't create any lumps or knock out too much of the air. Finally, add the spices and orange zest, then the blended fruit. Fold again until well incorporated, then set aside while you make the browning.

Preheat the oven to 160°C fan (350°F) and line a 20 cm (8 in) cake tin (pan) with baking parchment.

Put the treacle and rum into a saucepan over a medium heat and bring to the boil, then reduce to a simmer and cook until reduced by a third. Remove from the heat, leave to cool, then add to the cake mix. Pour the mixture into the prepared tin, then bake for 1 hour 40 minutes, or until brown on top and a skewer inserted into the centre comes out clean. Remove from the oven and allow to cool in the tin.

Once fully cooled, remove from the tin, but don't remove the baking parchment. Place the cake on a plate or in the container you will store it in, then make small holes across the top of the cake using a cocktail stick (toothpick) or skewer. Slowly pour over some rum a little at a time, then cover and store in an airtight container until ready to serve.

PASTELITOS DE GUAYABA

SPANISH CARIBBEAN GUAVA PASTRIES

MAKES 9

The specific origins of this dish aren't quite clear. Some say it was Lebanese immigrants trying to recreate baklava. The addition of the cheese is said to have been influenced by the American expansion into Cuba as a result of the Spanish-American war until communism in 1959. Now, these pastries are enjoyed beyond the island and can be found in *panaderias* (Puerto Rican bakeries) in Little Havana, Miami and New York where there are large Puerto Rican and Cuban populations. The cheese isn't essential for this recipe at all, they're just as delicious with the guava jam only.

Ingredients

Pastry

300 g (10½ oz/2⅓ cups) plain (all-purpose) flour, plus extra for dusting

¼ teaspoon sea salt

½ teaspoon sugar

160 ml (5½ fl oz/⅔ cup) water

250 g (9 oz) salted butter, at room temperature

Filling

270 g (9½ oz) guava paste or guava cheese

170 g (6 oz) semi-hard cheese, such as manouri, cut into 9 pieces (optional)

Glaze

1 medium egg

1 tablespoon whole (full-fat) milk

2 tablespoons Demerara sugar

To finish

2–3 tablespoons icing (confectioners') sugar

First, make the pastry. Combine the flour, salt and sugar in a large bowl. Mix together then gradually pour in the water to bring together and form a dough. Shape into a ball, wrap in cling film (plastic wrap), then chill in the refrigerator for 30 minutes.

Put the butter in between 2 pieces of greaseproof paper. Press with a rolling pin to begin to flatten the butter, then roll out to approximately to the size of an A6 piece of paper (10 × 15 cm [4 × 6 in]) and set aside.

Next, roll out the dough into a circle to approximately 30 cm (12 in) in diameter and place the butter in the centre. Fold the left side into the middle followed by the right, covering the butter and allowing the dough to overlap in the centre. Holding the rolling pin horizontally across the dough, press the dough to seal over the butter. Then fold the excess dough from the bottom upwards towards the centre, then fold the excess from the top, down towards the centre. Again, holding the rolling pin horizontally across the dough, press the dough to completely seal over the butter. Give the dough a quarter turn, roll out the dough into a long rectangle, approximately 15 × 40 cm (6 × 16 in). Using a knife, lightly mark the dough into thirds, then fold the bottom third up into the centre and the top third down into the centre and press with the rolling pin again to seal. Wrap the dough in cling film (plastic wrap) and chill in the fridge for 30 minutes before rolling again. Repeat this process 3 more times, giving the dough a quarter turn each time.

Preheat the oven to 200°C fan (425°F). Roll out the pastry to 5 mm (¼ in) thick, then divide into two large rectangles. Lightly mark lines on both sheets of the pastry using a knife to create 9 squares. Place 2 tablespoons or 30g square of the guava paste/guava cheese and a square of cheese (if using) onto each square. Lightly brush water in between the gaps of the pastry sheet, then place the second sheet of pastry on top (with the lines facing up). Press lightly with your fingers along the lines to seal the 2 pastry sheets together, then slice along the lines to create the 9 pastries. Use a fork to crimp the edges all around.

Whisk together the egg and milk for the glaze and brush this over the tops and edges, then sprinkle with the Demerara sugar. Place on a baking sheet, then bake for 20–25 minutes, or until golden brown, flaky and puffy. Allow to cool for at least 10 minutes, then sprinkle with the icing sugar.

POLVORONES/POLVORÓN

PUERTO RICAN/CUBAN SHORTBREAD BISCUITS

MAKES 12

What makes these nutty, butter cookies unique is their distinctive crumbly, cracked texture and shape. *Polvorones* translates to polka dots, referencing their roundness. They originated on the Spanish island of Andalucia, where they often used pork fat (lard), giving the biscuits their crisp bite. As part of their evolution, the addition of guava jam is what now makes them uniquely Caribbean. As the Spanish also colonised parts of the far East too, these cookies are also found in the Philippines.

Ingredients

120 g (4¼ oz) salted butter, softened

60 g (2 oz) vegetable shortening

100 g (3½ oz/scant ½ cup) golden caster (superfine) sugar

1 egg yolk

200 g (7 oz/1⅔ cups) plain (all-purpose) flour

70 g (2½ oz/generous ⅔ cup) ground almonds (almond meal)

¼ teaspoon sea salt

½ teaspoon ground cinnamon

guava jam (jelly), to garnish (optional)

Preheat the oven to 190°C fan (400°F) and line a baking sheet with baking parchment.

Put the butter, vegetable shortening and sugar into a large bowl and beat until light and fluffy, then whisk in the egg yolk until well incorporated. Sift in the flour, ground almonds, salt and cinnamon. Fold through until well incorporated, being careful not to over mix – the texture should be grainy. Form spoonfuls of the mixture into 12 balls, then place on the prepared baking sheet. Press a small dent into the top of the biscuits using your finger, then repeat with the remaining dough. Bake in the oven for 15 minutes, then remove from the oven and place 1–2 teaspoons of the guava jam (if using) into the dents. Return to the oven and bake for a further 5 minutes. If you're not using guava jam, skip this step. Once baked, remove from the oven and leave to cool on the baking sheet. They will be a little soft to touch and the jam may be hot, so allow them to firm up slightly before serving and eating.

SALARA
GUYANESE COCONUT ROLLS

SERVES 8–10

The look and feel of salara are a special symbol of Guyana. In Queens, New York, there is a large diaspora community of Guyanese and Trinidadians within the Richmond Hill area. Sybil's has been in business since 1976 and serves handmade, freshly baked salara among many other baked treats, daily. The slightly sweet dough is lined with sweetened coconut, similar to that within the plate tart recipe (see page 255) before being dyed its iconic red, making it uniquely Guyanese. As with many immigrant communities, it's these iconic food items that evoke those nostalgic feelings of home.

Ingredients

7 g (¼ oz) fast-action dried yeast

25 g (1 oz) raw cane sugar

80 ml (2½ fl oz/5 tablespoons) lukewarm water

400 g (14 oz/scant 3¼ cups) strong white bread flour, plus extra for dusting

5 g (¼ oz) sea salt

120 ml (4 fl oz/½ cup) whole (full-fat) milk

85 g (3 oz) salted butter, melted, plus extra for brushing

Coconut filling

75 g (2½ oz/generous ⅓ cup) Demerara or raw cane sugar

75 ml (2½ fl oz/5 tablespoons) water

100 g (3½ oz) dried coconut, freshly grated or desiccated (dried shredded)

¼ teaspoon freshly grated nutmeg

¼ teaspoon ground cinnamon

1 teaspoon vanilla extract or vanilla bean paste

2–3 drops or 1 teaspoon red food colouring, depending on type used

Put the yeast, sugar and water into a bowl, then mix and set aside in a warm place for 5–10 minutes to allow the yeast to activate. Put the flour and salt into a separate bowl, then once the yeast mixture starts to bubble and froth, add it to the flour along with the milk and 55 g (2 oz) of the melted butter. Bring together into a dough, then tip out onto a clean surface and knead for 8–10 minutes. Alternatively, you can do this in a stand mixer. Return to the bowl, cover and set aside in a warm place to prove for 1 hour, or until doubled in size.

Meanwhile, make the filling. Put the sugar and water into a saucepan and whisk until the sugar has dissolved, then bring to the boil. Add the remaining ingredients except the food colouring, then reduce to a simmer, cover and cook for 8–10 minutes, stirring continuously, until the moisture has been absorbed by the coconut and the mixture becomes rich and sticky. Remove from the heat, then set aside to cool. Once cooled, add the food colouring and mix well – you want an even red colour throughout.

Once the dough has risen, roll it out on a lightly floured surface into a rectangle, about 1–2 cm (½–¾ in) thick. Brush the dough with the remaining butter, then spread the coconut filling on top evenly, leaving a 1 cm (½ in) border around the edge and pressing down to ensure it stays in place. Starting from one of the long edges, roll up the dough tightly and carefully to create a log shape. Gently place the roll onto a baking sheet lined with baking parchment, then cover with a dish towel and leave to prove again for 1 hour, or until doubled in size.

Preheat the oven to 180°C fan (400°F).

Once risen, bake the roll in the oven for 40–50 minutes, or until golden brown and hollow-sounding when tapped underneath. Remove from the oven and brush the top with more melted butter to glaze, allow to cool, then slice to serve.

PINE TART

GUYANESE PASTRIES WITH PINEAPPLE JAM

MAKES 8–10

Pastries are very popular in Guyana. Cheese rolls, meat pies and pine tarts are a sample of the many snacks you'll find in Guyanese bakeries. The country credits pastries as a contribution from the Madeiran Portuguese who settled briefly during the 1800s, just as they were in Trinidad and Tobago around the same time following their mass socio-economic and religious migration from Europe. Although their communities don't have a strong presence now, their influences can still be felt.

Ingredients

Filling

800 g (1 lb 12 oz) fresh pineapple, crushed or blended

150–200 g (5½–7 oz) raw cane sugar (depending on acidity and ripeness of the pineapple)

juice and zest of 1 lemon

¼ teaspoon sea salt

½ teaspoon freshly grated nutmeg

½ teaspoon ground cinnamon

1 teaspoon vanilla extract or bean paste

Pastry

500 g (1 lb 2 oz/4 cups) plain (all-purpose) flour, plus extra for dusting

½ teaspoon sea salt

225 g (8 oz) salted butter, frozen

60 g (2 oz) vegetable shortening or lard

125 ml (4 fl oz/½ cup) cold water

1 medium egg, beaten

First, make the filling. Combine all the ingredients in a saucepan over a medium heat and bring up to a low boil, then simmer for 40–50 minutes, or until the liquid has evaporated and the fruit has become a sticky, thick jam. Remove from the heat and set aside to cool.

Meanwhile, make the dough. Combine the flour and salt in a bowl, then grate in the frozen butter and crumble in the vegetable shortening or lard. Mix so that the fat is coated in the flour and starts to resemble breadcrumbs, then gradually pour in the water while stirring to gently bring together into a dough. Wrap the dough in cling film (plastic wrap) and transfer to the refrigerator to chill for 30 minutes.

Preheat the oven to 190°C fan (400°F) and line a baking sheet with baking parchment.

Once chilled, remove the dough from the refrigerator and roll out on a lightly floured surface to 5 mm (¼ in) thick. Use a 9 cm (3½ in) pastry cutter to cut out as many circles as you can. You can re-roll and reuse the pastry offcuts as well, but they will lose a little of their puffiness once baked.

Mark a triangle on each of the pastry circles, then add 2 tablespoons of the pineapple jam in each triangle. Brush the edges of the pastry with a little water, then fold the edges inwards to form a triangle, leaving a small hole in the centre revealing a little of the filling. Place on the prepared baking sheet, then brush with the beaten egg. Bake in the oven for 25–35 minutes, or until golden brown. Allow to cool a little on a wire rack before serving.

PONE

CASSAVA & SWEET POTATO CAKE WITH COCONUT & SPICES

SERVES 8–10

The history of *pone* bread is an interesting one that is said to have evolved from the Indigenous Amerindians on the American mainland and the baked bread cake they made from corn. Upon arrival in the Southern parts of North America, namely, Chesapeake Bay, the enslaved African communities are said to have taken on this recipe and continued it. How it made its way to the Caribbean is unknown, however, there was a lot of custom and people exchange between both regions. Instead of using corn, sweet potatoes, pumpkin or cassava are often used in addition to the raisins, spices and sugar for sweetness.

Ingredients

400 g (14 oz) cassava, peeled and finely grated

120 g (4¼ oz) white sweet potato, finely grated

80 g (2¾ oz) pumpkin, finely grated

70 g (2½ oz) dried coconut, freshly grated, or desiccated (dried shredded) coconut

1 teaspoon baking powder

200 g (7 oz/generous ⅓ cup) light muscovado sugar

1 teaspoon ground cinnamon

1 teaspoon freshly grated nutmeg

10 g (½ oz) fresh ginger root, finely grated

60 g (2 oz) salted butter, melted, plus extra for greasing

325 ml (11 oz/1⅓ cups) evaporated milk

100 g (3½ oz/generous ¾ cup) raisins or sultanas (golden raisins; optional)

Preheat the oven to 170°C fan (375°F). Grease a 27 × 14 cm (10½ × 5½ in) (or equivalent) rectangular baking dish or tin (pan) and line with baking parchment.

Put the cassava, sweet potato, pumpkin, coconut and baking powder into a large bowl and mix together, then add the sugar, cinnamon, nutmeg and ginger and mix again. Pour in the melted butter and evaporated milk, then mix again to bring everything together.

Pour the mixture into the prepared dish or tin and bake in the oven for 35–40 minutes, or until a skewer inserted into the centre comes out clean. Serve warm or cold.

Note

This can be made vegan by substituting the butter for vegetable shortening and the evaporated milk for coconut milk.

EASTER SPICED BUN

SERVES 8–10

In the mid-seventeenth century, the British colonised Jamaica, taking over from Spanish rule. Their introduction of Christianity also brought along the customs associated with the religion. As it was believed Jesus was resurrected on Good Friday, hot cross buns were made to commemorate this. Spiced bun is an evolution of these little, yeasted molasses rolls. Throughout Jamaica, in particular, it is served sliced with the thickest slice of canned, processed cheese. I have no idea as to why or how the two were paired together, but, it's the most classic way to enjoy it.

Ingredients

600 g (1 lb 5 oz/4¾ cups) strong white bread flour

2½ teaspoons baking powder

2 teaspoons ground cinnamon

2 teaspoons freshly grated nutmeg

1 teaspoon ground mixed spice

½ teaspoon sea salt

15 g (½ oz) fast-action dried yeast

155 g (5½ oz/generous ¾ cup) dark muscovado sugar

50 ml (1¾ fl oz/3½ tablespoons) lukewarm water

50 g (1¾ oz) salted butter, melted, plus extra to serve

100 g (3½ oz/generous ¼ cup) black treacle (molasses)

2 teaspoons vanilla extract or vanilla bean paste

330 ml (11¼ fl oz/1⅓ cups) Guinness, porter or non-alcoholic malt drink

75 g (2½ oz/scant ⅔ cup) raisins, roughly chopped

30 g (1 oz/scant ¼ cup) mixed candied peel, roughly chopped

45 g (1½ oz/scant ¼ cup) glacé (candied) cherries, roughly chopped

15 g (½ oz) fresh ginger root, finely grated

1 medium egg

zest and juice of 1 orange

1½ teaspoons browning (optional)

Glaze

4 tablespoons molasses (black treacle)

2 tablespoons water

To serve

salted butter, for spreading

mature Cheddar cheese, sliced thickly

Preheat the oven to 150°C fan (350°F) and line a 900 g (2 lb) loaf tin (pan) with baking parchment.

Combine the flour, baking powder, cinnamon, nutmeg, mixed spice and salt in a large bowl. In a separate bowl, combine the yeast, 10 g (½ oz) of the sugar and the water, then mix and aside in a warm place for 15 minutes to allow the yeast to activate.

Melt the butter in a saucepan over a low heat, then add the remaining sugar, the treacle, vanilla and Guinness or porter. Stir until the butter has totally melted and the sugar has dissolved, then set aside to cool.

Add the raisins, mixed peel, glacé cherries and ginger to the flour mixture and combine, ensuring the fruits are evenly distributed throughout. Add the egg, orange zest and juice and browning (if using) and slowly stir together. Gradually pour in the cooled yeast mixture, then the Guinness mixture. Mix well to create a silky brown batter. Pour the batter into the prepared loaf tin and bake for 1½ hours, or until a skewer inserted into the centre comes out clean. Remove from the oven and leave to cool in the tin.

Meanwhile, prepare the glaze. Combine the treacle and water in a small saucepan and warm over a low heat until it begins to bubble. Using a pastry brush, spread the glaze over the top of the bun, then leave to set. Once no longer sticky, slice into thick pieces and serve with butter and thick slices of cheese.

KURMA/MITHAI
SWEET SNACKS

SERVES 8

Indian snacks are a big part of the eating culture across the subcontinent. Whether sweet or savoury, deep-fried, boiled or roasted, these foods hold particular meaning and are eaten for specific purposes or functions. Kurma (khurma) or mithai are common in Trinidad and Guyana, thanks to the East and South Indian communities who emigrated in the 1800s. They're a traditional, crunchy deep-fried dough made with ginger and spices before being coated in a sugar syrup to create a sweet crust on the outside. Originally, they were reserved for Diwali celebrations, however, now they can be found throughout the regions all year round.

Ingredients

240 g (8½ oz/scant 2 cups) plain (all-purpose) flour, plus extra for dusting

50 g (1¾ oz/scant ¼ cup) golden caster (superfine) sugar

1 teaspoon ground cardamom

¼ teaspoon ground cinnamon

¼ teaspoon ground nutmeg

10 g (½ oz) fresh ginger root, finely grated

60 g (2 oz) salted butter, cubed, cold

70 ml (2¼ fl oz/⅓ cup) whole (full-fat) milk

1 litre (34 fl oz/4¼ cups) vegetable oil, for deep-frying

Glaze

60 ml (2 fl oz/¼ cup) water

150 g (5½ oz/generous ⅔ cup) golden granulated sugar

Put the flour, sugar, cardamom, cinnamon, nutmeg and ginger into a large bowl and mix well. Add the butter and use your fingers to rub it into the flour until the mixture resembles breadcrumbs, then slowly pour in the milk and bring together into a dough. Knead until firm and springy, then wrap in cling film (plastic wrap) and freeze for 10–15 minutes.

Once firm, remove from the freezer and roll out on a lightly floured surface into a 5 mm (¼ in) thick rectangle. Slice this in half lengthways, then cut into 7–8 cm (2¾–3¼ in) wide strips.

Pour the oil into a deep saucepan and heat to 140–150°C (275–300°F), then carefully lower a few pastry strips into the oil. Deep-fry for a few minutes until golden brown, stirring and moving around the pan as they cook. Remove from the oil with a slotted spoon and drain on paper towels. Continue until you have fried all the kurma. Once drained, remove the paper towels.

To make the glaze, combine the water and sugar in a small saucepan and boil for a few minutes until a syrup forms. While the sugar syrup is hot, pour over the kurma and toss quickly to coat them in the syrup, moving the bowl around to ensure the kurma don't stick together. When the syrup cools, it should look like a white icing. Serve immediately.

MAMBA

HAITIAN PEANUT BUTTER WITH SCOTCH BONNET

SERVES 8

Along with people from the Dominican Republic, who also call this peanut butter mambá, it's clear this recipe has African roots. The Congolese word for peanut is *muamba* and this recipe has evolved from that. Peanuts are grown abundantly across Cap-Haitien, and Haiti's own peanut butter is unlike no other. Traditionally, raw peanuts are roasted in a large vat, turned continuously until the skins release themselves from the nut. They are then ground to form a smooth paste before sugar and hot pepper are added. Some say mamba is an evolution of American peanut butter, which is easy to produce with the abundance of nuts grown on the island. Locally made mamba has become a great way of helping communities and small-scale farmers in Haiti build wealth following recurring natural disasters and political unrest. Serve this with cassava bread (casabe/kassav) (see page 161).

Ingredients

320 g (11 oz/2 cups) whole raw unsalted peanuts (with skins)

30 g (1 oz/scant ¼ cup) light or dark brown muscovado sugar

½ teaspoon sea salt

2 tablespoons coconut or rapeseed (canola) oil

1 Scotch bonnet

Preheat the oven to 180°C fan (400°F). Put the peanuts onto a non-stick baking tray (pan) and toast in the oven for 20–25 minutes until you can smell their warm peanut smell, some of the skin has peeled back a bit and the peanuts are a slightly darker brown. Check towards the end to ensure they don't burn. Once toasted, set aside to cool. While the nuts are cooling, sterilise the jar to store the mamba in.

Put the jar to a deep saucepan, then fill it with cold water until the jar is covered. Bring to the boil and boil for 10 minutes. Remove from the heat and allow the jar to cool in the water. Once cool enough to handle, carefully remove the jar from the pan with a clean dish towel and leave to dry on another clean dish towel until ready to use.

Once cooled, put the peanuts into a colander over a baking tray and stir them continuously until all the skins have been removed. Transfer the skinned peanuts to a food processor and blend until smooth, scraping down the sides periodically. The mixture will start off crumbly but will eventually become smooth. After a few minutes, add the sugar, salt, oil and whole Scotch bonnet. Continue to blend for a further few minutes, stopping and scraping occasionally, until a smooth butter forms. Once smooth, transfer to the sterilised jar and store in the refrigerator for up to 1 month.

TEMBLEQUE
SET COCONUT PUDDING

SERVES 6

A beloved Puerto Rican sweet of coconut milk set simply using cornflour. When translated, *tembleque* means wobbly in Spanish due to its jelly-like texture.

Ingredients

60 g (2 oz/4 tablespoons) cornflour (cornstarch)

130 g (4½ oz/scant ⅔ cup) golden caster (superfine) sugar

¼ teaspoon sea salt

800 ml (27 fl oz/3⅓ cups) good-quality coconut milk

zest of 1 lime

1 vanilla pod (bean), split open, or 1 teaspoon vanilla extract or vanilla bean paste

2 teaspoons rapeseed (canola) or olive oil for greasing

90 g (3¼ oz/1⅓ cups) toasted coconut flakes

ground cinnamon, for dusting

Combine the cornflour, sugar and salt in a bowl, then slowly pour in the coconut milk and whisk until smooth. Add the lime zest and vanilla, then pour the mixture into a saucepan and simmer over a medium–low heat for 6–7 minutes, stirring constantly until the mixture thickens. Remove from the heat, then set aside briefly.

Grease 6 ramekins or glasses well with the rapeseed (canola) or olive oil, then pour in the mixture. Leave to cool a little, then transfer to the refrigerator to chill. Once set, carefully loosen the edges by running a knife around, then turn out onto a plate. Garnish with the toasted coconut flakes and a light dusting of ground cinnamon.

Note

You could make this into one tembleque rather than using smaller individual ramekins. Use a shaped or patterned, bundt-style baking tin, ensuring it is greased well so the pudding doesn't stick when turned out to serve.

NUTMEG ICE CREAM

SERVES 6–8

Nutmeg is precious to Grenada and this ice cream is a local favourite. This recipe is very easy to make even if you don't have an ice cream maker.

Ingredients

300 ml (10 fl oz/1¼ cups) double (heavy) cream
200 ml (7 fl oz/scant 1 cup) full-cream (or whole/full-fat) milk
2 teaspoons freshly grated nutmeg
3 medium egg yolks
2 teaspoons vanilla extract or vanilla bean paste or 1 vanilla pod (bean), split and seeds scraped out
100 g (3½ oz/scant ½ cup) raw cane sugar
1 teaspoon cornflour (cornstarch)

Gently heat the cream, milk and nutmeg in a saucepan over a medium heat until it just starts to boil.

Meanwhile, whisk together the egg yolks, vanilla, sugar and cornflour in a large bowl. Once the milk is steaming, pour a little into the egg yolk mixture and whisk to temper it, then slowly pour in the rest, whisking continuously. Pour the mixture back into the saucepan, then cook over a low heat for a further 5–10 minutes, stirring continuously, until the mix thickens. Once the mixture has thickened, remove from the heat and set aside to cool before churning.

Churn in an ice-cream maker according to the manufacturer's instructions, or scrape the mixture into a freezer-proof container and freeze. Every hour, remove from the freezer and stir, ensuring you get all the ice crystals around the edges. Repeat three or four times, or until the ice cream is thick and smooth.

SORBET COCO

COCONUT SORBET

SERVES 6–8

You'll find this across both islands Guadeloupe and Martinique, by the beach or in the markets. *Sorbet coco* is freshly churned by hand the old-fashioned way with all local ingredients – coconut milk, vanilla and sugar.

Ingredients

125 g (4½ oz/generous ½ cup) granulated sugar
⅛ teaspoon sea salt
½ tablespoon cornflour (cornstarch)
250 ml (8 fl oz/1 cup) good-quality coconut milk
250 g (9 oz/¾ cup) evaporated milk
1½ teaspoons vanilla extract or vanilla bean paste or 1 vanilla pod (bean), split and seeds scraped out
½ teaspoon ground nutmeg
zest of 1 lime

Combine the sugar, salt and cornflour in a bowl, then set aside.

Pour the coconut milk into a saucepan and warm over a low heat. Add the evaporated milk to the rest of the ingredients and whisk, then add the warmed coconut milk and whisk until dissolved. Return the mixture to the pan and warm slowly for a few minutes until thickened. Keep whisking to ensure the mixture doesn't stick and burn on the bottom of the pan. Once thickened, remove from the heat and set aside to cool.

Churn in an ice-cream maker according to the manufacturer's instructions, or scrape the mixture into a freezer-proof container and freeze. Every hour, remove from the freezer and stir, ensuring you get all the ice crystals around the edges. Repeat three or four times, or until the sorbet is thick and smooth.

DRINKS

LOCAL NON-ALCOHOLIC DRINKS
RUM AND RHUM AGRICOLE
PUNCH, TONICS AND WINE
HOT

henever I'm away, I hunt down 'local drinks'. They're the ones made with all the produce that naturally occurs on the islands. From tamarind, ginger and sorrel, to soursop, June plum, mauby bark, pommecy there and guinep, the list goes on. Here you can try a few for yourself. For the most part, they simply require boiling and steeping of the main ingredients, then straining and sweetening to taste.

These natural ingredients and plants have been held closely by the communities that grew them. Sorrel (hibiscus), originally native to parts of Asia, made its way to Africa, where it is known as *bissap, wonjo, foléré, dabileni, tsobo, zobo*, or *sobolo*, before being transferred to the Americas. Sorrel has a special connection to the Caribbean, in many ways. It is the national flower of Haiti and now a Christmas tradition due to the flower coming into season around November and December. During the 1800s, it experienced a second migration following the period of indentured enslavement from Indian communities. They used the plants for daily worship, self-care and offerings, as it was carried by Kali – the goddess of power within Hinduism. The connection both communities had to the earth and their spiritual beliefs informed a large part of their survival, which has allowed particular cultural practices to stand the test of time.

The bark of the Snakewood tree makes the bittersweet drink known as *mauby* in Trinidad and Barbados, *mabi* in Haiti and the Dominican Republic and *mavi* in Puerto Rico. It is popular across the islands, and within the region, also, and sold dried with other spices to be boiled at home, as a syrup or fresh in coolers on the roadside, ready to drink. In the early 1900s, 'mauby women' were known street traders who carried vats of the homemade brew on their heads and sold them around town. Still made in the same way today – the bark is boiled with whole spices such as cinnamon, nutmeg, cloves, citrus peel and vanilla before adding sugar. It is said, some would make a fermented version which I have never tried but would be very curious to, as mauby already has a very distinct taste, which you'll either love or hate.

GINGER BEER

SORREL

SERVES 8–10

Homemade ginger beer is a common local drink you'll find sold on the roadside of many of the islands. The best variety to use is African ginger as it's much stronger giving a lovely layer of extra spice and heat once steeped.

SERVES 8–10

I love sorrel, it was a staple on the menu at my restaurant and a must have on the table every Christmas. The subtle warmth from the ginger, clove and cinnamon is so comforting, even with the slight sourness from sorrel leaves. You can definitely enjoy it as it is, but it's even more delicious with a shot of rum, in my opinion!

Ingredients

300 g (10½ oz) fresh ginger root
2 unwaxed lemons
10 g (½ oz) cinnamon sticks (about 4)
5 g (¼ oz) cloves
3 litres (101½ fl oz/12⅔ cups) water
750 g (1 lb 10 oz/3⅓ cups) golden granulated sugar

Rinse the ginger under cold running water to ensure it is thoroughly clean, then grate it into a saucepan and set aside.

Using a vegetable peeler, remove the lemon zest from the lemons and set aside. Squeeze the juice into the saucepan with the ginger, then discard the remaining flesh. Add the cinnamon sticks, cloves and water to the saucepan and bring to the boil. Once boiling, reduce the heat and simmer for 20 minutes. Remove the pan from the heat, add the reserved lemon rind and set aside to cool.

Once cooled, strain through a sieve (fine mesh strainer) or muslin (cheesecloth), squeezing out as much of the juice as possible. Finally, whisk in the sugar and then decant into sterilised bottles (see page 275). Store in the refrigerator for up to 3 days. Serve chilled.

Ingredients

200 g (7 oz) fresh ginger root
2 unwaxed lemons
100 g (3½ oz) dried sorrel (hibiscus flowers)
10 g (½ oz) cinnamon sticks (about 4)
5 g (¼ oz) cloves
2.5 litres (84½ fl oz/10½ cups) water
750 g (1 lb 10 oz/3⅓ cups) golden granulated sugar

Rinse the ginger under cold running water to ensure it is thoroughly clean, then grate it into a saucepan and set aside.

Using a vegetable peeler, remove the lemon zest from the lemons and set aside. Squeeze the juice into the saucepan with the ginger, then discard the remaining flesh. Add the sorrel, cinnamon sticks, cloves and water to the saucepan and bring to the boil. Once boiling, reduce the heat and simmer for 20 minutes. Remove the pan from the heat, add the reserved lemon rind and set aside to cool.

Once cooled, strain through a sieve (fine mesh strainer) or muslin (cheesecloth), squeezing out as much of the juice as possible. Finally, whisk in the sugar and then decant into sterilised bottles (see page 275). Store in the refrigerator for up to 3 days. Serve chilled.

RUM PUNCH

SPICED RUM

SERVES 6

Rum punch at Carnival or a lime (party or gathering) always goes down well and it's a drink that is a notable part of our culture. The term punch in the context of drinking, is said to originate from India and the Hindi word *paanch* meaning 'five', in reference to the amount of ingredients in a recipe. As Bajans are the original rum producers, their saying for the best punch goes 'One of sour (lime juice), two of sweet (simple syrup), three of strong (rum) and four of weak (water), a dash of bitters (Angostura bitters is delicious!) and a sprinkle of spice (nutmeg), serve well chilled, with plenty of ice'.

Ingredients
ice cubes, as needed
150 ml (5 fl oz/scant ⅔ cup) dark rum
75 ml (2½ fl oz/5 tablespoons) white rum
500 ml (17 fl oz/generous 2 cups) orange juice
400 ml (14 fl oz/generous 1½ cups) pineapple juice
100 ml (3½ fl oz/scant ½ cup) grenadine
2 limes, cut into wedges
Angostura bitters, to taste
freshly grated nutmeg (optional)

Fill a large jug (pitcher) with ice, then add the rum, juices and grenadine. Mix well. Pour into six glasses, then finish each glass with two lime wedges, a few dashes of bitters and a little nutmeg.

SERVES 6

In St. Lucia, almost every market trader in Castries sells mixes for spiced rum batches or sells bottles of it made already with the spices in it. This spiced rum recipe gives you the opportunity to try it yourself. All you need is a bottle of your preferred rum and the spices below. It's best to use a golden rum; dark and white won't work as well.

Ingredients
500 ml (17 fl oz/generous 2 cups) golden or dark rum
a few pieces of bois bande bark
a few cinnamon sticks
a few blades of mace
5 cloves
2 star anise

Combine all the ingredients in a large sterilised jar (see page 275), ensuring the spices are fully submerged in the rum. Close tightly, then leave to steep somewhere dark and cool for at least 6 weeks before drinking – the longer it is left, the strong the flavour.

TI' PUNCH

PETIT (SMALL) PUNCH

SERVES 1

Tí Punch is the national drink of Martinique but is also found across the French Caribbean in countries such as Haiti. Using only four simple ingredients – *rhum agricole* (Martinique) or *rhum Barbancourt* (Haiti), lime, sugar cane juice and ice. The name *tí punch* evolved from the Kreyòl term *petit punch* meaning 'small punch' due to its size. The ingredients in the drink speak to the time. Sugar production had peaked and limes had been imported by the Spanish from Polynesia and heavily cultivated in Haiti since the 1520s. In the early nineteenth century, Franz Karl Achard succeeded in breeding the white beetroot into a so-called 'sugar beet'.

This was groundbreaking for the French at the time, as early simmers of the Haitian revolution meant disruption to sugar cane production, thus, affecting the importation of refined sugar into France. Following the end of the revolution, sugar cane growers had no purpose for their matured sugar canes that were ready to be processed. The system had been built around the European desire for refined sugar, which meant refineries and distilleries on the island for rum production from molasses were redundant. As there was still a market for rum to be sold locally, someone (it is not known who exactly) came up with the smart idea of taking the sugar canes straight to the distillery, pressing their juice and making rum from the liquid sugar itself rather than the molasses. It was then that rhum agricole was born. This process and fast thinking created a whole new product. Rhum agricole and rhum Barbancourt have a unique earthy and grassy taste in comparison to other molasses-based rums made across the Caribbean which are richer and more caramelised. Naturally, the age, cask type and location the sugar cane crops are grown will influence the flavour profile of the rhum. For example, the cane harvested near the Demerara River in Guyana has a sweeter and bolder taste than French Guyanese rum due to the difference in the sugar used.

In Martinique, the most traditional preparation would be called '*chacun prépare sa propre mort*', translating to 'each prepares their own death'. In essence, upon drinking ti' punch, you would be served a glass, rhum, limes, and sugar cane juice to prepare the drink to your preference, and only you are responsible for the effects it may or may not have.

Ingredients

60 ml (2 fl oz/¼ cup) rhum agricole

30 ml (1 fl oz/2 tablespoons) sugar cane juice (or 15 ml/1 tablespoon sugar syrup)

¼ lime, little juice, mostly skin and pith squeezed and left in the cup for the oils to permeate

ice cubes, as needed (optional)

Put 3–4 ice cubes (if using) into a short glass, then add the rhum agricole, sugar cane juice and lime juice. Mix well to combine.

HAITIAN CREMAS

SPICED COCONUT MILK & RUM PUNCH

SERVES 6

Cremas is Haiti's milky Christmas drink. Eggnog style drinks were originally developed in the US, however, in 1900 a Venezuelan chemist and perfumist – Eliodoro González – began developing his own version. Native to Caracas, it is said he wanted to create a drink, *ponche cremas*, similar to eggnog that people could enjoy without the alcohol. The idea made its way into the islands and has stuck ever since.

Ingredients

270 g (9½ oz/generous ¾ cup) evaporated milk
150 g (5½ oz/scant ½ cup) condensed milk
250 ml (8 fl oz/1 cup) coconut milk
2 teaspoons vanilla extract or vanilla bean paste
zest of ½ lime
125 ml (4 fl oz/½ cup) rum (dark, spiced or white)
ice cubes, as needed

Syrup

50 g (1¾ oz/scant ¼ cup) Demerara or raw cane sugar
50 ml (1¾ fl oz/3½ tablespoons) water
1 star anise
1 cinnamon stick
3 cloves

First, make the syrup. Combine the sugar, water, star anise, cinnamon stick and cloves in a saucepan and boil until the sugar dissolves and a syrup forms. Set aside to cool overnight and allow the spices to flavour the syrup. The next day, place all the remaining ingredients in a jug (pitcher) and whisk until well combined. Remove the spices from the syrup and set aside, then add the syrup to the drink and mix until well incorporated. Return the spices back to the cremas, then serve over ice.

TRINI PUMPKIN PONCHE DE CRÈME

SPICED PUMPKIN, MILK & RUM PUNCH

SERVES 6

Comparatively to Haitian cremas, Trinidadian *ponche de creme* uses eggs, giving it an extra silky, smooth texture. Ponche de creme can be made with calabash pumpkin, giving it a bright orange hue and extra velvety feel. Today, the recipe has evolved to include rum and there are many variations of it, such as Cuban *crema de vie* and Puerto Rican *coquito*, which uses coconut milk.

Ingredients

200 g (7 oz) pumpkin, peeled and diced into medium chunks
2 medium eggs
140 g (5 oz/scant ½ cup) evaporated milk
200 g (7 oz/scant ⅔ cup) condensed milk
¼ teaspoon ground cinnamon
¼ teaspoon ground nutmeg
1 teaspoon vanilla extract or vanilla bean paste
zest of ½ lime
250 ml (8 fl oz/1 cup) rum (dark, spiced or white)
a few dashes of Angostura bitters

To prepare the pumpkin purée, place the pumpkin in a pan and cover with water. Place over a high heat and bring to a boil. Once boiling, reduce the heat to a high simmer and cook the pumpkin for 10–15 minutes or until the pumpkin is soft and breaks easily with a fork. Once cooked, remove from he heat, strain and place the pumpkin in a bowl. Crush with a fork until smooth to make a purée then set aside.

Next, crack the eggs into a heatproof bowl set over a pan of simmering water and whisk for a few minutes until frothy. Be careful they don't get too hot and start to overcook. Once frothy, remove from the heat, then whisk in the evaporated milk, condensed milk, cinnamon, nutmeg, vanilla and lime zest. Whisk in the pumpkin purée or add to a blender and blitz until smooth. Once evenly incorporated, whisk in the rum and bitters. Add the poncho de creme to a sterilised bottle (see page 275) allow to fully cool before serving chilled over ice. Keep refrigerated and use within 3 days.

GUAVA WINE

SHRUBB
SPICED CITRUS LIQUEUR

SERVES 6

SERVES 8–10

Prior to rum establishing itself and the effects of drinking, *mobbie* from sweet potatoes or *ouicou* from cassava, were common ferments. This one with guava is an easy one to make and try for yourself.

Shrubb is a homemade liqueur made with spices, citrus peel and rhum agricole, exclusive to Martinique. Families commonly make the drink around Christmas time and recipes are often passed down through families over generations.

Ingredients

235 g (8¼ oz) guavas, washed thoroughly
5 g (¼ oz) fresh ginger root, washed thoroughly, then grated
400 g (14 oz/generous 1¾ cups) Demerara sugar
3 g (⅛ oz) fast-action dried yeast
1.25 litres (40 fl oz/5 cups) lukewarm water
2–3 star anise (optional)
1 cinnamon stick (optional)
3 cloves (optional)

Ingredients

5–6 unwaxed oranges (or 60 g/2 oz dried orange peel)
1 cinnamon stick
1 vanilla pod (bean), split in half
5 cloves
1 litre (34 fl oz/4¼ cups) rhum agricole (or white rum)
500 g (1 lb 1 oz/2¼ cups) Demerara sugar or raw cane sugar

Put the whole guavas into a clean bowl and crush to break up. The more broken the fruit, the better they will ferment. Carefully transfer the crushed guava to a large sterilised jar or wide-mouthed bottle (see page 273) and add the ginger, then set aside.

Next, put 200 g (7 oz/scant 1 cup) of the sugar and yeast into the bowl, then add the water. Whisk until the sugar has dissolved, then pour the mixture over the fruit in the jar. Add any spices you're using, then cover the opening with cling film (plastic wrap) to allow the gases to build and release. Leave to ferment in a cool, dark place for 6 weeks, checking periodically.

After 6 weeks, carefully open the container and double strain the mixture into a bowl using a muslin (cheesecloth) and sieve (fine mesh strainer). Depending on how ripe and sweet your guavas, you can add the remaining (7 oz/scant 1 cup) sugar to finish. Leave to sit, then serve chilled. Store in an airtight bottle in the refrigerator for up to 1 month.

Using a vegetable peeler, remove the skin from the oranges, being careful not to go too deep into the bitter pith. Place the peel on a plate with the inside of the peel facing up, then leave to dry in a sunny, well-aired place for 48–72 hours, or until they are completely dry and have curled up.

Put the peel into a large sterilised jar (see page 275) along with the cinnamon stick, vanilla pod, cloves and rhum agricole. Leave to infuse for at least 72 hours, or up to a week in a cool, dark place – the longer it is left, the strong the flavour. You'll notice that the orange peel will change the colour of the rum quite quickly.

Strain the rhum through a sieve (fine mesh strainer) into a bowl. Discard the peel, but reserve the spices. Whisk in the sugar, then pour into a sterilised bottle (see page 275), adding the reserved vanilla pod and whole spices. Serve chilled over ice. Use within 3 months.

GUINNESS & SEA MOSS PUNCH

SERVES 4–6

The Irish seem to have heavily influenced the use of Guinness and Sea Moss in the Caribbean, it's just ironic I've featured them both in the same recipe. I always wondered what the heavy connection between the Caribbean and Guinness consumption was, being that it's brewed in Ireland. Many of the males in my family love a nice cold Guinness, malt or stout, especially Guinness Foreign Extra Stout, because it is stronger. By 1799, Guinness was mostly known for brewing ale before it began focusing solely on producing porter. West Indies porter was the perfect brew for the islands because it was made robust enough to withstand the heat and humidity of the tropical climate, brewed stronger and fortified with extra hops.

Guinness was particularly popular with the Irish communities in the Caribbean because of their shared origins. As a community, the Irish found their position within the British Empire quite complicated as they were both colonisers and the colonised. In Montserrat, the Irish had managed to elevate their social class moving from indentured servants to plantation owners and managers when communities from the African countries then began to be enslaved.

The Irish also had experience using sea moss. The potato famine of 1845–1849 left masses of the community without food, over one million lost their lives and many others were on the brink of starvation. During this time, the reddish moss that grows in abundance along the Irish coasts became a major source of sustenance. The variety common in the Caribbean is more of a yellowish colour but they behave relatively the same.

Milky punch drinks with a little spice are very popular, especially in the anglophone islands of Jamaica, Trinidad and Tobago, whether it's with peanut, soursop or pineapple 'sky' juice, they're great over ice.

Ingredients

Punch base
1 × 397 g (13¾ oz/1¼ cups) tin condensed milk

1 × 410 g (14½ oz/generous 1¼ cups) tin of evaporated milk

½ teaspoon freshly grated nutmeg

½ teaspoon ground cinnamon

1 teaspoon vanilla extract or vanilla bean paste

ice cubes, as needed

Guinness and sea moss gel
50 g (13/4 oz) dried sea moss, rinsed twice

juice of ½ lime

1 litre (34 fl oz/41/4 cups) water

a few cinnamon sticks

Guinness and sea moss
4 tablespoons sea moss gel

330 ml (11¼ fl oz/1⅓ cups) Guinness Foreign Extra (or another stout)

30 ml (1 fl oz/2 tablespoons) rum

a few dashes Angostura bitters (optional)

Put the sea moss into a large bowl along with the lime juice and water, then leave to soak overnight. The next day, transfer the sea moss and water to a saucepan and add the cinnamon sticks, then boil for 20–30 minutes, or until the liquid has reduced by at least a third. Remove from the heat and allow to cool a little, then remove the cinnamon sticks and transfer to a food processor. Blend until smooth, then transfer to a sterilised jar or airtight container (see page 275) and refrigerate for up to 1 month (or freeze for up to 3 months). Ensure you use a clean spoon each time you use it.

Combine all the base ingredients in a jug (pitcher) or blender and mix until smooth. Add the Guinness and sea moss ingredients and mix again. Serve over ice. Keep refrigerated and use within a few days.

COCOA TEA

BUSH TEA

SERVES 4

Almost like hot chocolate, this is the best tea recipe you'll ever taste. The tradition of cocoa tea drinking is said to have originated in the West Coast town of Soufriere, St. Lucia around 1833, following abolition. As tea leaves were harder to source but cocoa was not, it became a new custom that has stuck ever since. I first tried this in St. Lucia with *bek fwi* (fry bakes), (see page 242), for breakfast and have never looked back. Boiling the raw cocoa with the spices (and bergamot peel, as my friend from Grenada does) before adding the milk and sugar gives the tea an extra warmth and hum. Cocoa has been grown and exported from St. Lucia, Grenada and Dominica, to name a few, for centuries. Along with sugar and coffee, cocoa was one of the main exports to Europe and beyond.

SERVES 1

Herbalists, persons who practised naturalist medicine with plants, were common during the colonial period and often used as the source for healing. The affinity with the land (provision grounds) and all it provided us, has become customary to our understanding of plants for centuries. I love the term 'bush tea' because the generality of it is equally very specific and unique. Bush tea, in my experience, was the hot tonic you started the day with, which referred to the leaves of various plants that would be foraged to make something to drink. Not only that, it was also the invisible remedy that 'fixed' every ailment I presented my grandparents with; from a cold to stomach ache – bush tea fixed it. When visiting my grandad in Barbuda, I did exactly this. He had a bush of fever grass growing in his front garden, ready to be picked and steeped every day.

Ingredients

60g (2 oz) raw cocoa stick, grated
1 litre (34 fl oz/4¼ cups) water, plus 1½ tablespoons for the flour mixture
3 cinnamon sticks
4 bay leaves
9 cloves
¼ whole nutmeg, freshly grated
2 teaspoon plain (all-purpose) flour
4 tablespoons Demerara sugar
180 ml (6 fl oz/¾ cup) whole (full-fat) milk or coconut milk
Fry Bakes (see page 242), to serve

Ingredients

a few strands of fever grass, bruised (or 1 thumb-sized piece of lemongrass stalk)
a thumb-sized piece of ginger, sliced (optional)

Place the fever grass and ginger (if using) in a cup or small tea pot, cover with hot water and leave to steep for 5–8 minutes before drinking.

Put the grated cocoa stick, water, cinnamon sticks, bay leaves, cloves and nutmeg into a saucepan. Bring to the boil, then simmer for 25 minutes. Strain the tea, discard the spices and cocoa residue, then return the cocoa water to the pan and set aside.

In a separate bowl, dissolve the flour in the 2½ teaspoons water to create a paste, ensuring there are no lumps. Add a tablespoon of the cocoa water and stir in to temper the flour mixture. Add the flour mixture to the pan, then bring to the boil. Once the pan starts to come up to the boil again, whisk in the sugar and milk, then cook for a further 5–10 minutes until thickened. Serve hot with the fry bakes.

AKASAN
HAITIAN CORNMEAL DRINK

SERVES 4

Many Caribbean islands (and South American countries) have their own cornmeal drink or porridge. Walking along the streets of Port-au-Prince, you'll hear street traders calling out, while they carry large buckets of this spiced beverage on their heads. The exact origins of akasan are unknown, however, it is said to have been consumed for centuries. The name alone holds some etymology, with akasan translating to 'ak-100', as 'san' is the creole word for one hundred. With corn once grown in abundance, it was an easy, filling and possibly comforting beverage to create.

Ingredients

800 ml (27 fl oz/3⅓ cups) water

¼ teaspoon sea salt

⅓ teaspoon freshly grated nutmeg

2 cinnamon sticks

3–4 star anise

125 g (4½ oz/generous ¾ cup) fine cornmeal

1–2 teaspoons vanilla extract or vanilla bean paste

60 g (2 oz) raw cane sugar

1 × 410 g (14½ oz/1⅓ cups) tin of evaporated milk

Pour half the water into a saucepan and add the salt, nutmeg, cinnamon sticks and star anise. Simmer over a medium heat for 3–4 minutes.

Meanwhile, put the cornmeal and remaining water into a bowl and mix into a smooth paste. Slowly add the paste to the simmering water, stirring continuously to avoid lumps. Reduce the heat to low and continue to simmer for 5–6 minutes, until the cornmeal is soft and no longer grainy. Add the vanilla, sugar and evaporated milk and mix thoroughly. Serve warm or chilled over ice.

PANTRY

**STAPLE SEASONINGS
CHUTNEYS AND CONDIMENTS
HOT SAUCE AND VINEGARS
OTHER CONDIMENTS**

GREEN SEASONING

MAKES 1 JAR

Sofrito, epis and green seasoning are fundamentals of cooking across the Caribbean, with influence based on the French and Spanish elements within the cooking or locality of ingredients. You'll see the recipes for these are very similar but have a few key differences that reflect the flavours of the island. The green seasoning uses chadon beni or culantro, a wild herb, native to parts of the Americas (including the Caribbean) with a beautiful fragrance of coriander and spring onion.

Ingredients

6 garlic cloves

60 g (2 oz) chadon beni (culantro/recao) or coriander (cilantro) leaves and stalks

4 spring onions (scallions)

10 g (½ oz) fresh ginger root, unpeeled and cleaned

a few sprigs of thyme

25 g (¾ oz) seasoning peppers (pimento/ají dulce) (or ½ a (bell) pepper or another mild chilli, any colour)

30 g (1 oz) parsley leaves

2 Scotch bonnets (optional)

200 ml (7 fl oz/scant 1 cup) water

2 tablespoons rapeseed (canola) or olive oil

Combine all the ingredients except the oil in a food processor and blend until mostly smooth, then stir in the oil. Store in a sterilised container (see page 275) in the refrigerator for up to 2 weeks.

EPIS

MAKES 1 JAR

Epis is Haiti's unique seasoning blend used
for flavouring meat stews, vegetables and fish.
The addition of bouillion, lime juice and vinegar
in the epis, speaks to the heavier use of acidity
in French cooking.

Ingredients

1 brown onion
4 spring onions (scallions)
25 g (¾ oz) pimento peppers or another mild chilli or ½ a (bell) pepper, any colour)
3 Scotch bonnet or piment bouc (goat peppers)
6 garlic gloves
30 g (1 oz) chadon beni (culantro/recao) or coriander (cilantro) leaves and stalks
60 g (2 oz) parsley leaves and stalks
10 g (½ oz) fresh ginger root, unpeeled and cleaned
a few sprigs of thyme
1 vegetable stock cube or bouillon cube
1 lime, juiced
2 tablespoons apple cider vinegar or white vinegar
2 celery stalks
200 ml (7 fl oz/scant 1 cup) water
60 ml (2 fl oz/½ cup) rapeseed (canola) olive oil

Combine all the ingredients except the oil
in a food processor and blend until mostly smooth, then
stir in the oil. Store in a sterilised container
(see page 275) in the refrigerator for up to 2 weeks.

SOFRITO

MAKES 1 JAR

Sofrito in mainland Spain would commonly
incorporate tomatoes, however, Spanish Caribbean
islands have evolved the recipe. Instead, they
use a similar base to green seasoning, often omitting
the tomatoes, then add cumin and annatto –
an ancient peppery, red seed, native to the islands.

Ingredients

12 garlic cloves
1 onion
2 spring onions (scallions)
140 g (5 oz) seasoning peppers (pimento/ ají dulce) (or 1½ (bell) peppers, any colour)
45 g (1½ oz) chadon beni (culantro/recao) or coriander (cilantro) leaves and stalks
30 g (1 oz) parsley leaves and stalks
15 g (½ oz) broad leaf thyme (Cuban oregano), or substitute for Mexican or Greek oregano)
1 teaspoon annatto seeds, ground
150 ml (5 fl oz/scant ⅔ cup) water
2 tablespoons Annatto Oil (see page 307)

Combine all the ingredients except the oil in a food
processor and blend until mostly smooth, then stir
in the annatto oil. Store in a sterilised container
(see page 275) in the refrigerator for up to 2 weeks.

TAMARIND CHUTNEY

MAKES 1 JAR

This chutney is fragrant, fresh and goes perfect with doubles (see page 99) or curry duck (see page 114).

Ingredients

200 g (7 oz) tamarind pulp (with seeds)
650 ml (22 fl oz/2¾ cups) warm water
1 Scotch bonnet
2 tablespoons roughly chopped coriander (cilantro) or chadon beni (culantro) leaves
3 garlic cloves
1 teaspoon ground cumin
2 teaspoons amchar masala
250 g (9 oz) raw cane sugar

Combine the tamarind pulp and water, Scotch bonnet, coriander or chadon beni, garlic, cumin and amchar masala in a saucepan. Bring to then boil, then reduce to a simmer and cook for 30 minutes. Strain, discarding the tamarind seeds, garlic, Scotch bonnet and herbs. Return the liquid to the pan along with the sugar, then simmer for a further 30 minutes over a medium–low heat until the sugar dissolves and the chutney thickens slightly. Pour into sterilised jars (see page 275) and allow to cool. Store in the refrigerator for up to 3 months.

CUCUMBER CHUTNEY

SERVES 8–10

This cucumber chutney is so simple to make. It's cool, fresh and is always eaten with doubles (see page 99).

Ingredients

1 whole cucumber
2 teaspoons sea salt
2 tablespoons green seasoning (page 301)

Grate the cucumber in a bowl then add the salt. Mix the salt well into the cucumber, then leave to sit for at least 30 minutes. After 30 minutes, a lot of the cucumber's moisture will have been released. Squeeze the cucumber to release as much liquid as possible, then discard all of the cucumber water. Finally, add the green seasoning and mix. Store in a container or airtight jar, use within 3 days.

CHADON BENI CHUTNEY

SERVES 8–10

This fresh, vibrant chutney goes well with pretty much everything, but is a key component of bake and shark (see page 112).

Ingredients

100 g (3 1/2 oz) fresh chadon beni (culantro) or coriander (cilantro), roughly chopped
4 garlic cloves
1 Scotch bonnet (seeds removed if you prefer less heat)
2 1/2 tablespoons lime juice
320 ml (11 fl oz/1⅓ cups) cold water
1 1/21 teaspoon sea salt
2 teaspoons raw cane sugar

Combine all the ingredients in a food processor and blend until smooth. Pour into a sterilised jar (see page 275) and store in the refrigerator for up to 7 days.

COCONUT CHUTNEY

SERVES 8–10

This roasted coconut chutney is smokey, savoury with a little heat and hails straight from Trinidad. It is another condiment that goes well on top of doubles (see page 99) or with kitchri served with smoked herring (see page 113).

Ingredients

1 dried coconut
1 teaspoon sea salt
1 Scotch bonnet
2 garlic cloves
1 tablespoon roughly chopped coriander (cilantro) or chadon beni (culantro) leaves

Pierce the eyes on the coconut carefully and pour out the water (reserve it to drink). Crack the coconut open, then separate the flesh from the shell. Over hot coals or in a hot, dry pan, roast the coconut pieces until the white flesh browns and blisters slightly. Once roasted, grate the coconut into a bowl. Put the salt, Scotch bonnet, garlic and coriander or chadon beni into a pestle and mortar and pound until roughly blended. Add to the grated coconut and mix well. Store in a sterilised jar or airtight container (see page 275) in the refrigerator for up to 3 days.

CHOW
TRINIDADIAN SPICED FRUIT SALAD

MANGO TALKARI
CURRY MANGO

SERVES 8–10

SERVES 6

Chow is a quintessential street food snack found in Trinidad and Tobago, made with fresh fruits, hot pepper, chadon beni and sometimes other ingredients to the vendor's style. It's such a unique eating experience, with sweet, sour, hot and fresh flavours all at once – I love it!

Mango talkari (mango masala) is essentially a green mango curry. The beauty of the Caribbean is the abundance of fruits that grow all over – along the roadside or in people's front gardens. When mangoes come into season, they make their presence known so much that you'll find them laid across the ground having fallen from the branches above. This recipe is great because it utilises them when unripe. The mangoes are cooked down in amchar masala – a dry mango spice mix, although they have a sharpness from being unripe, they still add a delicious sweetness when served with roti.

Ingredients
2 mangoes, peeled and cut into 2 cm (¾ in) cubes
1 pineapple, peeled, cored and cut into 2 cm (¾ in) cubes
handful of chadon beni (culantro/recao) or coriander (cilantro) leaves, roughly chopped
2–3 garlic cloves, crushed
1 Scotch bonnet, finely chopped (deseeded if you prefer less heat)
juice of 2 limes
sea salt

Ingredients
2 litres (68 fl oz/8½ cups) water
1 kg (2 lb 4 oz) green (unripe) mangoes (about 3–4), peeled and chopped
4 teaspoons sea salt
100 ml (3½ fl oz/scant ½ cup) rapeseed (canola) or olive oil
3 tablespoons amchar masala
120 g (4¼ oz/generous ½ cup) Demerara sugar
1 Scotch bonnet, split in half (or left whole if you prefer less heat)
8 garlic cloves, crushed
2 tablespoons chadon beni (culantro/recao) leaves or coriander (cilantro), roughly chopped

Put the fruit into a bowl, then add the chadon beni, or coriander, garlic, Scotch bonnet and salt to taste. Mix well, then allow to sit for 30 minutes before serving.

Pour the water into a large saucepan and bring to the boil. Add the mango flesh and 2 teaspoons of the salt, then cook for 30–40 minutes until the mango is a little tender but still firm to touch. Drain, then set aside.

Next, heat the oil in a saucepan over a low–medium heat, then add the amchar masala. Cook out the spices for a few minutes, ensuring they don't burn, then add the sugar. Stir a little so the sugar doesn't stick, then allow it to caramelise for a few minutes. Once the sugar has melted and is bubbling, add the mango, Scotch bonnet, garlic and chadon beni or coriander. Cook for 5–7 minutes, stirring regularly, until the mangoes are covered in the spices and have broken down somewhat, creating a spiced, syrupy sauce. Store in a sterilised jar (see page 275) or airtight container in the refrigerator and use within a few days.

HOT PEPPER SAUCE

PIKLIZ
HAITIAN PICKLED VEGETABLES

MAKES 1 JAR

This recipe is one I make at home for everyday use. When writing this, I couldn't help but reference Montserrat and our very own calypso royalty, Alphonsus 'Arrow' Cassell. Born and raised in Plymouth, via Trinidad, his 1982 international release of *Hot Hot Hot* brought calypso to the masses. Him along with many other calypsonians, have used their artistry to share the wider political message of the Caribbean.

Ingredients

160 g (5¾ oz) Scotch bonnets
4 garlic cloves
120 ml (4 fl oz/½ cup) apple cider vinegar or distilled white vinegar
20 g (¾ oz) coriander (cilantro) or chadon beni (culantro)
juice of 2 limes
½ teaspoon sea salt
½ teaspoon sugar

Combine all the ingredients in a food processor and blend until smooth. Transfer to a sterilised jar (see page 275) and store in the refrigerator for up to 1 month. Ensure you use a clean spoon each time you use it.

MAKES 1 JAR

A condiment of cabbage, carrots and hot pepper brined in a vinaigrette. Pikliz is a derivative of the French word *piquer*, which means to sting or burn, due to the strong vinegary, chilli flavours within it.

Ingredients

320 g (11 oz/scant 1½ cups) granulated sugar
1½ tablespoons sea salt
320 ml (11 fl oz/1⅓ cups) water
320 ml (11 fl oz/1⅓ cups) distilled white vinegar
200 g (7 oz) white cabbage, thinly sliced
2 carrots, julienned
2 red onions, thinly sliced into rings
2 garlic cloves, crushed
juice of ½ lime
2–3 sprigs of thyme
1–2 Scotch bonnets, sliced
5 cloves

Combine the sugar, salt, water and vinegar in a jug (pitcher), stir to dissolve the sugar and salt, then set aside.

Put the cabbage, carrot, onion, garlic and lime juice in a sterilised jar or airtight container (see page 275). Add the thyme, Scotch bonnet and cloves. Pour over the vinegar mixture, then seal and leave to pickle for at least a few days in the refrigerator before using. Store in the refrigerator for up to 1 month. Ensure you use a clean spoon each time you use it.

AGRIO DE NARANJA

SPICY BITTER ORANGE VINEGAR

SERVES 8–10

The combination of oil, vinegar, fresh citrus juice to marinate, hot peppers, onions and garlic as a hot, spicy fragrant condiment is a common mix throughout the region. This agrio de naranja steeps hot peppers and fresh herbs in citrus juice, the longer it is left the more intense the flavour and heat will be. Similarly, Puerto Ricans call theirs *pique*, made with the above ingredients and the addition of pineapple skin.

Ingredients

5 Scotch bonnets, split in half
3 garlic cloves, halved
3 sprigs of oregano
1 sprig of thyme
1 teaspoon sea salt
1 teaspoon peppercorns
juice of 4 oranges, sieved
juice of 2 limes, sieved

Put the Scotch bonnets, garlic, oregano, thyme, salt and peppercorns into a sterilised jar (see page 275), followed by the orange and lime juice. Leave to infuse for at least 3 days before using. Store in the refrigerator and use within 7 days. Ensure you use a clean spoon each time you use it.

TI' MALICE

DEVIL SAUCE

SERVES 8–10

Similar to Agrio de naranja, this hot vinaigrette from Haiti is named after Ti' malice and Bouki from an old Haitian folklore. Ti' Malice is said to have been a prankster, yet smart. Whereas Bouki was hardworking and greedy. Both played tricks on each other. This hot sauce goes wonderfully with fritay (see page 35).

Ingredients

7–8 round shallots, diced
juice of 1 sour orange (or juice of 1 orange and 1 lime)
90 ml (3 fl oz/⅓ cup) apple cider vinegar
3 garlic cloves
4 Scotch bonnets, roughly chopped
1–2 teaspoons sea salt
2 tablespoons olive oil
2 tablespoons water

Put the shallots, sour orange juice and vinegar into a bowl, cover and set aside to marinate overnight.

The next day, crush the garlic and Scotch bonnets in a pestle and mortar, then add to the shallots along with the salt and oil. Transfer to a saucepan with the water and simmer over a medium heat for 5–7 minutes. Remove from the heat and set aside to cool. You can use it as it is or blend into a smoother sauce. Transfer to a sterilised jar (see page 275) and refrigerate for up to 2 months. Ensure you use a clean spoon each time you use it.

ANNATTO OIL

MAKES 125 ML (14 FL OZ/½ CUP)

Annatto seeds are a naturally occurring, 'ancient' spice, used by the Indigenous communities across the Caribbean and South Americas. Their bright red colour and slightly peppery taste is now used to infuse oil or ground to form part of the base flavours of many Spanish Caribbean dishes.

Ingredients

3 tablespoons annatto seeds
125 ml (4 fl oz/½ cup) rapeseed (canola) or olive oil

Put the annatto seeds and oil into a saucepan and warm over a low heat. As the oil heats up, the colour from the seeds will seep into the oil, turning it red.
If the annatto seeds start to turn dark red or black, they are burning, so remove from the heat immediately. When bubbles start to form around the annatto seeds, remove the pan from the heat and leave to steep for 1–2 minutes. Strain the oil into a sterilised jar or airtight container (see page 275). Store in a cool, dry place for up to 3 months. Ensure you use a clean spoon each time you use it.

MANGO SOUR

SERVES 8–10

Mango sour is a popular condiment from Guyana, usually served with dhal puri roti (see page 237) or snacks such as egg ball and cassava ball recipe (see page 77).

Ingredients

1 green (unripe) mango, peeled and sliced
2 garlic cloves, crushed
½ Scotch bonnet
½ teaspoon sea salt
1 teaspoon apple cider vinegar
600 ml (20 fl oz/2½ cups) water

Combine all the ingredients in a saucepan over a medium heat and simmer for 20 minutes until the mango is soft, then remove from the heat and allow to cool.

Transfer everything to a food processor and blend until roughly smooth. Scrape into a sterilised jar (see page 275), then store in the refrigerator for up to 1 week. Ensure you use a clean spoon each time you use it.

REFERENCES

ACADEMIC JOURNALS

The Codrington Papers. 'Papers of the Codrington Family, Antigua, 1700-1869. Bodleian Library, University of Oxford.

Udo, Emem Michael (2020). 'The Vitality of Yoruba Culture in the Americas.' Ufahamu: A Journal of African Studies, 41(2).

Maryam Ogunbiyi (2016). The Influence Of Yoruba Religion And Gastronomy On The Yoruba Diaspora Of Cuba And Brazil: A Transnational Analysis.

Karin Vaneker (2010). From Poi to Fufu: the fermentation of taro. Cured, Fermented and Smoked Foods: Proceedings of the Oxford Symposium on Food. Prospect Books: 216-224.

Carney, Judith (2013) Chapter 2: Seeds of Memory: Botanical Legacies of the African Diaspora.

Snooks, G & Boon, S. (2017) Salt Fish and Molasses: Unsettling the Palate in the Spaces Between Two Continents. European Journal of Life Writing. Volume VI (218-241).

W. Herold, Marc (2015) Nineteenth-Century Bahia's Passion for British Salted Cod: From the Seas of Newfoundland to the Portuguese Shops of Salvador's Cidade Baixa,1822-1914. University of New Hampshire. Commodities of Empire. Working Paper No.23.

Francis, Shrinagar I. (2022). The Journey of Saltfish across the Atlantic to the West Indies and its Movement through the Culinary Landscape of Trinidad and Tobago. Dublin Gastronomy Symposium. Food and Movement.

Ramlachan, Nicole, et al. (2007). "Two Reflections on Making Callaloo in Trinidad: An Interview with Betty Laban and Angella Ramlachan." Callaloo, vol. 30, no. 1, pp. 347–50.

Hidalgo, Dennis (2012). Africa and the Caribbean: Overview

Ohman, Alexis (2014) Saltfish vs. Parrotfish: The Role of Fish and Mollusks in English Colonial Foodways at Betty's Hope Plantation, Antigua, West Indies. Department of Archaeology Faculty of Environment.

Lowenthal, David and Clarke, Colin. G. (1977). Slave Breeding in Barbuda: The Past Negro Myth. Annals of the New York Academy of Sciences.

Chatland, Jan (1990). Descriptions of Various Loa of Voodoo.

Berleant, Riva (1991).Hidden Places and Barbudan forms: Naming the Creole Landscape. Professional Geographer. 43.

(1). Pp. 92-101.

Pfeifer, Julia (2016). "The Loa as Ghosts in Haitian Vodou." Ghosts - or the (Nearly) Invisible: Spectral Phenomena in Literature and the Media, edited by Maria Fleischhack and Elmar Schenkel, Peter Lang AG, pp. 137–46.

Berleant, Riva (2012). Beans, Peas and Rice in the Eastern Caribbean. IN Rice and Beans: A Unique dish in a hundred places. Richard Wilk and Livia Barbosa, eds. London and New York. Berg: pp. 81-100.

Smart, Cherry-Ann (2019). African oral tradition, cultural retentions and the transmission of knowledge in the West Indies. Volume 45, Issue 1.

Ralph R. Premdas (1996). "Ethnicity and Identity in the Caribbean: Decentering a Myth," Kellogg Institute for International Studies. 234.

Mika Miyoshi (2016). 'Representation of African Heritage in Trinidad Carnival'.

Mehta, Brinda J., and مهتابريندا. "Indo-Trinidadian Fiction: Female Identity and Creative Cooking / الكتابة الروائية الهندية - الترينيدادية: الهوية النسوية والطبخ الإبداعي." Alif: Journal of Comparative Poetics, no. 19, 1999, pp. 151–84.

Riggio, Milla C. (1998) "Introduction: Resistance and Identity: Carnival in Trinidad and Tobago." TDR (1988-), vol. 42, no. 3, pp. 7–23.

Brereton, Bridget (2007) Contesting the past: Narratives of Trinidad and Tobago History. NWIG: New West Indian Guide / Nieuwe West-Indische Gids, vol. 81, no. 3/4, 2007, pp. 169–96.

Turks and Caicos Islands, 1878-1891. British Online Archives.

Estiman, Edward (2014) A survey of Ackee fruit utilization in Ghana. University of Health and Allied Sciences.

RUNDOWN. Richart Price, Sally Price. NWIG: New West Indian Guide / Nieuwe West-Indische Gids, Vol. 67, No. 1

After Emancipation: Aspects of Village Life in Guyana, 1869-1911. Barbara P. Josiah. The Journal of Negro History, Vol. 82, No. 1 (Winter, 1997), pp. 105-121

Jamaican Versions of Callaloo. B. W. Higman. Callaloo, Vol. 30, No. 1, Reading "Callaloo"/Eating Callaloo: A Special Thirtieth Anniversary Issue (Winter, 2007), pp. 351-368 (18 pages)

Esposito, Eleonora (2019). Callaloo or Pelau? Food, Identity and Politics in Trinidad and Tobago: Linguistic Insights in Transcultural Tastes. Food Across Cultures (pp.43-70)

F Pillai, Suresh. Food Culture of Indo Caribbean

erreia, Jo-Anne (2012). Madeiran Portuguese Culinary Heritage in Trinidad and Tobago. The Culinary Story of Trinidad and Tobago.

ARTICLES

Plant of the Month: Hibiscus – daily.jstor.org

A brief history of ackee and saltfish – theculturetrip.com

The story of green turtle soup – georgehbalazs.com

The culinary culture behind turtle stew – brasseriecayman.com

Cayman island sea turtles – saveur.com

Eating turtles – uncommoncaribbean.com

Akasan Haitian cornmeal drink – imbibemagazine.com

In the Barrio, a flurry of snow cones – ediblemanhattan.com

Lechon Puerto Rico – atlasobscura.com

Puerto Rico's pork highway – bbc.com/travel

What is Adobo – foodandwine.com

Clarin Rum Haiti – atlasobscura.com

The Plantation system – nationalgeographic.org

BOOKS

Rita G. Springer –*The Caribbean Cookbook*, Pan Books, 1989

David and Gwendolyn Daley – *Caribbean Cookery Secrets*, Little, Brown Book Group, 2013

Ranin Ganeshram – *Sweet Hands*, Hippocrene Books, 2018

Vanessa Bolassier – *The Creole Kitchen*, Harper Collins, 2015

Yvonne John – *Guyanese Seed of Soul*, R & M Pub Co., 1983

Yolande Cools-Lartigue – *The Art of Caribbean Cooking*, Koolart Publications, 1998

Dr. Jessica B. Harris – *High on the Hog*, Bloomsbury, 2012

Professor Hakim Adi – *African and Caribbean People in Britain: A History*, Penguin, 2022

Appleby, Sue – *The Cornish in the Caribbean - From the 17th to 19th centuries*, Matador, 2023

Dookhan, Isaac – *A History of the Virgin Islands of the United States*, Canoe Press, 1994

INDEX

ACKNOWLEDGEMENTS

As many of you may (or may not) know, this book has been many, many years in the making. Not only does it compile a lifetime's work but particularly over the past few years I've been writing, researching and traveling the islands to learn and explore as much of our beautiful culture as possible. I've been so fortunate to meet so many wonderful people along the way who have quietly inspired many parts of this book. Whilst there were moments when I couldn't wait for it to be completed, nothing happens before it is ready and the time it took allowed for so many bonus life moments to inspire and influence it further.

To everyone who worked on this book, thank you for bringing your best and bringing this to life!

To all my close loved ones, family and friends - you know who you are. I'm so grateful for all of your enthusiasm and belief in me and this work and for appreciating its importance and necessity as much as I have. Whether you've come along to eat my food or we've shared a conversation about life and the world, it has quietly influenced so many elements of this book in ways I never realized it would, so thank you.

Thank you to my literary agent Emma Bal and the team at Madeleine Milburn TV and Literary agency. Working with you Emma has been wonderful from day one, you understood this work and me, which ultimately brought the best out of both so thank you again for all of your knowledge and expertise!

Thank you to my lovely editor Eve Marleau (and Isabel Gonzalez-Prendergast) and the team at Hardie Grant. Eve, it has been such a joy to work with you on this. You are just a wonderful, funny and patient person who has also encouraged me so much during this process to be open, get my thoughts onto paper and bring out the best of me. I truly am grateful to have worked with you on this.

To my Grandmothers, Eleanor Beatrice (7/8/1927-30/12/2021) and Othella Fernalla (20/4/1935-27/12/2017), both of you kept me rooted in my culture through our shared love of cooking and eating food that's made with love. Without these precious moments, this book would not have existed and I thank you eternally.

To my Grandfather, William Henry (7/2/1926-4/11/2014) for always being a safe and peaceful place for me. In the short time we shared, you taught me so much which I am forever grateful for.

To Mum, you're my number one supporter and affirmation whatsapper! You're always there to support me (even when you didn't fully understand this food thing) and through that I'm glad to have shared many of my experiences in the food world with you. Lots of love x

ABOUT THE AUTHOR

Keshia Sakarah is an outstanding self-taught chef, food educator, recipe contributor and food writer. She currently teaches cooking in schools and prisons, focusing on matters such as culture, identity to explore how heritage and history has influenced how we eat what we eat. As a lover of food and travel first and foremost, she loves to explore ingredients and develop an understanding of their relationship to various communities around the world.

As such, she has written pieces for *Time Out*, *National Geographic Traveller*, *Conde Nast Traveller*, *MOB Kitchen*, *Vittles*, *Eater* and *Resy*. Her passion for creativity with ingredients has found her contributing recipes to publications such as the Guardian: *Feast*, *BBC Good Food*, *Twisted*, Phaidon, *Ocado*, *Great British Chefs*, *BBC Food*, *Sainsbury's*, *Waitrose*, *Delicious Magazine* and *Olive Magazine*. She has been featured on BBC World Service, Woman's hour and *Masterchef: The Professionals 2021* and 2022 as a guest street food expert and was named one of the 100 influential women in food by CODE Hospitality in the same years.

Alongside food writing and teaching, Keshia runs her supper club Baruru, specifically taking diners on a food journey throughout the Caribbean. The event is hosted by a historian, who tells stories alongside an ever changing menu, with dishes from the revolutionary creole island of Haiti all the way south to the afro-indian cultures of Trinidad and Tobago. Her food has depth, context and makes every effort to explore who she is and where she is from in all of its beauty. Baruru supper club evolved from her container restaurant Caribe' - to which this book has been named after. Caribe' started as a pop up and residency in kitchens across London in 2018, before growing into a local eating spot based in Brixton, serving a modest 24 covers and receiving a glowing review in the Evening Standard in 2021.

Keshia's goal has always been, and continues to, celebrate the diverse food culture that exists in the Caribbean, here in the UK food scene and future work will explore deeper connections between Africa and its diaspora.

Quadrille, Penguin Random House UK, One Embassy Gardens, 8 Viaduct Gardens, London SW11 7BW

Quadrille Publishing Limited is part of the Penguin Random House group of companies whose addresses can be found at global.penguinrandomhouse.com

Penguin
Random House
UK

Published by Quadrille in 2025

www.penguin.co.uk

A CIP catalogue record for this book is available from the British Library

ISBN 978-1-78488-683-7

10 9 8 7 6 5 4 3 2 1

Publishing Director Kajal Mistry

Senior Commissioning Editor Eve Marleau

Copy Editor Grace Wynter (Tessera Editorial) and Lucy Kingett

Proofreader Sarah Prior

Designer Evi-O.Studio | Evi O, Eloise Myatt and Katherine Zhang

Photographer Matt Russell, Yvonne Maxwell and Michael Lovell

Food Stylist Benjamina Ebuehi

Prop Stylist Tabitha Hawkins

Production Director Stephen Lang

Production Manager Sabeena Atchia

Colour reproduction by p2d

Printed in China by C&C Offset Printing Co., Ltd.

The authorised representative in the EEA is Penguin Random House Ireland, Morrison Chambers, 32 Nassau Street, Dublin D02 YH68.

MIX
Paper | Supporting
responsible forestry
FSC® C018179

Penguin Random House is committed to a sustainable future for our business, our readers and our planet. This book is made from Forest Stewardship Council® certified pape